Aug 9 2006

Barb,
It was a pleasure meeting you at the
Sacred Harvest festival. It is my
hope that the Lady will guide
your journey as you walk the
Sacred Path.
Blessings
DdMc

COURTING THE LADY
A WICCAN JOURNEY

BOOK ONE:
THE SACRED PATH

THE SACRED PATH

The Sacred Path is an age old oral tradition steeped in Magic and mystical lore, which reveals the secrets of nature and the nature of the universe as it explores the very nature of Magic itself. Initiates on the Sacred Path, are instructed by mentors who utilize the walking of a path in the forest as a guidebook presented by the Divine to answer the humanity's most pressing questions about the creation of the universe and our place in it.

Unlike many other traditions, the Sacred Path tradition provides clear answers as to why Witches do what they do, and explains in detail the complex origins of our sacred ceremonies, Magical tools, and rituals. Beyond that, it ties together the practices of today, with those of the ancient past, and reveals secret connections never before revealed in print.

For the novice Witch or the accomplished Elder, the Sacred Path tradition brings to light information that will illuminate and validate every tradition, and which will prove valuable to all who seek to understand the ancient mysteries. And for those who are just curious about Witchcraft and its underlying spirituality, the Sacred Path will provide the fundamental tools necessary to clearly understand those who choose to walk that path, and to better understand the impact that these ancient traditions have had on religion, science, art, and civilization.

About the Author

Patrick McCollum, a nationally recognized Wiccan elder and High Priest, has been in the craft for over forty years. Originally initiated as a Witch in the early 1960's, Patrick began his mystical journey following a near death experience, and has been walking the Sacred Path ever since.

In 1997, Patrick became the first government recognized Wiccan Chaplain in the United States. In 1999, he received a Certificate of Recognition from the California State Senate, for his spiritual work with inmates. Following that, Patrick became the first Wiccan in history to become a professional member of the American Correctional Chaplains Association.

Patrick has lectured at various colleges and universities, and has been interviewed on both radio and TV. He also served as a technical director and participant in both the History Channel's and Lifetime TV's, prime time specials on Witches. Patrick teaches workshops nationwide on Magic, herb lore, and Witchcraft, and has been a primary presenter at the Pagan Spirit Gathering in Ohio for 6 years.

Patrick also serves as a Priest of Brighid and is a nationally acclaimed goldsmith and jewelry designer. His pieces have been worn by many celebrities over the years and his work has been featured in Fred Segal, Henry Bendels, and the famous Forum Shops at Caesars Palace.

To Write to the Author

If you wish to write the author or would like more information about this book, please write to the author in care of Our Lady of the Wells Press and we will forward your request. Our Lady of the Wells Press cannot guarantee that every letter written to the author will be answered, but all will be forwarded. Please write to:

Patrick M. McCollum
c/o Our Lady of the Wells Press
450 Center Street #133
Moraga, CA. 94556
Please include a self-addressed, stamped envelope with your letter.

COURTING THE LADY
A WICCAN JOURNEY

BOOK ONE:
THE SACRED PATH

PATRICK M. McCOLLUM

2006

Our Lady of the Wells Press
Moraga, CA. 94556, U.S.A.

For information, address Our Lady of the Wells Press,
450 Center Street #133, Moraga, CA. 94556

FIRST EDITION
First Printing 2006

Cover design by Patrick M. McCollum

Cover photo by Daniel Kaufman from his book *Ireland: Presences* (St. Martin's Press, 1980), used with permission.

Edited by Barbara A. McGraw

Library of Congress Cataloging-in-Publication Data
McCollum, Patrick M.
        Courting the Lady; a Wiccan Journey; Book One: The Sacred
        Path / Patrick M. McCollum – 1st ed.
        ISBN 0-9777986-8-2 (pbk)
  1. Witchcraft.   2. Magic.   3. Nature Spirituality
  4. Herbs—Miscellanea.

Printed in the United States of America

This book is dedicated to my wife
Barbara McGraw,
who kept me on track while I wrote, and pushed me toward
excellence at every turn

and to

the members of the Cauldron of Cerridwen, who walked the hills
and valleys in search of infinite wisdom

Contents

Acknowledgements

This book could not have been possible if not for the support and encouragement of my wife Barbara McGraw. At a time when I was frustrated by the rapidly changing face of Paganism in America and the noticeable loss of traditional wisdom as it was conveyed during the early Fifties and Sixties, she encouraged me to write it all down. Then as I struggled to figure out how one conveys an entirely oral tradition through a written manuscript, without falling into the common trap of just summarizing ritual and providing brief descriptions of the tools of magic and the traditions practiced, i.e., Wicca 101, she suggested the solution.

Her wisdom, editorial suggestions, and faith in my writing, paved the way for this final manuscript, which I feel provides exactly what I sought to produce when I first started this project -- the opportunity for the reader to take a journey down the Sacred Path, and to hopefully discover that that which appears to be hidden, is in truth -- merely unseen.

I would also like to thank the talented Daniel Kaufman for providing me with the wonderful photo for my cover from his book *Ireland: Presences* (St. Martin's Press, 1980), which precisely captures the essence of the secret places where ancient wisdom resides.

In addition I would like to thank Professor Richard Keady for his help in editing, and for his friendship and support in the finalization of this book.

And lastly, I would like to thank those in the coven who taught me, and who took the time in a changing world to introduce me to the sacred.

The Sacred Path

As thorn and stone and unknown turn,
await the traveler beyond.
A lantern sits among the lilies,
in a place that's filled with song.

Yet no light beams through darkest night,
nor bell rings to guide one there.
For the place lies far beyond our dreams,
in a world as elusive as air.

Yet a walk on a path through forest or glen,
or herb filled creek they say.
May open the door to that fairy place,
that eludes the light of day.

And if it's magic you seek, you'll find it there,
in fern and oak and willow.
When you lay your head in the soft sweet duff,
that serves as nature's pillow.

And while its secrets may in shadows lie,
they are not hidden, but merely unseen.
And the key that unlocks the magical world,
is held by heaven's queen.

So walk the path and touch the green,
the water, the air, and the earth.
And bask in the fire of the new born sun,
for in this, lies the secret of rebirth.

XIII

PROLOGUE

THE PAGAN SUMMIT
March 1st, 2001
Bloomington, Indiana

"So, moving to the first item on the agenda, what are the most important issues facing the Pagan movement during the upcoming year," the Summit chairman inquired of the fifty-or so leaders present during the opening of the Summit. I looked around the room at the diverse congregation of participants who had traveled from various locations around the country to represent their constituents, and I wondered what might come of this groundbreaking meeting. Even more so, I wondered if anything could actually be accomplished here, considering the significant differences between the congregations and their beliefs, which covered a wide gambit of Pagan faiths, from the Feminist Dianic Separatists to the Fellowship of Isis, to the Church of All Worlds. The last few stragglers meandered in and took their seats, joining us in the Georgian Ballroom of the Memorial Union Hotel, which was neatly centered in the meticulously groomed campus of the University of Indiana. And I found myself overwhelmed by the mere fact that this was happening at all. Who would have thought that we would have come so far, certainly not me? But here we were — representing close to a million men and women, as we met at the heart of this respected center of learning. Each of us, in one way or another, had played some important role in the establishment of our religion here in the United States, and we had all come together this day to assure a safe and secure future for generations of Witches to come.

"We'll break up into smaller groups," the moderator continued, "and each group can independently discuss the issues that those in that particular group feel are paramount to them. That way we can have more intimate discussions about these issues and it will be easier to come up with a summarized list for the larger group. Once we have the lists, we'll get together again tomorrow as a whole and flesh out what we agree are the most important issues from the small group lists. Then we'll use our last day together to see if we can come up with a plan to address them."

We broke up into four small groups, each with a facilitator, and each named after one of the four elements: fire, water, earth, and air. Once we were assigned to a group, we diligently began our deliberations which lasted a full day, and yielded blackboards full of ideas and suggestions. In the evening, we met socially, many of us meeting for the very first time. Even though most of us had heard of one another or worked together long distance by phone or e-mail, it was nice to put a name to a face, and I made several new friends and reconnected with some old ones from the early years. We talked through the night about Magic and religion and current social trends, and I didn't get to bed until after 2:00 am. When I finally hit the sheets, I was thoroughly exhausted and the warm cozy colonial quilt supplied by the hotel, provided a welcome introduction to an unfamiliar bed, as I drifted into a quiet and peaceful sleep in Bloomington Indiana, 2,000 miles away from home.

The following day, we met once again in the elegant Georgian and arranged our chairs to form a giant circle, in the manner most common among Wiccan congregations. There was a long fold-out table against the southern wall, filled with a multitude of doughnuts, croissants, assorted fruits, and hot steaming coffee and tea, and as the participants brought their selections back to their seats, the room gradually became filled with their wonderful scent. I helped myself to a doughnut and a cup of black tea and I returned to my chair, just as the moderator signaled that it was time to start. When the moderator wheeled a rolling blackboard into view and allowed it to settle in a place where we all could see it, the circle of leaders dominating the floor in the otherwise empty ballroom, quieted to a hushed whisper. As the meeting progressed, representatives from each of the smaller groups began reading their lists, one after another, and new categories were added to the board, while like categories were combined. After a short while, a list of a dozen or so of our most important issues appeared before the whole community, and I was taken back to see that everyone seemed to be in agreement on the main issues for the first time in close to twenty-five years.

Professionalism in leadership and increasing the level of understanding in the national community were on the top of the list. A pagan prison ministry program, and discussing the Bush administration's new Faith-Based Initiative, followed as a close second and third. There were suggestions about how to create unity between the different traditions and how to train clergy to take a responsible role in society. There was also a keen interest in how to promote fund raising, and there were discussions about how to educate the press about our religion. The list went on and on, and eventually, we came to the round-table discussion part of the program.

"We have to develop professionalism in our leaders and clergy," one woman began, "if we want to have the rest of the world see us as being serious."

Everyone nodded their heads and many spoke out in approval.

"Establishing a national prison ministry is critical," a well known leader across the room from me spoke up, looking directly at me, as I was already working on that.

"Yeah, and Patrick already has a great start on that one," someone else joined in, and I was taken back for a moment or two, finding myself the center of everyone's attention.

"We also need to take the necessary steps to participate actively in the new faith-based social programs," another woman chimed in in a serious voice, removing the focus from me.

"I agree," a man on my left joined in. "It's important to be recognized right from the beginning so that the new President and his administration can't claim that we're not a religion."

"How could he claim that?" another man far across the room shouted back. "Of course we're a religion. We're the oldest religion!"

"You're not going to start that again," a long-haired middle aged man who I knew from his name tag was a well know Pagan writer. "Most everyone now agrees that we've only been around since the seventies," he continued, a certain degree of cynicism obvious in his voice.

"But what about Gardner?"[1] another man across the room returned, leaning forward as the debate began to escalate. Everyone was familiar with this long standing battle as to whether we were a new religion, born of the sixties and a couple of books written by Gerald Gardner, or whether we were a continuation of a long unbroken line of Witches tracing its history back through ancient civilizations.

"Okay, so if you consider Gardner, maybe we could push that back to the early fifties," the writer continued, but the first Witches in this country didn't even get here until sixty-eight or sixty-nine, so it really doesn't make much difference."

"And that was on the east coast," someone else joined in.

"Okay, now everyone, we're getting off the subject here. Let's get back to the agenda," the chairwoman interrupted, tapping on the floor with her bottle of Aqua Fria spring water to get our attention.

Things gradually turned back to the agenda at hand. But I had already been moved by the momentary flurry off the subject, and I found myself needing to speak up, but decided to hold my tongue. Instead, my mind drifted gradually out of the conversation at hand, and I found myself transported back into my past — to a place and time 36 years before. And, as the now distant circle of leaders moved on to the subjects of returning to nature and where our morals and ethics came from, for me the room faded away into a gray and swirling fog. When finally I reached

---

[1] Gerald Gardner, author of the first book on modern Witchcraft.

XVII

that now familiar place, both within my mind and within my spirit, the flood gates opened, and a powerful stream of memories flooded in. Once they started, all contact with the Summit was washed away, and I sat once again on my 1962 Triumph on a California street in 1965, awaiting my destiny. . . .

XVIII

CHAPTER 1

The Accident

I looked to my right as I started into the intersection and saw that the way was clear. As I turned to my left, I saw a blue and gray Chevrolet bearing down upon me. I tried to turn my "bike" to the right, but it started to slide sideways in front of the oncoming car, so I tried to hit the rear break to stop my slide, but my foot slipped between the brake peddle and the shifter and hit the ground, snapping the bone in my right ankle. Just as the pain of the break hit me, I heard a terrible scraping sound and looked up to see my front tire strike the front fender of the speeding car. All of the sudden, everything slowed down and became incredibly clear.

My motorcycle started to spin like a top. The left side of my body slammed into the car, and I felt another stabbing pain; something in my left leg gave way as it was crushed between the car and my Triumph. Somehow, I managed to push myself upward, avoiding having my leg torn off as the car and my bike collided for the second time. I remember flipping on my back as I smashed through the passenger side window of the car and landed face up on the top edge of the car's bench seat. I clearly saw the dome light inside of the car as a piece of glass sliced down the side of my nose, and I distinctly remember my vision turning red as blood sloshed across my face.

Apparently, about this time, the woman driving the car reacted to the initial crash and she hit the brakes. I know this because the momentum of my body violently changed direction, and I felt a momentary tug against my left ankle as it snapped, apparently wedged between the doorpost and the base of the passenger window for some reason. The first time I hit the windshield I didn't penetrate all the way through. I recall watching an incredible amount of blood travel in a wave across the glass and actually thought how beautiful it looked as it cracked into thousands of light filled spider webs, and myriad prisms of red sunlight shone intensely through. An instant later, I hit the windshield a second time. This time the pain was overwhelming. My body seemed to explode, and a tremendous sense of acceleration overtook me. There were flying shards of glass, loud scraping sounds — almost prehistoric in nature — and intense cold as I exited the vehicle through the front windshield. The last conscious thing I recall was seeing the hood ornament speeding toward me. There was a second tremendous explosion, then absolute and complete silence. . . .

There was no sense of feeling, no sensation, no smell — or any sense that there should be. No pain, no sound . . . nothing. And yet there was a vague sense that I had existence. There was nothing above me or below me or around me — just darkness.

From above and to the right, if there had been such a thing as the right, there began a tiny distant point of light. It was as tiny as the sharpest point of a needle. Even as small and distant as it was, its intensity was unequaled by anything I had previously experienced. Gradually, the tiny point expanded and seemed to travel directly toward me. As it grew in size and proximity, I began to experience what would be akin to senses, yet they were deliciously different than those we experience in life.

The first was an overall sense of calm and security. I was absolutely unafraid or concerned about anything. The second was a unique sense of warmth. It was like being in a warm bath, slightly warmer than body temperature but not hot. I was completely suspended in this warmth; there was no sense of floating and there was no sense of relationship between the warmth and anything else, that is, no sense of the warmth being contained as in a pool. There was no up or down.

The third sense was similar to sound. It was like music, yet there wasn't any particular tune. It was more like the sound of snow flakes falling; you know that soft tinkling sound that you really can't quite hear but that sounds like little ice crystals striking each other in the breeze. Or perhaps it was more like the sound of the grass on the prairie, when the wind coaxes each blade to move, and the rippling waves produce a sound made up of a million vibrating stalks — like faint, almost imperceptible, but countless voices, each sustaining a single note, which lends a part to a kind of hymnal chord that is not musical in any ordinary sense, but resembles the harmony that you feel you hear just above or behind the sounds of a babbling brook, deep in a silent forest, as the sparkling water navigates its way through tiny waterfalls and swirling pools. Yes, it was like that, only even a hundred times quieter. And, of course, with no other sound in existence, as quiet as it was, it was significant — haunting — overwhelmingly beautiful.

The warmth began to move. Imperceptibly at first and then with definite motion, it began to rotate clockwise. The bright light — which was dazzling white — began to envelope me. There was a sense that it was made up of wisps of light rather than a single beam. They seemed to swirl around me as if I were inside a funnel upside down. As the warmth continued to turn extremely slowly, my body seemed to be drawn into the tunnel of light. Looking back, it is very hard to say if I was moving up into the light, or it was moving down to surround me. While this point may not seem significant, there was a sense on the edge of my perception of this experience that told me the difference was incredibly important.

The light completely surrounded me, and though I could not see behind me, I knew that there was no longer darkness there, but rather the infinitely long tunnel of the same wispy light that extended before me, continuing on. While I can't exactly remember seeing it, the light began to take on a different characteristic. It began to incorporate color — many different colors. A soft flash here, then there — never remaining long enough to actually perceive it. Kind of like a strobe whose flash is quick, but only repeats itself occasionally — there and gone before you can register it.

Next there was a sound — something faint and off in the distance — ahead in the tunnel. Sort of like the sound of the sea. At the same time there was a scent: musty, earthy like fallen leaves after an autumn rain. Pleasant, calming, reassuring, comforting, agelessly ancient — and familiar.

The center of the tunnel dissipated, or became more diffused, mist like. . . . and a hand and arm extended toward me out of the mist, waif like. They were translucent, shimmering — like the foam on the sea on a moonless night, like the radiance of the inside of an abalone shell when it is still damp with saltwater and lit by the light of the first crescent of the moon on a misty shore, like the very first moment of light you see when silver is heated by a torch and it begins to roll as the metal becomes liquid. When you pull the torch away, there is a soft light radiating from the surface of the molten metal which is silvery and pinkish and similar to the surface of a pearl. The hand and arm were illuminated much like that.

I reached out with my hand, prompted by an unspoken gesture. The act seemed natural, absolutely right. It was with the warmth and untrained absolute naturalness of a baby drawing to its mother's breast, and the mother responding in kind without knowing what is expected of her. As my hand joined the one extended to me. . . . I experienced connection. The gentle grip was yielding and welcoming like a handshake with a dear but long lost friend. It is difficult to describe the sensation, but it was as if in connecting with the outstretched hand, there was no sense of trade-off. No feeling as though by grasping it, I was something less or that I had to give up something or that the extended hand was something more. It felt neither powerful nor intrusive, neither warm nor cold, strong nor weak, but rather — exactly right. It became an extension of me or me of it, equal, complete — as in the act of scribing a circle. You know what I mean — when the line you start with finally connects with itself and you know the figure is complete. Anything less would appear unfinished, undone, but when the line reconnects with itself, it becomes the beginning and the end, and each and every point in

4

between. As the illustrator, you know at that moment that the figure is finished, and you move on to the next task without another thought. That acknowledgment of completion was what I experienced when I accepted the outstretched hand and was accepted in return.

There was a distinct change in the tunnel of light when I took hold of the waiting hand. The mist from which the hand had extended gradually disappeared, and the tunnel seemed to expand outward slowly. The farther away it got, the more rapidly it receded, until it was almost as though I was watching one of those films where they take a picture of clouds in the sky and then they speed it up. At the same time, directly around me all sense of movement stopped, and it was as if time stood absolutely still. Only a soft, misty gentle barrier remained surrounding the arm before me. It was shimmering and slightly domed like a very shallow bubble, both luminescent and fragile. At the same time, far out on the periphery as the mist retreated, it dissipated into tongues of wispy blackness until I was left floating, seemingly suspended in infinite blue black space – – connected only by the arm and hand which gently but firmly held me. There was no sense of fear of the blackness behind me; rather, the lack of anything below, intensified my sense of security and connection to the hand above.

The bubble began to break up. There are no words to describe the actual physical or spiritual sensation accompanying this transition. It could not be described in physical terms because it was unlike anything we can ever experience on earth or even conceive of. Probably the best analogy would be to imagine blowing a bubble with one of those little kits you can buy at the grocery store. As you continue to blow, the bubble eventually reaches a point where you know that any moment it's going to explode. Then, as the tension builds on the surface, hundreds of rainbows form, and it becomes more and more fragile until at the last possible moment, when the tension is at its very highest — it shatters into a million pieces, with each fragment carrying a small piece of the rainbow puzzle. That was what it was like when the barrier disappeared. Once

5

the explosion took place, the fragments traveled their zigzag paths in a million different directions with each diminishing in size like a melting meteor until they all ceased to be — leaving only the memory of their existence on the surface of my mind. The incredible thing about this experience was that I was aware of and experienced each and every individual fragment's life span, from the moment of the explosion, until each ceased to exist.

When the bubble shattered, there stood before me — a woman of indeterminate age. Her features were young, yet old, and there was the same translucent quality that I described in the hand. There was also a faint luminescence surrounding her, which was different than that of the tunnel. While there was nothing behind me it seemed that *everything* was behind her. Her features reminded me of a grandmother. Not the dilapidated form of an old woman near death, but rather the grandmother image brought to mind when we think of the aroma of cookies baking in a Victorian kitchen, or the one you run to as a small child. You know, the one that takes you into her arms and pulls you to her breast, hugging you until you feel like you are safely surrounded in a warm snugly nest smelling of laundry soap, coffee, bacon and eggs, and vanilla all rolled into one.

Her eyes were gray, or perhaps faded blue. It was hard to really put a finger on it. Perhaps they were both. Either way, there was a deep sense of understanding, of knowledge hidden below the surface of her glance. I'm not sure exactly how to describe it, but there was a feeling in my heart that she knew my every thought, my every joy, my every pain.

Perhaps the most striking and memorable of her features was her hair. It was incredibly long. I don't mean long by the standards that we usually use to measure long hair as in waist length or down to the floor, but rather it was so long that it was infinite. It twisted and tangled and seemed to be everywhere. It was gray in color, yet it seemed to contain all the colors of growth and life and all living and breathing things — including the rocks and the

6

earth and the sky. As my eye followed the spiraling mass of waves and curls beyond that space where she stood directly before me, her hair became everything that was. In this secret and hallowed place, her hair was the sky and the mountains and the very ground itself.

"Are you ready to come?" she asked.

I was confused. I couldn't understand what she was talking about.

She asked again. "Are you ready to come with me?"

I still didn't understand her question. I didn't even know who I was.

"Who are you?" I asked.

"I am God," she replied. And when she spoke, I knew absolutely for sure that what she had said was true. There was no question that she was God.

Instantly, all of my memories returned to me. I knew who I was and how I came to be before her. I also understood her question for the first time. She had asked me if I was ready to die!

My thoughts raced before me, and I relived all of my dreams for the future. I was only fifteen years old. I wanted to live, grow up, get married — and have a family. I wanted to experience sex. I wanted to move to a remote island — maybe somewhere in the south Pacific and build a home there with my own hands.

"I don't want to die now," I pleaded. "There are too many things I want to do now in my life. I'm not ready!"

There was a subtle but distinct change in her face. It was more the sort of thing that I felt rather than saw. She smiled at me. Not the beaming smile one lights up with when some wonderful event takes place in one's life, but rather just the corner of her mouth on one side curled up. I had the sense that perhaps there might have been tears forming in her eyes — but I did not actually see them. Rather, there was an aching feeling of sadness in my heart. I remember thinking that the whole moment was much like the time I told my first real girlfriend that I wanted to break up and she looked at me with a hurt look but did not cry. After she'd she walked away, I knew that she was sobbing

7

alone in some secluded hallway in the back of the school yard and I shared her pain.

"There will be pain," God said very softly — the same sense of sadness in her voice.

"I don't care," I said.

Just then she let go of my hand — and I began to fall down the tunnel, which seemed to be straight up and down now with me falling toward some distant point I could not see. I fell faster and faster, reaching incredible speed. The tunnel was black now with no definition to the walls or sides. While there was nothing to be seen, there did seem to be a definite path that I followed as I fell. It was like being in the middle of a force field that went on and on and on. As I fell, I could feel the walls moving in closer and closer until they felt so close that it was as though I was being suffocated. I fell face first with my arms and legs extended, and, as I neared what I perceived to be the bottom, I could feel the air compacting against my body until I felt I was going to be crushed by the velocity. All of the sudden there was light ahead . . . . . There was ground ahead . . . . . "I'm going to hit!" I screamed to no one. There was impact . . . . . Everything exploded! And then someone spoke.

"We've got him back," a man's voice said.

I heard many people talking all at once. I opened my eyes and saw two men bending over me. There were red and yellow flashing lights and many people I did not know crowded around me. Within an instant, I was in excruciating pain.

"I've changed my mind," I called out, deciding that I *did* want to die. "Please God, please let me die!" But God did not respond. She had left me now and I was alone in my pain. I could not speak out loud to the paramedics because I had a large chunk of concrete jammed in my mouth, which I later learned had broken off the curb when I hit it. A few minutes after I came to, a second emergency vehicle pulled up and a technician got out and used some kind of miniature jack hammer to break the concrete out of my mouth. I choked and gagged as the dust from the concrete

8

went down my throat. I tried to reach up to stop them, but they held my arms, and I suffered instead. As soon as the man was successful in getting the concrete out of my mouth, even though I was gagging and in terrible pain, I felt compelled to tell him: "I've seen God," I said. "I saw God!"

"I'm sure you did," he answered, throwing an odd glance at the paramedic that had revived me.

"God was a woman," I told him.

"Don't worry son, your going to be okay," was all he had to say.

"We've been working on him for quite a while," the first paramedic told the second man.

"He's a lucky guy," the technician responded and then some other men came over and moved me onto a board of some kind and strapped me on. Next they picked me up and loaded me into an ambulance with people crowding all around. "I saw God," I cried one last time, and then there was only blackness as I passed out from the pain.

❧⊰⊱☙

I have no recollection of what took place over the next three days. Finally, when I woke up, both my parents were there. They told me what had happened to me, and when they were done I told them that I had seen God. I did not tell them that God was a woman because I was worried they wouldn't believe me. Next the doctor came in. He told me I was lucky to be alive. He told me that my legs were broken in several places and so were both wrists. In addition, my eye had also been partially pushed out, but they were able to fix that while I was still unconscious. My skull had been fractured and a long laceration on my head created by the offending blow required quite a few stitches to seal the wound. My jaw had also been dislocated and several ribs had been cracked. He told me that the paramedics had performed C.P.R., but they had had quite a difficult time reviving me.

9

I told the doctor that I had seen God, and he said he believed me. He told me that it was a real miracle that I had survived.

I stayed in the hospital for quite a while and spent a lot of time thinking about what had happened to me. As I lay in my hospital bed, I reviewed my near death experience and tried to reconcile it with my religious beliefs. Nothing seemed to fit. I had always been told that God was a man, and that a person could not be admitted into heaven without being saved, yet it was obvious to me that this was not the case. The reality of my experience challenged everything I believed, and my mind was in turmoil trying to sort out the truth.

After I got out of the hospital, I went to church and discussed what had happened with the minister there. When I told him that God was a woman, he responded by telling me that God was not and had never been a woman. I argued with him and told him that I knew for sure that she was. He told me that no one could see God and that it was evil to entertain even the possibility. He told me I was being tempted by Satan and that I needed to pray for forgiveness. I went home that night and got down on my knees and prayed to Jesus, asking for him to clear up my confusion or to show me that he was real and that what I had seen wasn't real. There was no response.

I spent the remainder of the year trying to resolve this disturbing conflict. Throughout that time, I approached several members of the clergy and presented them with my story. My girlfriend's Catholic priest listened to my account with some interest, but denied the possibility that God could be a woman. He told me that many people had seen visions of the Virgin Mary, but none of the visions had ever claimed to be God. He rationalized my experience by telling me that I was young and that it was common for young people to have overactive imaginations. I asked him if he had ever actually seen God. He said that he had not.

Next, I talked with a rabbi at the synagogue where my best friend attended services. Surprisingly, he told me that in the early history of their religion, there were people who worshiped a female Goddess, but that she wasn't really God. I asked him if he'd ever seen God and he told me that he hadn't, but that he'd read the Torah and that he knew through the words of the prophets who *had* seen God and who had been personally spoken to by him, that God was a man.

The more members of clergy I spoke to, the more I came to the realization that very few people, if any, especially within the clergy, had actually seen God, and that it really seemed to bother them that someone else might have done so. This surprised me as I had always just assumed that all members of the clergy were people that were personally called by God. It seemed from my conversations that the general consensus was that God was not directly available to people in the sense that he did not manifest himself before them, except in ancient times. Rather, he was reachable only through prayer, and he would respond to you only if you were worthy, according to various religious doctrines that often conflicted with one another. Very few of the clergy members I spoke to seemed to be in agreement as to what was necessary to be worthy of God's presence.

For me, having actually seen God, and having heard her speak, much of what these clergy had to say appeared incorrect. Finding few answers, I decided to review my experience and try to determine what, if anything, I could conclude or learn about God from my own experience — considering that she did not reveal or command anything of me. Here are some of the conclusions I reached. These are not necessarily revelations from God, but rather just observations gleaned from my intimate personal experience of her.

1) There is God. I saw Her!

2) You do not have to be particularly worthy or follow some specific doctrine to go to her. I wasn't and didn't.

3) There is somewhere that you go after you die. Life here on earth is not the end of our existence. And God takes you there.

4) At least some people have a choice whether they are ready to leave this world and go with God.

5) She is compassionate and loving, not someone to be feared, not someone who is demanding.

6) Dying is not a terrible or frightful experience. Instead, it is calm and peaceful, and you feel like you are going home. Everything seems just right — and it is.

✌︎ଔଷ୭ஒ

I was very troubled as to why I had the experience I did during the accident, and I was particularly confused as to why God appeared to me as a woman. I was perfectly happy as a Methodist, and I surely wasn't seeking any religious revelations. I couldn't seem to find anyone around me that had any answers, and I appeared to be all alone in my experience.

The following year, just before Easter was coming up, I had been talking with the minister of my church, hoping for guidance. He suggested that what I really needed to do was to pray to Jesus for help. Even though I'd already tried that, I decided to try again and I came up with great idea. I'd often heard about sunrise services for Easter where a minister takes his congregation out to a natural setting and holds a spiritual service when the sun first rises in the morning. I didn't want to be in a big crowd of people, so I decided I would go up on a hill close to my home and have a sunrise service of my own.

I got up early on Easter morning, about four o'clock or so, and began the steep climb to the summit of a low series of foothills that overlooked my town, Granada Hills, near Los Angeles. The air was cool and crisp, and I could smell the dampness on the leaves, as they gave off that peculiar odor we all associate with an early wilderness morning. As I made my way up the steep trail that led to the summit, the unusually clear sky was blazing with stars and there was just the tiniest hint of the coming dawn, caressing the horizon to the east. About halfway up the slope, the trail veered to the right in order to circumvent a large white rock that protruded from the hillside. I worked my way around the obstruction, feeling that inherent chill one finds within

12

natural stone when you take hold of it to gain stability. The trail became steeper now, and I had to grab onto a thick branch wedged between a couple of stones in order to pull myself up to the next level. Just before reaching the top, I slipped on a patch of silvery moss and nearly went off the edge, bringing a rush of adrenaline when I finally reached the summit.

As I came out over the top, I dropped to my knees and prayed and asked God to give me guidance in the quandary I found myself in. I asked him to resolve my conflict and for him to show me the right way. I asked that he clarify my experience and help me understand what it all meant. Then I got up and walked over to a mound of earth that was several feet higher than the surrounding area, and laid back against it, resting my head in the soft wild grasses growing there. I turned my attention to the enormous sky, tracing the patterns of stars suspended there in the blackness, waiting in anticipation for the dawn.

Sometime before sunrise, I fell asleep lying on the mountaintop. While I was sleeping, I had an amazing life-like vision. It began with me standing in a dusty field on the outskirts of some primitive village. The houses were built of mud and the weather was dreadfully humid and hot. There was a small crowd of people in the field closer to the edge of the community, and there was a robed woman there addressing them. I began to walk toward where they were, but my feet were bare, and there were lots of rocks and stickers on the ground. I wasn't used to walking bare-footed and the cutting thorns made my progress very slow. The woman was facing away from me, and I couldn't hear exactly what it was she was saying, yet I felt drawn to her conversation even so. The people who stood all around her moved in closer and knowingly nodded their heads as she spoke. But, as hard as I tried, I couldn't reach her, so I still couldn't hear what it was that she said.

When I finally did reach the outer edge of the crowd, the people as a group began walking away from me. At this point the mysterious woman was leading them back toward the town in the distance, and the small congregation hovered close to her as they moved away from me across the field. I wasn't sure exactly what to do because my feet were really getting cut up without any shoes, so I just stopped where I was and gave up in despair.

Once I gave in, the vision faded away and clarity became just a fog. When the vision cleared up again, I was in a different place, and it seemed to me to be a different time. I stood among the buildings of a city, whose facades were constructed of carved stone. Perhaps it was ancient Greece or the early beginnings of Rome. In any case, the civilization was far more advanced than before. Instead of mud huts and dusty fields, the buildings were intricate and crafted by skilled labor. The people there appeared much more organized, and the city was well kept and clean. Once again, there were people gathered around a robed woman that I could not clearly see. There were many more people involved this time, and they were tightly crowded around her as she spoke. I tried to work my way through the large crowd, but there were just too many people in the way. I could hear the sound of her voice off in the distance, but I still couldn't make out her words. When I finally got to the center of the group, the mysterious woman had already left, and the people who had gathered to listen, were breaking up and going home. There was something compelling about the woman, but I couldn't figure out what it was. All I really understood was that I had a tremendous desire to know her, but something was keeping me away. I considered trying to follow her, but it was too difficult, so I decided once again to give up, for I was tired and she had moved beyond my sight.

My vision faded again, and swirling mists once more prevailed. When the churning fog finally receded, I found myself in yet a third new place. I was wandering down a maze of twisting streets in what seemed to be a Medieval European city. It was very difficult to find my way through the narrow corridors, and I couldn't seem to find my way out. I walked and walked until I was nearly exhausted, and when it seemed I couldn't walk any farther, I came upon a quaint yet ample plaza — paved with foot worn stones.

14

There was a fountain sporting a statue, holding a chalice from which water flowed. And the courtyard was filled with people, their attention focused, as one, on a woman standing near the fountain, lit by the afternoon sun.

Once again she was robed, and I couldn't see her face or hear what she was saying. I tried desperately to reach her but when I got close; she started walking down a narrow passageway on the other side of the crowd. And try as I would — even pushing and shoving — I just couldn't make my way through all the people. Once again, I was ready to give up but this time I decided to press on. I pushed through the crowd and started down the passage, but she was nowhere to be seen. I continued on faster and I caught a glimpse of her turning a corner at one of the many intersections entering the narrow street. I could feel her slipping away, so I started to run. The streets became like a maze, and I had trouble trying to decide which way to turn. Every so often I would catch a glimpse of her, and I would know which way to go. Finally, when I thought I had no strength to go on, I called out to her, and she stopped. . . .

I felt my heart soar, and I got tears in my eyes at the thought of finally catching up with her. I was so overwhelmed with emotion and desire to be with her that just the thought that she might acknowledge me was almost more than I could bear. In that moment, that tiny instant in time just before she turned around to face me, I came face to face with my greatest fear. What if she rejected me? What if after all my effort — my all consuming desire to be with her — she just turned away and walked on. It was in this state of emotion and turmoil that I waited for her response. She turned to face me now, hooded — enveloped in her flowing robes. Her face was hidden, concealed by the cowl and the cape that surrounded her, as it tousled lightly in the breeze. Her garment was of a plain and coarse weave — perhaps wool or some other homespun material. Yet, with all its homeliness, there was a quality about it that made a substantial impression on me. For in all its coarseness and apparent weight, it shimmered like

15

sunlight on a calm sea, and as the wind blew gently through the corridor, even with its weightiness, the material took flight — like the finest silk.

"I've been chasing you forever," I blurted out, as the words literally poured from my heart. "I was so afraid that I'd never catch up to you and that I'd never get a chance to express how I feel," I went on — overcome by the feelings that had built up inside as I pursued her from place to place.

"And what feelings are those?" she asked in a soft yet vibrant voice.

I paused for a moment, unsure of myself, and I considered how much I really wanted to reveal to her. I felt very vulnerable and somewhat embarrassed at the idea of opening up my thoughts and heart to her.

"I love you, and I want you to always be with me," I cried out, succumbing to the emotions that had been building inside. The raw words echoed down the narrow corridors gradually losing their intensity as they sought their way out of the twisting labyrinth, finally ending their short life in an uncomfortable moment of silence as I awaited her reply.

"It was right of you to pursue me," she returned gently, her voice still soft, yet powerful and clear. "It is also fitting that you should love me," she continued, and in doing so, she took a step forward toward me.

"But how shall I show my love for you?" I asked, confused by her answer and not knowing how to respond.

She stood up very straight, and everything around us seemed to freeze in time. She reached up with both hands and gracefully pulled back the hood of her robe releasing long gray hair that shimmered with its own light. She looked directly at me with a glance that was so filled with love and compassion that it pierced to the very center of my being. I recognized those same blue gray eyes that I had first seen in the tunnel of light, and I realized that it was the *Lady* who stood before me.

She smiled at me, and all my fears were immediately dispelled, and I found myself filled to the point of bursting with her spirit.

16

"You can serve me," she replied.

And with those words the vision faded, and I found myself lying back in the deep soft grass on the top of the hill where I had gone to hold my Easter service. My clothes were slightly damp from the tiny droplets of morning dew that had formed on the grass, and I could smell the reassuring scent of damp earth as the sun reawakened the waiting world.

I looked around. The sun was just breaking the horizon and everything looked crisp and clean. And I knew in that moment that I would dedicate my life to her. As I got up from the ground I wondered how this turn of events would affect me and my future — although at that particular moment it didn't really seem to matter any more. I had been touched and my heart was filled with wonder. I walked back down the path I had taken to reach the mountain top, and I noticed all the little markers I had referenced on my way up. There was the white rock, where the trail veered to the right, the broken branch, wedged between two stones, even the patch of moss that I had slipped on working my way to the top. Yet, the path I now walked was deliciously different. For it was illuminated by the light of a new dawn, and the shadows that had existed when I made my way in the darkness had now dissipated, leaving the way clear to see.

As I continued on my way back to the road, I was filled with a new confidence, for I could see all the obstacles that stood in my way on the path, and I knew that from that day on the Lady would walk with me. I also knew that I had nothing to fear, for in the end, I now knew, she would be there waiting for me at the end of that tunnel — and the thought of her being there and greeting me with her outstretched hand gave me a new perspective on the world. I walked on to my car, considering the possibilities for the future and opened the door knowing full well that nothing in my life would ever be the same again.

CHAPTER 2

Witches

Several weeks after my vision of the Lady at Easter, I was driving down the highway in Granada Hills when I saw a man hitchhiking on the side of the road. I pulled over and stopped to pick him up. He was tall and slender and about twenty years old with slightly curly brown hair and green eyes. He had an infectious smile, and I liked him right from the start. When I resumed my trip, we struck up a conversation together and eventually our discussion turned to religion. I told him about my near death experience, and he listened intently as I revealed what I had seen.

"I'm not surprised at all that you saw the Goddess," he responded, attributing an unfamiliar word to the woman in my vision. "In fact," he continued, "I believe in her, too."

Up 'til that time, I had not considered her as a "Goddess," but rather thought of her as God, who for whatever reason, chose to appear to me as a woman. Actually, by this point in time, I had stopped referring to her as God altogether and instead spoke of her quite simply and fondly as *"The Lady."*

My passenger went on to tell me that he belonged to an ancient religion that worshiped both a Goddess and a God and that, in fact, he was a Witch. At first I considered that he was pulling my leg, but as he went on, I realized that he was serious. I confronted him regarding traditional images of Witches found in religion and popular lore, and asked him in an accusatory tone how he could belong to a religion that revolved around the worship of evil. He informed me that while some of the images portraying Witches were accurate though misrepresented and that others were misunderstood, most were just propaganda created by the Christian church in Europe centuries ago to demonize his faith. He told me that Witches didn't worship evil at all. He went on to say that my description of the Lady was very close to the Witches' idea of the Divine. I was so intrigued by his explanation and by the other claims he made that, just before I dropped him off, I asked if I could learn more. It occurred to me, as he described the Goddess Witches worship, that she and the Lady I'd seen at the end of the tunnel might be one and the same, and if that were so, I wanted to learn all that I could about her. It also crossed my mind — considering that I was seeking a religion that saw God as a woman — that it was just too much of a coincidence that shortly after my whole experience of the Lady, I should just happen to pick up a hitchhiker who belonged to a religion that worshiped God as a woman. I really felt that my path was being directed by the Lady and that, perhaps through this connection, I might find a way that I could serve her.

"I'm pretty sure that everyone in the coven would be very interested in meeting you, and there is even a possibility that you could join us," the man responded seriously.

I felt a flash of excitement pulse through my body at his suggestion.

And just at that moment, a poem by Robert Frost raced through my head. It was the one about a path not taken, where a man is presented with a fork in the road and has to choose which path he'll take — the one normally traveled, or the more mysterious one, which is unknown. After he's made his decision, which was to take the road less traveled, he is pleased with himself. He realizes that by limiting the paths we travel to those most taken, we also limit our experience of the world and our knowledge of life. Before my experience of the Lady, I *never* would have thought of asking my passenger to consider me for his group, but I decided in that moment, prompted by some unexpected intuition, to choose as Robert Frost did — the road less traveled. Once my decision was made, I moved quickly to seize the moment — because somehow I knew deep in my heart, that *this* was one journey that I definitely did not want to miss.

19

"I really am interested," I responded in an excited voice, hopeful that he wouldn't leave before I could convince him of my sincerity. "Please, consider me."

"Why don't you give me your phone number," he returned, in a friendly, yet somewhat reserved tone. "I'll talk with the others in my coven and see if they might at least consider a meeting with you. But you need to understand that ours is a very secret tradition and that, unless everyone in our group agrees that they're willing to meet with you, nothing else is going to happen. But I will tell you that I'm pretty sure they'll at least discuss it, and I think that they'll be just as interested in learning about your experience as you are in learning about us.

I pulled the car over to a concrete curb in front of a gas station where my passenger indicated he wanted to be dropped off. As he opened the door to exit, I reiterated one more time my interest in meeting with the Witches and wrote my number down and handed it to him. He told me that if they did agree to see me, and the meeting went well, it was likely that I'd be invited to join their coven.

As he got out of my car he turned to me and said:

"If you don't hear from me within three days, then you should just forget that you've ever spoken with me." And with that he turned around and walked away from my car, heading toward a housing tract to the west. When he finally disappeared around a corner several blocks away, I put the car in gear, took a deep breath, and drove away — filled with a million questions.

I was on pins and needles for two days after meeting the man on the road. By the morning of the third day, when I still hadn't received a call from him, I became worried that I might never hear from him again. It seemed that each time I had turned to someone for answers; they had failed me in the end. When I asked for help from the clergy, instead of really looking at my experience and trying to help me sort it out, they just automatically recited scripture or avoided the issue all together. Some even indicated that mine were the sort of questions that were blasphemous to even ask. I was fearful now that these Witches — or whoever they were —

might also leave me hanging, while at the same time it was becoming increasingly important to me to take the next step — whatever that was — in the service of the Lady.

On the evening of the third day, just after dark, the phone finally rang. It was the man I'd met on the road, and I was so relieved that he was getting back with me that I could hardly wait to hear his response. He told me that he'd spoken with the other members of his coven, and that they were very interested in meeting me. He asked if I could be available to see them on the following Friday night, which was only two days away. I was so elated that his coven had come to a decision that I could hardly contain my enthusiasm. My heart was literally pounding so fast that I felt like I was on a roller coaster just starting down the first giant drop. If you've ever been on a roller coaster, you know exactly what I mean. There's that point when you just top the first big hill and see the drop in front of you. Your body tells you you should be frightened, but at the same you want to go on. Then once the coaster starts down the hill, it's out of your hands — and one way or the other you take the ride. On the way down, whether you choose to laugh or scream, your heart beats out of control. And for those few moments, you aren't exactly sure if the decision you made to take the ride was a good idea or a mistake. Yet at this point, it doesn't really matter, for the ride has already started and you won't know the outcome until you get to the very end. That was exactly how I felt when I received the call. I already knew that I was going to commit to the ride, but I just wasn't sure where it would lead. On the one hand I was filled with fear, and on the other, exhilaration, excitement and an intense desire to know. So I went ahead and took the first step — I told him I would come. As excited as I was, I tried my hardest to contain myself and keep my voice level and calm. I didn't want to scare this guy away or seem unworthy of the coven's attention. I made a great effort to sound as if the invitation was just an everyday occurrence — but I'm sure he knew the truth.

He suggested that we meet at Stony Point, which was a giant outcropping of rock located in the northwest corner of the San Fernando Valley, near the intersection of Topanga Canyon Boulevard and the old Santa Susanna pass in the city of Chatsworth. He went on to tell me that the best time for us to meet was just before dark, because by that time most of the people in the area would have gone home, and we would have more privacy. I immediately agreed to meet them there and as we hung up the phone, I felt a growing level of pleasurable anticipation fill my heart. I knew that this meeting, this rendezvous with destiny, no matter what the outcome, would be a meeting I would never forget. . . .

I couldn't help but wonder what the people I was about to meet would be like. Would they wear black robes and pointed hats like I'd seen in movies? Would there be ugly old women with warts on their noses like the Witches portrayed at Halloween? Would there be both women and men involved? It hadn't occurred to me until just then, but I realized that the first Witch I met was a man. I had always thought that Witches were all women. I wondered if they did spells — could they really fly? Would I learn to fly too?

My mind was boggled with so many questions. How did all this fit with the Lady? Was she the Goddess the man spoke about? Hopefully, I would find out the answers to all my questions soon. I went to bed that night, filled with wonder. Everything seemed almost dreamlike and surreal, when I considered the period of my life since I'd been touched by the Lady. There was even a point just before I fell asleep where the thought crossed my mind that I had actually died in my motorcycle accident rather than survived it, and that all of this, the visions and meeting the man on the road, were some kind of weird dream world like you'd see on the Twilight Zone.

For the next two days I was extremely nervous. I was both frightened and excited about the upcoming meeting. Up until the time I met the man on the highway, one of the main things I had heard about Witches was that they ate babies and did evil things. But looking back in contrast as

I was growing up, there were also underlying themes in literature and fairy tales that gave me a sense that Witches were sometimes good. In fact, even today most any child, if you ask them, will tell you Magic itself is something very special. In any case, after my conversation with the hitchhiker, it was clear to me that he just didn't fit the negative image. All of these contradictions left me somewhat confused, and I didn't know exactly what to expect at our upcoming rendezvous. My hope was that the people I was about to meet were just what my strange passenger professed them to be — but I wasn't absolutely sure. All sorts of conflicting pictures played through my mind. And it wasn't until the afternoon of the day of the meeting that reality actually hit me: I was going out to meet a coven of Witches, in a very remote place by myself — *in the dark!*

As I prepared to leave for the coven meeting, I paused for a moment on my way out the door and reviewed the reality of my situation. I was feeling a little uneasy at the time, so I turned around and made my way back into the kitchen. I opened the drawer next to the stove, looking around to see if my parents were watching, and retrieved my mother's favorite butcher knife out of the drawer. I hid the weapon carefully in the sleeve of my jacket and walked out to my car, trying to look as casual as possible. I put on a front as though I was going to the store or perhaps out on a date, but as I covered the distance between the front door and my Dodge, I was sure that my family, and every neighbor and person on the street knew what I was up to. I was especially conscious of the knife riding within the folds of my sleeve, and I was sure that everyone in the world could see the outline of the huge blade under my jacket and were running quickly to their phones to call my parents or the police. When I reached my station wagon, I slid the knife carefully out of its hiding place and transferred it gently under the driver's seat for protection — just in case. The closer it came to time for me to leave, the more nervous and frightened I became, and finally, resigned to the fact that I had already made my decision, I took a deep breath, started my car, and headed down the long road that would lead me up into the foothills and the destiny that awaited me.

❧☙ℭℜ℞❧☙

I drove to the appointed meeting place and followed a narrow unmarked dirt road into small grove of abandoned orange trees — just to the south of the rock tower. Giant boulders of sedimentary origin, fifty feet in diameter, had long ago fallen off the towering stony point, creating a series of watchful guardians that formed a rough circle around the natural megalith. Beyond those, rose a four hundred foot rock outcropping with vertical faces — filled with caves and wind carved sculptures, looming ominously amid the advancing shadows, which were instantaneously born of the battle between the retreating sun and the surrounding moonscape. I rolled down the window and took in a deep breath of the cool dry air and waited anxiously to be contacted by my former passenger.

A short while after I arrived, just as it was getting dark, the man I'd met on the highway worked his way out of the rocks following a powdery footpath up to the car. He nodded his head in acknowledgment and motioned for me to roll my window down.

"Hello," he said in a friendly voice.

"Hi," I answered, nervously, making no effort to leave the security of my Dodge. My voice was wavering, and I was pretty sure that he could tell that I was scared.

"There's nothing to be afraid of," he said in a soothing tone. "Just relax and everything will go just fine."

I took a deep breath and let it out slowly, laboring to take his advice.

"There's absolutely nothing to be concerned about," he went on. "I know this seems like a weird place to meet, but there's a good reason for that. None of the coven members want you to know where they live until they meet you and make sure that you're someone we can trust. It also works for you too. If things don't pan out, they won't know where you live either."

I was somewhat relieved by his explanation and felt more at ease as soon as he spoke. There was so much tension that had built up inside me by this point in time that my muscles had been in the fight-flight mode since early that morning. As he continued his explanation, I noted a unique calmness in his voice, and I could feel the tension leave my body in waves as his clarification reduced my concerns. I also noted a certain confidence in his manner that I hadn't noticed during our previous conversation several days ago. There was something very unique about this man, especially within this particular setting, with its giant rocks, orange trees and oaks, and even the small sounds of animals scurrying in the surrounding brush — that caused me to reassess my perception of him. It took me a moment to determine what was different about him, and then it came to me. *He fit perfectly here.* There was a certain sense of ease about him in this natural setting that you seldom see in most people in the wilderness. He seemed acutely aware of everything around him, while at the same time being completely comfortable being surrounded by nature. He suggested I get out of the car, and I complied, leaving the security of the butcher knife tucked discreetly under the seat as we began to move away from the car and on into the rocky fortress. It may have been my imagination, because there were so many things going on in my head at the time, but I'm pretty sure that the crickets and other small insects didn't quiet down as we worked our way into the brush, like they would have if other intruders had invaded their realm.

As we walked along, the man finally introduced himself and told me his first name was Ron. Ron led me on through the rocky terrain at the base of the point and started up an overgrown path that led to the backside of the sandstone promontory. We worked our way up a steep slide covered with underbrush and began to literally climb up the northern face of the monument. The stone was cold, gritty, and filled with hundreds of finger sized holes, probably the remains of some prehistoric sea life that had long ago abandoned the rock. We followed narrow ledges, clinging to the coarse surface and gradually worked our way up through a series of interconnected chimneys and small caves carved millennia ago by the action of the sea on the then submerged sandstone.

Eventually, we came to a large cavern, probably twenty-five feet in diameter and about 100 feet above the ground with concave walls and a low blackened ceiling. As we entered the tunnel, seven other people became gradually visible, huddling around a small flickering fire — awaiting our arrival. Ghostlike patterns conjured by serpentine flames, which eventually revealed the faces of three women and four men occupying the inner depths of the chamber, danced upon the cavern walls. As Ron ushered me into the center of the room and began to introduce me to the members of the coven, the man directly opposite me, on the other side of the fire, threw several small delicately leafed branches into the flames. Immediately, the chamber lit up with the addition of new fuel, and I could now clearly see all of the people in the room. Ron made introductions, telling me a little about each member beginning with the woman on my immediate left.

"Patrick, this is Stephanie. She is our High Priestess, and she's also in charge of our coven." Stephanie, who was probably in her late twenties, leaned forward and offered me her hand. Her grip was firm, but gentle. She had very long chestnut hair that fell almost to her knees, and when she leaned forward to greet me, it tumbled off of her lap where it was originally tucked and spilled out on to the cavern floor, forming shimmering waves as it reflected the nearby firelight. She wore leather sandals and a simple heavy long cotton dress, which was somewhat coarsely woven, topped with a macramé bodice.

"Hello, Patrick," she said, in a soft British accent. Her greeting felt sincere, but somewhat reserved, and I could tell that she was trying to get a sense of who I was, without making me feel uncomfortable. She withdrew her hand after a moment, and Ron told me that she was originally from a place called Chelsea in England.

Next to her sat a lightly bearded man, somewhat older than the Priestess. Ron introduced me, telling me that his name was Jack and that he was the High Priest of the coven. Jack also took my hand, and nodded a greeting, but didn't say anything. He seemed much more reserved than Stephanie, but he was still cordial. Ron told me that Jack was also from Britain, and that Stephanie and Jack were a couple who'd originally met in England, and then later moved to Ireland with a friend named Michael who was their High Priest. I also learned, through the course of the evening's conversation, that while Jack and Stephanie had never married, they had lived together for many years. Ron also told me that around 1960, after living in Ireland for about three years, the two of them had moved to the U.S. and settled in the San Fernando Valley.

Next to Jack was Eldon. Eldon was about twenty years old and kind of quiet. He reminded me a little of a young Dean Martin, very handsome with dark features. Eldon greeted me with a smile, and acknowledged me with a shy nod from across the campfire, but did not attempt to shake my hand.

Next came Nicky. She was a seventeen year old girl with short sandy hair and the tiniest spattering of freckles around her nose. Nicky was almost the exact opposite of Eldon. She talked constantly during our initial introduction, and she was really quite friendly. I found her bubbling personality to be almost infectious, and I noticed she seemed to have a similar effect on the others in the cave once she began to speak. She was positioned almost directly across the fire from me next to Eldon who tended the fire, so we weren't able to actually shake hands, but she did stand up and acknowledge me as we were introduced, and I felt sure that she would have made physical contact, if it weren't for the other people and obstacles in her way.

To the right of Nicky, and back on my side of the fire, sat Karen. Karen was about eighteen and was Ron's fiancé. She had shoulder length dark hair, an olive complexion, and cat-like green eyes. She also was quite friendly, and I found her to be quite attractive. Karen and I spent several minutes in conversation, and we shook hands as we met.

Also on our side of the fire, sat James, a forty-something year old red haired man from Canada, and another guy who was also named Ron, but whom everyone addressed as R.J. He was about nineteen or twenty years old, with long brown hair tied in a pony tail.

Finally, sitting directly on my right, was the last member of the coven — Derek who was about my age. Derek was actually quite standoffish, and I wasn't sure at all that I liked him. He was quite slender, a little shorter than I was, with hair about the same color as mine — brownish blond. He greeted me with just a nod.

When the introductions were complete, the High Priestess directed me to sit next to her. Once I was settled, everyone started asking me questions all at once. It was actually a little overwhelming for me at first, but I felt I did a pretty good job of responding. They asked me where I was from and what kind of education I'd had. They asked about my family and our religion. But mostly they asked about my experience with the Lady. Often through the course of the questioning, they would ask me to go into more depth about such things as the color of her hair or what her voice was like. Eventually, I think they were convinced that I actually had seen their Goddess, and I sensed a gradual positive change in the way they spoke to me. Even so, the meeting turned out to be quite different than I had expected, and I was a little disappointed at the lack of mystical or magical quality to the experience. There were no black robes or smoke filled rooms and, while the conversation did give me a great deal of insight into their beliefs, deep down I had sort of hoped that something more special would happen. Mostly my feelings were a direct result of my own expectations rather than a lack of performance on their part.

When I was a child, my father used to read fairy tales to me nearly every night from a thick green collection of beautifully illustrated volumes called *My Book House.*

There were many stories about Witches, both good and bad ones. The one thing that they all had in common, however, was that most of them wore black pointed hats, heavy robes, or beautifully woven capes, and the majority of them could fly and perform all kinds of miracles, and they were constantly doing magic of some sort or other. The overall experience of the evening wasn't anything close to ordinary, in fact, it was anything but normal. After all, meeting Witches in a cave, high above the valley floor, in the dark of the night, was definitely not a daily occurrence. It's just that I had hoped they might do something magical, even though I didn't have a clear understanding of just what that was.

We continued to talk and stayed around the fire for a couple hours more with the conversation moving back and forth between us — mostly talking about our lives. But woven into what seemed to be ordinary conversation, I later realized, were my very first lessons. I learned that Witches practice a nature oriented spirituality that honors the Mother of all creation, and sees nature as a divinely inspired guidebook for our instruction, which lays the foundations for Witches' ethics and spirituality. Furthermore, they eluded that there are secrets revealed in the forest that unlock the mysteries of the universe and that the discovery of these, coupled with Witches' connection with the Goddess as a touchstone, place us on a path that leads to understanding our spiritual and mundane duties as human beings. Eventually, Jack suggested that we'd talked long enough, and he brought the meeting to an abrupt end. He instructed Ron to see me back to my car and told me that they would be in touch with me shortly. As Ron and I descended the cliffs and walked back to my car together, he told me he could tell that everyone liked me and that I would probably hear from them all soon.

I drove home feeling very happy and excited. While the meeting in the cave lacked that particular mystical quality I had been hoping for, I could feel that that mystery existed below the surface of our conversations. It was apparent to me that the coven members were being intentionally reserved, especially in the early portions of the meeting. I did notice, however, that once they got to know me, they opened up considerably more concerning mystical and magical topics. I could tell from comments made by Jack and Stephanie that ours was not a typical coven meeting. Underlying the entire conversation, there was a certain implied assurance that if I were accepted into the group, there would be magically exciting experiences ahead.

Overall, I felt the meeting was a success. I liked most everyone I'd met, and I was pretty sure that after our lengthy discussions and the evening we'd spent together, the coven felt the same about me. It was as though I was on some unshakable course toward a mysterious destiny, and underlying it all was the surety that one way or the other, I would reach my destination. I was really hoping that they would ask me to join them, and even though they told me they were going to have to discuss it, I had a strong feeling that their conclusion was inevitable.

I was excited by what I'd learned during the discussions in the cave, and much of what the Witches told me fit right in with my own personal experience of the Lady. I think out of all the things that I learned that night, the one that most struck me was how absolutely different these Witches were than the image portrayed by my church. I was still unsure just exactly who these people would turn out to be in the end, but so far I was impressed by what I'd seen and heard. It seemed obvious to me that the accusation that Witches were evil, and that their intent was to cause harm, was totally unfounded. In fact, after spending an evening with them, and listening to numerous examples that showed guidelines they appeared to follow, I got the sense that they had a vision of what was right and what was wrong that was more concrete and made more sense than the views of most of the other people I knew at the time.

Several days after the meeting at Stony Point, I received a phone call from Ron.

"Everyone really likes you," he said. "We had a meeting, and they all agreed that they want you to join our coven."

I was elated to hear from him. Yet, somehow, I already knew in advance that they would ask me to join.

"That's great; this is incredible," I replied. "I really wanted to join your group, and I'm so happy about your decision. So what do we do now? What's the next step?"

"We'll have to get together for another meeting," he replied enthusiastically. "How does next weekend look for you?" I told him that that sounded just fine. We continued on with our conversation, discussing what would be the best time to meet and where we should get together. We finally agreed to meet at his house on the upcoming weekend at around four o'clock just before evening.

"We'll have a short meeting and an informal ritual to commemorate the occasion," he told me. "There'll also be time set aside for you to ask more questions and learn more about our beliefs. In any case, it'll be a great opportunity for you to get to know each of us a little better and to see first hand what it is that we do." We talked on for a few minutes more about the meeting at Stony Point and the people in the coven, and then we said our goodbyes.

I was even more excited about the upcoming meeting than the first one. The more I thought about it, the more I really felt that the Lady had directed me on this path, and I was anxious to see where it would lead me. It was hard for me to believe that I'd actually met real Witches, but it appeared that I had. I found myself fantasizing about what it would be like to be a Witch. I wondered if I could actually learn to do Magic, and just what Magic was. But there was still some small concern on my part. Although I must admit that that concern began to seem completely ridiculous — considering that there was absolutely nothing in their actions so far that might cause me to feel that way. Yet I still found it difficult to cast off all the prejudices I had

31

been taught by my Christian upbringing. I also had a hard time shaking the stereotypical vision presented throughout my childhood, through movies I'd seen and stories I'd been told, and some component of that indoctrination still lurked on the fringes of my imagination.

Even though I entertained these concerns to some small degree, my gut feeling was that these were good people. Unconsciously my mind returned to my earlier conversation with Stephanie in the cave where she answered my concerns regarding Witches supposedly worshiping Satan.

"Satan is actually a Christian or Hebrew deity," she said. "He isn't included in our pantheon — and never will be. Basically, Witches consider Satanists to be Christians or Jews that have chosen to worship evil and to go against the biblical vision of God. We do not worship evil, and we are not against the Christian or Hebrew God. In fact, we see most versions of the Divine as just being different manifestations of the Goddess. The only disagreement we have with most of the new religions, like Christianity, is the terrible violence its people have imposed on everyone through history who sees God in a different way than they do. As Witches, we believe in balance between all the diverse peoples of the world, and, in fact, we see the diversity of all life as being sacred. For us, most people's vision of the Creator is sacred, if that vision brings harmony and peace to the world, and the people who hold that vision show a desire to acknowledge that type of higher power."

I considered her words for a second time and found them to make sense. Now that I'd had time to really think about it, my degree of concern lessened considerably, and I found myself relaxing a little as my head worked its way gently into the soft folds of my pillow. I reached out for the knurled switch on the pole mounted floor lamp next to my bed, feeling the resistance as the tiny cylinder gave way with a click between my fingers. And as the image of the bright bulb with its little 100 watt label faded from my memory, I turned comfortably onto my side and surrendered myself to a world lit only by the light of my imagination.

CHAPTER 3

The Journey Begins

The morning of the second meeting, I got up just after dawn, and went out into my back yard. After a few moments of silence, during which I collected my thoughts, I looked up to the sky and made my very first prayer to the Goddess. It was still very early and dew drops nestled in all the nooks and crannies in the grass, waiting for the full force of the sun to swoop down and give them flight. I wasn't sure if there was any special way to address the Lady, so I just spoke my feelings as they came from my heart and hoped that she would hear me. I asked her to guide me and to keep me safe, and to help me make the right decisions about this Witch thing. And most of all, I reminded her that I wanted to serve her, and I prayed that she would keep me pointed in the right direction. A soft morning breeze awoke as I conversed with the Goddess and the leaves in the neighboring trees began to rustle in response to my heartfelt prayer. I took the soft gust as a sign that the Lady heard my request, and I felt secure and fulfilled, knowing that she was there with me.

It was a sunny spring afternoon when I left for the meeting at Ron's house that first week of May 1966. When I arrived at his home, which was near the area where I had dropped him off the first day I met him, everyone was already there to meet me. As I got out of the car, I felt a pang of anxiety, and I was also somewhat nervous, albeit not so much as for our first meeting. I really hoped that choosing this direction would lead me to a stronger connection with the Lady. But at this point, I still didn't know exactly what I was getting into.

As I started up the concrete walkway leading from the street, I saw Ron's home for the very first time. It was a large blue and white two story house, located in one of the new tracts recently built near Canoga Park. There were two small trees on either side of the walkway leading up to his porch, and an ornate oversized double door providing entry into the house. Upon my arrival, Ron directed me through the double doors — only one of which was open — and on through a slate floored entry way to a large slightly darkened room in the back portion of the house. All of the other coven members, who were originally standing in the front yard when I arrived, followed us closely behind. I could feel my heart beat increase as I made my way through to the back of the house. I wasn't really sure just exactly what was going to happen, and I remember repeating to myself quietly, "These are Witches, Pat — real Witches. I mean, *real Witches!*"

As I entered the room, I was met by an earthy smoky smell that emanated from a small charcoal burner which sat on a built-in bar to my left. The room was dimly lit by four candles that were placed in odd locations, considering the several accessible tables in the room. One was high on top of a bookshelf which was fastened to the wall directly facing me as I entered the room. Another was on the floor next to an overstuffed wing back chair with a piece of aluminum foil placed under it to keep the melting wax from dripping on the braided rug. The third candle sat on a small oriental style octagonal table, which had been placed in front of a hallway that appeared to lead back into the bedrooms near the Western side of the house. The last candle, which was larger than the other three, sat precariously on a footstool, which was to my left as I walked into the room. That candle also had a piece of aluminum foil underneath it. I remember wondering why the candles were in such odd locations and made a mental note to myself to ask when the time seemed appropriate.

In the middle of the room sat ten mismatched chairs — arranged in a tight small circle facing one another. Stephanie pointed to the chair closest to the larger candle and directed me to sit there. Everyone else sat down after me except Jack, who instead walked over to the bar. He picked up the smoldering dish sitting there and carried it back over to the circle of chairs and presented it carefully to Stephanie, who was seated next to me. She opened a small pouch she carried around her neck and emptied the contents into the burner. There was an immediate reaction, and a pungent, yet pleasant, cloud of smoke rose immediately to the ceiling like a mushroom cloud, and then made its way outward, following the contours of the acoustic ceiling until it gradually drifted gently back down to envelop us. The scent was sweet and intoxicating, not in the way one is intoxicated through the use of alcohol or drugs, but rather like listening to a symphony. It was earthy and pleasurable and uplifting and definitely nothing like any incense I'd ever smelled before.

As the soothing smoke settled around us, forming a fragrant fog, Stephanie said something quietly in a language that I couldn't understand. It seemed as though it were some kind of incantation, although I wasn't really sure. When she finished, everyone in the room responded in unison with a single word, *"Dukaat!"* Stephanie paused for a moment and there was silence throughout the room. Then she gently closed her eyes and took in a soft but deep breath. She held it for a moment, visibly allowing all tension to leave her body, and then she exhaled and rose eloquently from her chair and turned to stand before me. She seemed taller now than I remembered her, and there was a special stateliness to her manner.

"Welcome to our coven," she said, breaking into a heartwarming smile that made me truly feel welcome.

"Thank you," I replied, in a wavering voice that came out of nowhere. All of a sudden without any warning, I was filled with unchecked emotion. I don't know where it came from, but I actually had to control myself to keep back the tears forming in my eyes. I guess I wanted to join this group even more than I'd realized. I took a deep breath, gained my composure, and waited for whatever came next. After a few awkward moments of silence, the Priestess reached out and placed her left hand on my forehead gently. Then she blew ever so softly on the coal in the censor, which she still held in her right hand, and directed a puff of sweet scented smoke toward me, reminiscent of fragrant pine duff, summer rain, and fields of wildflowers

35

mixed with swaying grass. The movement was graceful, spellbinding, and very sensuous. For a brief moment our eyes met, and I was in awe of her — for I could see, looking into her eyes, that she too was filled with the spirit of the Lady.

"May the Mother of all things be with you," she said. "May the God of the forest keep safe your path, and may there always be a spring near your home." Her words fell upon me like a warm down quilt on a cold winter's night. I felt safe and welcome in this new circle of friends. As the echo of her words became lost in my mind amid a hundred growing questions, the other coveners responded to her blessing.

"*Dukaat,*" they said, once again in unison.

Stephanie then asked me to rise and face the large candle behind me. As I turned, I noticed for the first time, now that my eyes had adjusted to the flickering candlelight, that there were symbols carved into the glowing wax. I faced the candle as she instructed, and once again she spoke.

"You stand now in the east, the place of beginnings. Know now that each direction holds within its domain certain gifts for you. But none is so precious as the gift of light. For even *lazra meck* — the light of darkness — illuminates our spirit, and reveals doorways into the other realms. Turn now and face me, for the beginning is behind you and all else stands before you."

I turned as she requested, and she reached out with open hands beckoning me to join her. I accepted her grasp, and as I did so, each of the coveners walked forward and welcomed me into their fold. Afterward, we sat back down in our chairs and, one by one, each told me something about their religion.

I learned that the faith of the Witches was thousands of years old and that Witches had practiced Magic since the beginning of time. I also learned that they cast spells and held eight major rituals to honor the turning of the seasons and the cycles of nature. I already had a sense that these were things associated with being a Witch, and I was very happy to have my hopes verified.

"Over time, we'll take you out into the forest and teach you the way things work," Ron told me.

"We'll also teach you what we call the 'natural laws'," Karen chimed in, explaining that it was necessary to understand these laws in order to comprehend how and why Magic works.

"Of course you'll have to be initiated before you can attend any of the actual ceremonies," Jack explained. "We call the main ones 'holidays' because the term originates from the words "holy days," which is what they are. The thing most people don't know is that the word holy actually derives from the word holly, which is a plant sacred to the Goddess. The real meaning of a holiday is a day involving the use of the plant holly in ritual to honor the Goddess and to acknowledge her fertility in the creation of all of nature. Other religions also use the term holiday, but most are not aware of its origins. In fact, there are many things celebrated by other religions that came to them through variations of our faith long ago. We actually have a lot in common with them, although most of them prefer not to acknowledge that tie."

"What about the Goddess," I asked. What do we call her and how does she fit into our practice?"

Everyone slid their chairs forward moving closer.

"Well," Stephanie began, "she's been worshiped under many names over time, but the name our coven knows her as is Arida."

"She's been known by that name for thousands of years," Jack joined in, shifting his chair slightly. "Our coven teaches that long ago her name was somewhat different, and might have been spelled with a "y" in the middle and possibly an "n" on the end, something like *Arydana* or *Arydanan*, but that was so long ago. Today we just call her Arida and keep alive her other names in our stories and our rituals as has been done since the beginning."

"You'll find that the names of the Gods have changed many times from one civilization to the next," Ron joined in,

37

"but the stories always change slowly, so there's lots of time for us to carry on the old within the guise of the new."

"How do you know all this stuff," I asked. "Are there books on Witches or the Goddess that I can read?"

"There are a few books that are supposed to be on Witches," Jack answered seriously. "But there aren't any about our coven. Most of the books available are about sorcery and certain forms of ceremonial magic, which have very little in common with us," he went on. "The big difference between the people using that kind of magic and us is that they have very little respect for nature and they know almost nothing about the mysteries hidden there. Several of the books even teach that you can control everything around you by knowing certain sayings or the names of particular beings. That kind of magic is against all we stand for, and so we don't practice it. Our Magic is based on understanding the natural laws — and our friendship with nature. We don't command anything, we only ask that our needs be met. In any case, the history of our path is long, and the only way to really understand it is to walk it yourself. I would discourage you from reading any of that other stuff, especially in the beginning, because it's irrelevant to our coven, and it'll only confuse things as you go along. The *only* way to learn *real* Magic is to walk the path with another Witch, and that's what you'll do with us.

"Let me give you a piece of advice, which you probably won't understand for many years, but it will be the most important lesson you'll learn from any of us. *Nothing is as it seems.* For Magic, you see, is composed of multiple layers — those that are obvious and seen on the surface, and those that are only seen with the wisdom of time and study. Even beyond that, there are further layers to be discovered, if you're diligent and the time is right, but those layers are so deep and hidden from view that they require a lifetime of study and, even with that, many seekers may still not find them."

"I don't understand," I questioned, wanting to know more.

"Let me give you an example of what I mean so you'll understand what it is that I'm getting at. Imagine that you're a primitive human being thousands of years ago with no knowledge of the world. Then one day as you are out walking, you discover a big red apple growing on a tree. After careful study, you pick the apple and take a bite discovering that it's delicious. From the Witches' point of view, you now are at the first layer of Magic — discovery of that which is obvious: Apples grow on trees and they're delicious to eat. This level of understanding is much like the sort of thing you might learn from a book or perhaps from a casual conversation with someone who already understands the subject.

"But now consider that another thousand years in time have passed and some future farmer accidentally discovers that, if he fertilizes an apple tree, the apples are more delicious. This analogy is equivalent to the second layer, which is more hidden from view than the first. In this example, we learn that there are things about the apple that can only be discovered through time and study. In this particular case, we can observe that there is another relationship in the overall scheme of things, which was not apparent at first. It was there all along, but it was hidden slightly below the surface, and because it didn't stand out like the big red apple in the first example, no one knew to look for it, and it was missed by everyone entirely.

"Once we've discovered this new relationship, we realize that, in truth, the unseen relationship between the apple, the tree, and the earth is far more important, and the consequences of understanding that relationship are much more wide-reaching than our original discovery ever was. In this example, we learn that it is only because the earth provides the tree's nourishment, and because of the specific quality of that nourishment, that we are given the end result: Apples grow on trees and they are delicious to eat. This process goes on and on, one layer after another.

"An even further example on this same line of thought would be that, in modern times, we now know that there is also a connection between the earth and the universe, and that there are weather patterns and ultraviolet light and cells that interact with their environment. And atoms and electrons and a myriad of other connections and cycles are connected to the apple. So, we can see over a long passage of time, even a third level has been revealed. This whole process of discovery, and this entire method of understanding the world surrounding us, is in essence what Magic is really about.

"Perhaps now you can see why it would be difficult to learn all this from a book. For the most part, only the first layer can be presented in that manner, and while you *can* learn something from this, you will most likely miss what is unseen. Not because it isn't there, but because you don't know to look for it out in the world or in nature. This is why ours is an oral tradition with very little written down. We have learned that walking the path with others that have gone before allows us to discover those things that are not obvious, and that this process is central to the successful understanding of Magic.

"You will also learn over time all about the history of our coven. This is critically important because through the study of our history, you'll discover those things that are hidden within the rituals themselves, and it is precisely those hidden meanings that the rituals are really about. That is why everything in Magic must be presented in the right time and space and context. For it is only through this method that a true understanding can be developed. That's why it's difficult for books to convey this kind of knowledge and why you should wait to read anything about all of this, until you fully understand where it all comes from."

Ron joined in, changing the subject. "I can't wait 'til you meet Arida in the forest. I'll always remember my first time, and it's an experience that will stay with me for the rest of my life." Everyone turned their attention to Ron, who was smiling and obviously excited to share his story with me. "I was out in the creek down by a small waterfall just below a place where we often do our rituals," he went on. "It was early in the morning and there was just the slightest hint of mist down by the water. I was searching for some herbs to make incense for spring, when a wonderful earthy scent wafted in on the morning breeze. The scent was very similar to that of our sacred oil, which is a special oil that we make to use in our rituals. Anyway, the smell made sense to me afterwards, since our legends say Arida wears oil created from the same plants we use to make our oil, and that you can often smell it just before she appears. At first I thought it was just one of the other coven members somewhere up in the trees, and that the wind was just carrying the scent of their sacred oil down to me. But then I heard the sound of tiny bells, so faint that I had to stand perfectly still to hear them. The sound they made was beautiful, and it was because of this that I knew *She* was coming.

"You wouldn't know this yet, but one of the first things you learn about the Goddess is that in addition to wearing the sacred oil, the sound of tiny bells usually precedes her coming. She is also the protector of the animals and loves and watches over all of the forest.

"Anyway, getting back to my story, I heard this wonderful tinkling sound, which is not quite like anything else in the world — and then I saw her. . . . She was in the trees just ahead — right where the creek makes an "S" shaped bend by a large cottonwood tree. I'll show it to you one of these days when we go down there. Anyway, it was just a momentary thing. First she was there, and then she was gone. But the scent of the oil remained long after. I went to the place where she stood, but there were no footprints, and no sign that anyone had ever been there. There was only that wonderful smell left to mark her presence. I found this black stone," he said, as he lifted up a smooth flat stone that he wore around his neck on a leather cord and showed it to me, "right where she had been. I've worn it ever since — to remind me."

Ron reached around his neck, slipped the necklace over his head, and held it out toward me.

"Go ahead, hold it in your hand," he prompted, grinning from ear to ear. I grasped the stone in my right hand and

41

an immediate sense of comfort fell over me. It fit perfectly within my grasp. There was something in the way it curved slightly, the way my thumb fit into the slight impression on the top that was indescribable. Just holding the stone in that moment was very reassuring. I actually felt filled with the spirit of his encounter.

"It's just right, isn't it?" he asked.

"It is," I answered truthfully, and I knew right then that it wasn't just another stone.

I could feel prickles going up and down my back as he continued his story. In fact, I found the whole conversation riveting because I, too, had heard the sound he was describing. For a moment I was drawn back to that place in the tunnel of light, just before I met the Lady. I recalled the haunting tinkling sound that I experienced as snowflakes, like tiny fairie bells on the edge of the wind, and I remembered the sweet misty scent of earth and rain and herbs all rolled into one that accompanied that sound. And I knew at that moment, in his heartfelt description of his own experience, that he, too, had been touched by the Lady.

"I also found another stone that I made into an amulet to carry in my pocket," Ron said, continuing the conversation. "I found it about a month later in the same spot, but that one was almost perfectly white. It must have washed down the creek from somewhere else, because it wasn't there when I found the first one. I'll show it to you some time too, it's really magical also."

The room gradually became quiet, and we all sat silently for several minutes, staring into the flame of the large candle in the east. I don't know what the others were thinking about, but I was thinking how lucky I was just to be there. Just having this conversation, and experiencing the little ritual that was held to welcome me, had transformed this ordinary living room into a truly magical place. As I sat quietly with the others, staring at that flickering beacon, I sensed that there were a million other mysteries still awaiting me. And I thanked my lucky stars that I was still alive, and that I was being given the knowledge now to go forward and learn — so that I could experience those mysteries first hand and enjoy all that stood before me.

"But above all and most important by far, in that moment, I first grasped what Jack was trying to explain when he told me about discovering the unseen and how the knowledge of Magic unlocked the layers, and how one must walk the path with someone who had traveled it before in order to know what to look for. For in his little story, Ron had connected me to a part of myself that I would never have found if I hadn't been here in this room, with this group, at this moment. And I thank the Goddess; saw the Magic in all that.

After awhile, everyone gradually leaned back in their chairs, and a more relaxed atmosphere permeated the room. When the moment seemed appropriate, I put myself forward and asked the question I had been dying to bring up since I first met the coven.

"Just what exactly is Magic," I queried, excited at the prospect of actually getting an answer.

Stephanie, who seemed fixed upon some unseen place that we couldn't see, began to respond quietly.

"Magic," she explained, "is a name we use to describe a number of different experiences pertaining to our religion. Probably the most common meaning we refer to when we use the word is our acknowledgment of the unseen force behind the laws of nature. While the force itself is seldom seen, the laws, which are a result of it, are a combination of things we know to be. Understanding and making use of these laws is another facet of what we call Magic. Basically, the laws themselves have been discovered by Witches through thousands of years of observation, and those laws form the foundation of our beliefs.

"Let me give you an example of one such law so you'll understand what I'm talking about. *If you don't eat you will eventually die!* Now this sort of thing might sound obvious to you, but at some point in history, there was a time when people didn't know this. Early Witches observed this particular phenomena and gave food to those who were

43

dying from malnutrition, and guess what? They were cured. Taking that type of action, in this particular case giving food to someone who's starving, is a good example of what we call Magic. The laws are like that. They're simple; they're basic; and for some reason, the majority of human beings either fail to observe what's going on around them, and so do not discover most of them, or they fear exploring the unknown.

"Now don't get me wrong," she went on, "while some natural laws are easy to spot — like the one I just made an example of — most of them take a great deal of observation to even notice, much less understand. We believe that one must begin by understanding that the potential for everything that we as humans accomplish is already there before we start. And it's been our observation that the Gods want us to discover the mysteries they've created so that we can participate in the beauty and wonder of the dance of life. That is why the Witches' faith teaches that to ask questions is holy rather than a sacrilege.

"Unfortunately, the majority of people in our culture are quick to pride themselves on their own great accomplishments, such as the ability to build a rocket and put a person into space. Yet they're seldom ever prepared to acknowledge the natural laws that really made it all possible. Have you ever considered that the metal for the rocket, and the fuel, and even the principles of aerodynamics that make it fly, existed long before human beings even conceived of the process. For that matter, even space itself, and the gravity we have to overcome, were here with their hidden potential — long before we ever showed up. It is only through study of what the Goddess has provided for us within nature that we are able to make these great steps forward. Magic, if you will, is the understanding of that potential available to us, combined with our desire for and connection with the Divine. When we use Magic, we tap this Divine potential, and in the act of utilizing it, and asking the Gods' intervention in our desires, we offer the highest form of worship — which is acceptance of the potential offered to us by our Creators."

"Wow, I never thought of it that way," I interjected. "But you're right. Most of us don't see much of what's right in front of us. I guess I just never realized that we could be so non-observant."

"Do you have any idea how many people don't even know where east or west are?" Jack continued. "Even though the sun rises and sets every day right in front of them, they somehow miss it. Many natural laws are obvious to some, and lost on others, primarily because of the lack of study. Witches study things far less obvious than the rising and setting of the sun, of course. The world is full of potential, and it's right here in front of us, if we take the time to look. I could go on and on, but the point is this: Magic is the art of understanding how things work and then using that knowledge in our lives. To others, some of the things we do seem like miracles, but to us they are just every day things. Even so, as simple and obvious as they may be to us, we always try to remain in awe of them. Because, to be so is to acknowledge the wisdom and power of the Mother of us all."

"I have a question about that?" I interrupted. "Just now, you referred to the Mother of us all. Yet earlier in our talk you referred to 'the Gods.' I've also noticed that you sometimes say 'the Goddess' and occasionally you refer to 'the God.' Then every once in awhile you use the term 'God,' just like everyone else does. Are they all the same or what? It's a little confusing to me."

"That's a good question," Nicky jumped in smiling, happy to add to the conversation. "It's a little complicated to explain, but I'll give you the abbreviated version for now. Basically, we believe that the Goddess created everything that exists, and that she is our spiritual Mother. We also believe that she gave birth to the God. So, when we say 'the gods,' we are referring to the God and the Goddess together. When we speak of God, rather than *the* God, we're using it as it is understood commonly in our culture, meaning the Supreme Being in any of her many manifestations. But, ultimately, we're talking about the Goddess. Does that help clear it up for you?"

45

"Yeah," I said.

The conversation gradually returned to that of our connection with nature and just how that connection plays a part in our beliefs. Jack explained to me that our religious observances follow the wheel of the year, and that each of our sacred holidays corresponded with some aspect of nature and our relationship to it.

"You'll see, as we observe our holidays," Jack explained, "that each one builds on the one before it, and they all relate directly to what is going on at that time of the season."

"And once you have studied nature," Stephanie joined in, pulling her long hair over her left shoulder and twisting it into a spiraling curl as she spoke, "you will learn to live with it instead of against it. When you have accomplished that, you'll be able to commune with it, and even talk with the plants and animals that live around us. Even the very elements that make up everything that there is can communicate, if you learn their language. Once you are able to accomplish this, you'll lose your fear of the unknown, and you will be at home wherever you go. Then you can walk in beauty the rest of your days and know truly in your heart that there is God."

We continued to talk on for hours. Each of the coven members, in time, told me of their own experiences with the Goddess and with magic. Their stories, although varied, each had a profound effect on me as they all carried within them a central theme — connection with the Goddess and a sense of belonging within the scheme of all things. I'd never really thought about it before, but my previous religious training — my Christianity — always stressed that living was something that we had to make our way through, something we all had to suffer until we could be with God. These people, on the other hand, talked about being with God here and now. They saw everything around us as part of the Divine. They felt that spiritual fulfillment was available to everyone all of the time. And most of all, they had a sense of where they fit in the scheme of things. I was awed by their sense of security, and I felt that I, too, wanted to be a part of it all.

As the evening came to an end, Stephanie decided that Ron would be my primary teacher. She explained that he would be the one to initiate my journey, and that the path he would lead me down had been traveled for eons before by those who sought to understand.

"It isn't that you'll walk in the exact same places as the rest of us or, for that matter, even have the same experiences that we've had. But what will be the same is the process you'll go through. You'll start at the beginning and use what you observe as a foundation for what follows. Over time, all of your experiences will come together and then all of a sudden, without noticing, one day you'll *get* it."

I was somewhat overwhelmed with all of the new things I was learning and contemplating, and it must have been showing because Ron reached over and placed his hand upon my shoulder.

"Don't worry Patrick," he added. "It sounds like a lot, and in fact it is, but I'll teach you everything you need to know to reach your initiation. It'll be a long road, but I think you'll really enjoy it. And, trust me; you'll learn more over the next year or so than you'd ever have imagined you could take in."

"I'm ready," I replied, inspired by all that I had heard. "I can't thank you all enough for allowing me to join your coven, and I promise I won't let you down."

Everyone stood up as though on cue and each agreed to help me out during my studies. I took down everyone's phone number and promised to call them if I needed their assistance, and they in turn agreed to call me if anything interesting came up that I might like to be a part of. When things settled down, Stephanie had us all join hands in a circle and we breathed together until our breaths and heartbeats joined together as one.

"Mother of all," she started, "we thank you for bringing us together and for helping us to discover your mysteries. And we pledge to honor the beauty of your creation and to

47

treat one another with respect. And as a family we go forward in our lives, *dukaat!*"

"*Dukaat,*" I repeated with the others, for the first time, even though I had no idea what the word meant, and then we broke up our circle and walked out into the front yard.

We all said our goodbyes and agreed to call it a night. But, as I was leaving, Stephanie pulled me aside and explained to me that they usually required a year of associating with a prospective new member before he or she could be initiated. I told her I wasn't sure just what initiation was, and she said that Ron would bring me up to speed on that during our lessons. She went on to tell me that they might consider initiating me sooner if I did well with my studies, but not to get my hopes up yet as we'd just have to take everything one step at a time, and that time would determine the outcome on this one.

I made a solemn promise to her to commit to study hard with Ron, and I told her how much this all meant to me. I also told her that if initiation was an important part of my learning process, then I was willing to do the work.

I said goodbye to Stephanie and then headed for my car.

"I'll call you in a few days," Ron called out, as I walked down the sidewalk. I turned and waved, acknowledging his offer and then walked the rest of the way to my station wagon and started for home. I was even more excited now than when I had arrived for the meeting, and I could hardly wait to get things started.

As I headed home, I said a little thank you to the Lady, looking upward slightly towards the starry sky above. I wasn't sure if that was where she was, but it seemed to me as good a place as any, and I wondered what she had in store for me tomorrow, considering today was already enough to last a lifetime.

CHAPTER 4

The Sacred Path

Ron and I spent many days in the forest over the next couple of months. It was a beautiful spring, and every day was bright, warm, and full of adventure. We began by visiting a wooded area near his home, which had a tenuous meandering creek that ran east to west across the western-most end of the San Fernando Valley. The place was filled with a multitude of diverse trees and plants, which created a perfect sanctuary for the animals that lived within its borders. It wasn't very far from the houses in the area, but with the babbling of the water and the singing of birds, it seemed like the most remote of places. Ron taught me that no matter how many cities sprang up or how many homes were built, if I had my heart in the right place, I would always be able to find a place like this.

"Take in a deep breath," he instructed me, as he inhaled an ample volume of the crisp scent-filled air. "What do you smell?" he asked.

I took in a deep breath as he directed, and then replied, "I can smell the trees — and dirt."

"What else?" he asked.

"I'm not sure what you mean," I returned, unclear what else he required of me.

"Close your eyes," he coaxed in a soothing, nearly hypnotic voice. "Start first with the trees. Do they all smell the same, or are they different?"

I did as he asked and discovered that there *was* a difference.

I took another whiff and tried to characterize the scent that predominated the area. It was minty and ever-present, permeating the air and even gently assaulting my tongue.

"Well, there's one that smells kind of pungent and little like mint," I told him.

"Very good," he returned, beaming me a smile of approval. "That one's called mugwart; however, it's not a

tree, it's actually a plant. See if you can make out the pine.
Can you smell it?"

I took in another breath and closed my eyes. I *could*
make out the pine, once I tried.

"Yes, I do smell it," I replied.

"Any others?" he asked.

"None that I can make out," I answered.

"That's okay. Two's a good start. Actually there are
about sixteen different trees and plants in this area that
you can identify just by their scent on the wind. Over the
next few months, I'll introduce them to you, one by one.
Then, pretty soon, you'll be able to smell them long before
you actually see them. Now, one more time — take in deep
breath, and remember the smell."

I did as he asked, noticing the pine and the mugwart
right away this time. There was also a musty smell, kind of
damp and earthy — a foresty smell made up of fresh earth,
leaves, water, and perhaps a few mushrooms. The scent
was quite pleasant and I found it to be very soothing.

"This   is   the   smell   of   Magic,"   Ron   commented.
"Whenever a place smells like this, it's full of the plants and
herbs we use in our rituals. Can you smell the water?"

I nodded my head.

"Water plays a very important part in our beliefs," he
said. Springs and other places where water runs out of the
ground are sacred to the Goddess. That's why we hold our
rituals here. This is sacred ground."

We walked on down the gradually sloping bank into the
creek bed, and I could feel the warm May sun on the back
of my neck as we moved on out of the trees. I knelt down in
the damp sand at the bottom of the ravine and put my
fingers into the bubbling water as it rushed by. It was
surprisingly chilly considering the time of year and the
shallowness of the flow.

"It's really cold," I said — looking up at my mentor.

"That's because it's fed by a series of springs all along
the bank there," he replied, pointing to a number of small
seeps and a couple of tiny pools several feet above the main
stream level. We walked over to the water laden bank and

stood examining the dozen or so tiny springs for awhile as Ron explained how the water worked its way up through the rocky aquifer and finally exited through small cracks and crevasses in the surface. As we examined the bubbling pools, he pointed out a few of the small plants that grew along their edges, and we talked casually for a while about our meeting with the coven.

When we finished our talk, we began to walk along the edge of the main watercourse, following the down-hill flow of the shimmering liquid. The sand was slightly gray, although it shown yellow under the meandering water. There were yellow-green water plants growing along the edges of the tiny stream, and their floating tubers bounced like corks where the water pooled, then continued — cascading over tiny waterfalls created by occasional deadfalls or protruding granite rocks. Crows called to us from high above, safely perched in the towering eucalyptus trees that Ron pointed out as we walked. The eucalyptus, with their smooth peeling bark and slender fragrant leaves, dominated the pine in this particular spot.

"The leaves," he said — reaching up and tearing off a few, which he handed over to me — "are used to make salves that are good for healing wounds. You can also boil them in water with sage, and breathe in the steam to alleviate the symptoms of colds and flu's. Witches mix them with other special herbs to create incenses for purification and healing, but we'll get more into that when we teach you how to make incense."

I bent one of the leaves, examining its waxy surface and accidentally snapped it in half.

"Go ahead, smell it," Ron prompted, so I brought it up to my nose and was surprised by the strong, almost overpowering medicinal scent.

"It smells very familiar," I told him, recognizing the smell even though I couldn't quite place it.

"They make lots of different medicines out of it," Ron informed me, "but what you're most likely being reminded of are cough drops."

51

"Yeah, that's it!" I replied excitedly, "It smells just like cough drops."

All of a sudden I felt special. *"I wonder how many people know that?"* I remarked quietly to myself. Somehow just knowing that one simple fact made me feel more connected to the giant trees.

Ron moved on and I followed, stashing the eucalyptus leaves in my front pocket. When we reached a large flat sandy area a couple of hundred feet past the eucalyptus, my teacher asked me to point out the four directions.

"Just point to where the north, the south, the east and west are."

I had a little trouble locating the directions because the sun was directly overhead and the trees blocked all the surrounding land marks. I'd been in the scouts as a kid, and I'd learned about the directions at the time, but this was a difficult call.

"I think that's the east," I said, pointing toward a rock embankment just to the left of the creek.

"Not bad," Ron returned." You are off a bit, but at least you're in the ballpark. The east is actually over there," he said pointing to a place about twenty feet to the right of my choice. Do you know how I know that?" he asked.

"No, how?"

"We'll, first, I looked at the shadows of the trees. Because this is May, I know that the sun travels across the sky slightly off center and to the south. I also know that it's just a little after noon, so the sun is pretty much directly overhead. That means it's approximately ninety degrees to the horizon right — are you following me so far?"

"Yeah," I answered, understanding his basic drift.

"Good. Anyway, if all I've said is true, then the shadows will be leaning toward the north because the sun is to the south of our location. Once I know where any particular direction is, it's easy to find any other since they're all ninety degrees apart. That spot over there that I said was the east is pretty close to ninety degrees from the shadows, so it has to be east, right?"

"Yeah, I see what you mean."

"But that's not the only way I know which direction is which," Ron went on.

"How else can you tell," I asked?

"See that ant hill over there — the one with the red ants crawling all over it?"

"Yeah."

"If you look closely, you'll see that one side of the hill is much steeper than the rest."

We walked over to take a look and I saw that what he said was true.

"Ants always build their hills with the steepest side facing north," Ron told me.

"Why do they do that?" I asked.

"Because that allows the longest side of their hill to face south, letting more sun fall on it during the winter. That's what keeps 'em warm during the cold weather. There are lots of other ways to tell the directions too, but for now, we'll just deal with the basics. I can see you already have some understanding of all this, but if you don't mind, I'm still going to start at the beginning. That way I'll know that we haven't missed anything. Is that okay?"

"It's fine with me."

"All right then — east is where the sun comes up. If you think of the earth as a great big clock laying face up on the ground, begin by making the east twelve o'clock. If you start from there and move around the dial in a clockwise direction until you're facing three o'clock, you'll be looking directly south. If you continue on to six o'clock, you'll be looking west, and if you go on to nine o'clock, you'll find the north. Understanding the directions and where they're located is very important in Magic, you know. Since one of our primary goals as Witches is to understand how things work and the natural laws that govern our world. Things like the movement of the sun and moon are critical observations. It's important to remember that these are the laws set in motion by the Goddess herself when the universe was created, and that acknowledging these forces is, in effect, acknowledging the wisdom and creativity of the Divine.

53

"Just think of it all as a great big giant painting in which the artist puts everything she has into its creation — her hopes, her dreams, and most important, her message to the world. In doing so, she offers her most precious gift — her artistry. If people then ignore the painting, and it sits packed away in some dusty attic, the whole purpose and act of creating it is wasted. That's why we must always pursue understanding what the Gods have given us. For within nature, hidden within its mysteries, reside the hopes and dreams and, most important, the message of our Creator. What's really sad today is that most people don't have even the most basic knowledge of the world we live in or how it works at all. Some even say that it's bad to try to understand the inner workings of nature. Can you imagine that? For us, understanding the things around us is the foundation of all Magic. We see all of nature as a guidebook, written by the Divine, full of metaphors and lessons for us all to live by."

I considered Ron's analogy of the artist and was inspired by it. He was right; everything around us is like an artist's creation. When I looked at it from that perspective, I felt sad for those who would miss it. But even more so, I felt compassion for the artist. And I realized, for the very first time, that it must be really difficult to be God.

My thoughts turned to the Lady as she held my hand. "There will be pain," she'd said. I remembered the look in her eyes when she said that, but it wasn't until now that I really understood. *She* knew pain! Somehow it had never crossed my mind that God could know pain, and I felt compassion for her — deep in my heart. My newfound knowledge brought me closer to her, and I made a promise to myself, right then and there, to learn all I could and to bring the beauty of her creation to all those who would listen.

We continued on down the sandy bottom bordering along the creek with my mentor pointing out this plant and that.

"Everything in nature has life you know," he brought up casually as we stopped before a man-sized boulder, which stood all by itself in the middle of the creek bed. The stone was covered with moss and the bottom was buried deep in the sandy loam. On closer examination, directed by Ron, I noted that there were tiny little insects — perhaps miniature beetles — crawling among the Lilliputian lichens.

"You see how tiny those guys are? You wouldn't even know they were there if I hadn't pointed them out to you. But that's not the point; the point I do want to make is that — they are there! There's a lesson in that. Just because you can't or don't see something, doesn't mean it doesn't exist. It often just means that it hasn't been discovered yet. Perception is just a particular way of looking at things, but not necessarily the truth. This is a good thing to remember as you make your way through the world, for there are many things yet to be discovered if you just keep an open mind."

I traced my finger through the tiny forest of algae in the water, scattering its minuscule inhabitants as they sought shelter in the tiny cracks and crevasses below the foliage. I considered Ron's lesson and saw the wisdom in it.

"I get what you're saying," I responded, moving my fingers to the coolness of the stone's uncovered surface. The truth was that I was totally amazed by the texture of the stone, itself, with its many faceted surfaces and its hidden colony of inhabitants. It'd been quite a while since I'd been out in the woods, and I guess I'd forgotten the wonder of it all. More and more I felt at home with nature and this was only my first day. I found myself wanting to just stay and enjoy the rock, but Ron's voice transported me back to the moment.

"Even the rock you're touching now is alive," he said. "Things don't have to move and breathe to have life; they just have to have that initial spark of creation bestowed by the Creator. There are many different kinds of life in our world, and the more you study Magic, the more you'll see what I mean. It will take you some time, but, in the end, I promise — you *will* understand. I looked around at the trees and rocks and the foliage that grew along the sides of the narrow canyon, taking in all the diversity of life that existed here. It was comforting to know that an even wider variety of life existed together in this special place than I was originally aware of.

"Everything also has a name," he continued as he prompted me to resume our walk up the creek. "The names might change with different times or different cultures, but this doesn't change our obligation to learn them. We learn the names of the plants and the rocks — and all the creatures of the forest, so they'll know we care enough to remember them.

"Have you ever gone to a party, where you were introduced to people whose names you didn't previously know? Imagine going a month later to another party, and seeing those same people again. If you don't remember their names when you see them, chances are they might feel somewhat slighted. But if you walk in and say 'hey Jim or hello Barbara,' the chances are that Jim and Barbara are much more likely to consider you to be a friend. In fact, this sort of a start usually leads to a far more intimate relationship as time goes on. This is exactly how it is with nature. I'll teach you the proper names of the things around you, so you can develop more intimate relationships with them."

I thought about what Ron said about making friends at a party, and I knew from personal experience that what he said was true. I actually had a reputation for forgetting the names of people I met, and I always wanted to change that about myself.   The idea of making an effort to remember the names of the plants and animals I came across was a welcome challenge for me. If what I was learning now was Magic, then I decided Magic was a good thing for me. Because everything I'd learned so far made perfect sense and, more importantly, it all led to a greater connection with the world around me and the Divine force within it. The truth was, I felt honored to be on this walk with Ron, and the more I learned from him, the more I liked the idea of becoming a Witch.

As we neared a bend in the creek, the canyon forming its sides grew steeper and taller. Ron led me up a trail that veered off to the left and we started up the bank toward the more level ground above. When we got to the top, I followed him to a tall slender tree with long tapering leaves shaped like feathers, and we paused there for a moment, catching our breath.

"This is a willow," he said fondly, "and it's very important in our religion. This tree, out of all the trees in the world, is most sacred to the Goddess, and it's almost always found near her holy wells. Touch it," he directed, taking my hand and placing it on the trunk just below the first cluster of branches. "Feel the texture of the bark and examine closely the color and texture of the leaves. File them away in your memory so that you'll recognize them later when I'm not around."

I did as he directed, noting that the outer side of the leaf was dark shiny yellowish-green and waxy to the touch. I also noticed, when I turned the leaf over, that the underside had a powdery texture that was almost gray-white in color.

Figure 1: Dried willow leaves collected on my walk with Ron

Returning to the bark, I noted that it was very smooth and green and seemed full of life, much the way the skin of a

57

young child shows a soft blue warmth below its surface — only the glow of this tree was green.

"This is where aspirin comes from," Ron told me.

"Really?"

"Yes," he replied. "It has been used for eons by Witches to overcome fever because we believe the tree controls things having to do with the element of fire. At some point scientists discovered it contains a particular acid, which combats pain and fever, so they distilled the plant to make a new drug which was later named aspirin.

I moved my hand down to a place where the tree's trunk had been slightly damaged, perhaps by an animal or a stick blowing in the wind. There was a small place where the bark was pulled back from the trunk and my fingers began to explore it gently.

"Go ahead, peel off a little piece," Ron directed. "It'll come off easily if you take your time." I pulled back the bark as he directed and tore off a small piece to examine as he suggested. The inside was white and moist and quite slippery to the touch.

"Taste it," Ron prompted, assuring me there was nothing to be concerned about. I put my tongue to the damp inner bark and was surprised by its biting taste.

"That's the acid," he said, responding to the face I made when I tasted the pungent willow. I recognized the tangy flavor from when I was a child. My mother used to grind up aspirin with sugar to give me on a spoon, before baby aspirin was invented, but no matter how much sugar she put in, the acidic taste still prevailed.

"It *is* aspirin," I returned gleefully — excited by my new knowledge.

Ron smiled, seeing my enthusiasm and he paused for a minute to let me get over myself.

"All Witches know that," he answered, bursting my bubble gently, "but don't worry, we all started somewhere." I looked up to see if he was laughing at me, but instead he seemed to be equally enjoying my discovery.

"The thing is," he went on, "most of the plants you'll find here are the original sources of many of today's medicines.

People forget, with all the new packaging and scientific evidence to back up our drugs, that Witches and medicine men and wise women around the world have been using this stuff since the beginning of time.

Ron paused for a moment to let that sink in, and then he continued with my lesson.

"If you take a couple of cups of that inner bark and boil it in a tea, you'll have the equivalent of a couple of aspirin. It's a little difficult to get it down, but a little sugar or honey helps."

Visions of my mother holding out a spoon flashed through my mind, and I made a solemn pledge to myself to stick to tablets I could swallow, unless I had no other choice.

"What's really important to remember out of all this is that the willow is sacred to the Goddess," Ron shared. "Because of that, we use willow branches to fashion our magic wands — which I'll teach you more about later. But as for the willow itself, you see, in ancient times when our religion first developed, it was extremely important to find water. People often had to go without food for extended periods of time, which was difficult but possible. But water was the one thing they just couldn't do without. Because locating water sources was absolutely necessary for survival, the willow, which was known to be a sign of water being close to the surface, played an important part in the formation of early civilizations. Because of this, it was considered sacred, and because of its association with sustaining life, it was also thought to be connected with the Goddess, who it was said created all life from water within her womb.

"Witches have a secret language called Elban, which has been passed down within our coven over the centuries. In Elban, the word that identifies the Goddess' womb is *na*. The word *na*, besides depicting her womb, also translates as a sacred vessel or a cauldron of water, which an artesian spring might well be seen to be. It is this sacred connection with *na*, the place of birth, which seems to be the primary connection between the willow and the Goddess. There are

59

a few others, but they don't seem to be as significant as this one. One thing that you should know right from the start is that much of our past is buried, and that nowadays, all we have to rely on are the stories that have been passed down from Witch to Witch, like I'm sharing with you now."

"Tell me more about Elban," I said, fascinated by the idea that there was a secret language connected to all this.

"Well, no one knows where it comes from, but we use a lot of the words in our rituals," Ron confided. "Basically, it's the language of Magic, and it carries within it a connection with the past that's important not to lose. Remember when Jack told you to look for what can be found below the surface, and how there are layers to our understanding? Well, Elban carries a connection to one of those layers, and if you study Elban long enough, it will help you discover mysteries I could never teach you.

"But for now, let's save our discussion on that subject for the future — when the time is right for studying Elban. Right now, I want you to concentrate on learning about the basics of nature, so you'll understand how everything is connected. After you're initiated we'll go far more into depth about Elban, but for now, just know that there is such a language, and that from time to time, I'll teach you a little as we go along. In the end, you'll have a better understanding of it all once you've actually joined the coven and see how it's used in the rituals and in our everyday Magic."

Ron circled the tree, working his way through the tangled brush and high grasses to the other side. I followed him gingerly, and we both stood together looking back through the maze of tree limbs to the creek beyond and the mountains far off in the distance.

"Getting back to the willow," Ron took up where he'd left off, "as I told you, we use a branch from it to fashion our wand. The wand, once it's made, is then considered to be a tool of fire. Now this may seem a little strange, since willows are always found near water, but because of the connection with the Goddess and *na*, the place of creation, we believe it also carries within its branches *lazra meck*, which you may recall Stephanie mentioning when we first met at my house. *Lazra meck* is the Elban word for the light of the Goddess and for the primordial fire that sparked creation, which we'll discuss in more depth later on.

"Personally, I find the belief that there is a connection between the willow and fire to be particularly interesting because, as I've already said, willow was used long ago to combat fever — which was also once associated with fire. There are also other reasons why the wand is associated with fire, but we'll discuss those later when you have a better understanding of Magic itself."

"When will I make my wand?" I inquired, as my teacher continued with its description.

"Well, assuming that you are initiated in time, we'll probably teach you how to make it in January; shortly after the holiday we call Yule, which is also the Winter Solstice. Once you learn the proper ritual for its creation, we'll go out on the morning of February 1st, the next seasonal holiday which we call Imbolc, and look for an appropriate branch. We consider Imbolc to be sacred to the Goddess; because it's the day she initiates the quickening of spring. It's also the time when herd animals first begin to produce milk, which for early humans provided one of the first accessible foods after winter. On this special day, when the first sap returns to the willows near sacred springs, each tree will be filled with the spiritual light of the Mother. For us, the sap returning in the willows marks the time when the Goddess reawakens the sleeping earth after the darkness of winter. When that happens, and you can see the first green hue of life returning to the holy trees, and the tiny new buds beginning to form on the surface of their limbs, it will be the right time to cut your wand. When that special day comes, one of us will take you into the forest, and help you to create your first magical tool, which will later become your most direct and personal connection to the Creator."

"Why do I have to wait until then to make it?" I asked impatiently, anxious to get started as soon as possible. "Can't we do it now, or at least sooner than February? The willows look green to me now, why won't that work?"

"There's a proper time for everything in nature," Ron replied, patiently as ever. "Over time, you'll more thoroughly understand that everything has its own time and place in the cycle of things, and that understanding these cycles is the greatest of all the mysteries. Things like birth, death, choosing a mate or even having a family are all critical parts of the circle of life. Witches see the transition of the willow through the 'Dark Times' of winter — where it appears to die, losing all of its leaves and any semblance of life — and its subsequent rebirth near Imbolc, as being a sacred component in the overall cycle of things. Because it is at this point in the cycle of the seasons that the Goddess has chosen to assure us that we'll return to the womb of creation and be re-birthed once again, we have chosen to create our magical wands at that time as a symbol of our commitment to her and to acknowledge our own new beginnings. That's why it has to be at the time of year when Imbolc falls that you cut your wand from her sacred tree and give it a new form of life in the ritual that follows. For by doing so, you'll be acknowledging your new beginning in the coven, and you'll also be dedicating yourself to the Goddess in the process. And from that day forward, you'll be guided by her infinite wisdom, until the time comes for *you* to return to her — at the end of your days in this world."

We left the willow together and walked on a short distance back down into the creek bed. My head was reeling from all the information I was taking in, and I was getting tired from standing. Ron, sensing my dilemma, asked if I would like to sit down for a few minutes. I nodded and followed him to the side of the creek bed where he sat down, leaning back against a large jutting rock. I joined him there, relaxing as I leaned back, and letting the cool solidity of the stone penetrate my muscles. Once I was settled, I began to run my fingers absently through the fragrant duff which had accumulated at the stone's base, disturbing fallen pine needles mixed with decomposing leaves. The scent of fertile earth wafted up, soothing my mind, and I began to really relax as I stretched out and let the sounds of the singing water lull my spirit.

"I know I'm sharing a lot," Ron started, "but there is so much to teach you and I want you to learn quickly. Take that tree over there the one with the roots sticking out from under the bank. That one's a cottonwood."

I looked at the giant tree, which was almost four feet in diameter at its base, and I acknowledged lazily that I saw it. It was huge with light yellow-green leaves and a rough course bark.

"That tree carries the heart of all magic," Ron continued, pulling a slender strand of grass from a nearby patch and placing the round end of the stalk in his mouth. "You can remember that fact by the shape of its leaves. See how they're shaped like a heart?"

I nodded affirmatively as he spoke, and then turned my attention to the leaves on the tree, noting that they were in fact shaped as he had said.

"Now look there," he pointed, "just below where the leaves join to the branches. Do you see those little buds, the ones that look like little acorns?"

I followed his finger, searching along the branch he pointed to, to see if I could find what he was talking about. Then I saw them, they were like little pointed green hats, and they appeared to be quite sharp.

"Those little buds are full of resin," he went on, "and they're the central ingredient in our sacred oil, which we wear in rituals and use to give life to the tools we use in magic. It's the same oil we talked about when you came to my house that first time to join the coven. The buds aren't quite ready yet, but they will be before we need them for Samhain."[1]

---

[1] The Witch's New Year, and first of the eight seasonal holidays or holy days. Samhain later became the secular holiday known as Halloween, and is celebrated on October 31st. The other holidays which we also call Sabbats, are Yule, which is the Winter Solstice, Imbolc, which is also known as Brigit, Eostre, which is the Spring Equinox, Beltane, which is also called May Day, Midsummer, which is the Summer Solstice, Lammas, and the Fall Equinox.

"What's Samhain?" I asked.

"Samhain is the holiday we celebrate at the beginning of the 'Dark Time,' which starts at the last quarter of the year before Winter Solstice, the darkest day of the year.

"Samhain is the holiday during which we acknowledge the mystery of death and talk about the world beyond the veil. Samhain is also the time when we hold a feast to honor those who have passed on, like our family or friends who have died. One of us will teach you more about that later when we are closer to that time in the season, but for now, we'll concentrate on learning about life, since that's where we are in the cycle of things. In any case, as I was saying, that's the tree that we make our sacred oil from, and the resin from its buds are the oil's main component. The cottonwood is also always found near water, and like the willow, it too represents the beginning of creation and is sacred to the Mother."

I looked again at the giant tree, noting how big it really was, and saw that the branches were literally burdened with the tiny cone shaped pods.

"Why don't you walk over there and pick a couple leaves and a few of the buds," Ron prompted. I did as he asked, making my way over to the tree that he said housed the heart of Magic, and pulled off a leaf from one of its low hanging branches. I turned the large heart tentatively between my fingers admiring the complexity of its design and the never-ending wonder of nature. Then I reached up and pulled off a couple of the buds, which required some degree of dexterity because the limbs were extremely flexible, and I found it hard to separate the buds from the branch. Once I had my treasures safely within my grasp, I returned to the rock next to my mentor and slid down its water worn surface, once again finding my comfortable place in the sand.

Each has its own unique significance, and plays an important part in the wheel of the year.

Figure 2: Dried cottonwood leaves and buds from my walk with Ron

      Ron prompted me to crush the leaf and smell and taste it. I followed his direction and found the taste to be very light and perfume-like with just a hint of flavor. It was a little like Chinese green tea — watered down with just a hint of celery and perhaps apple. The scent of the leaves was minimal, yet present, with a kind of fresh, clean smell that was something like the skin of a not too tart apple.

"The leaves are used to reduce fever like the willow," Ron interrupted, pointing to the leaves in my hand. "They were once used to draw out the venom in poisonous snake bites and such," he added. "However, we don't use them for that purpose any more. We do still use them as a poultice sometimes to draw out an infection when we encounter a nasty wound but, mostly, we make use of them by bruising the leaves slightly and then placing them on the forehead to bring down a fever."

I smelled the leaves one last time, storing away the memory for future use and moved on to the buds.

"That's it, try the buds now," Ron coaxed, obviously pleased that I was about to explore them. "Don't taste 'em," he emphasized, just crush them between your fingers and breathe them in."

I looked at the small half-inch long green buds, which reminded me of an upside down ice cream cone and began to roll them determinedly between my finger tips, gradually applying more pressure until the resin inside began to ooze through. The buds had a resilient gum-like quality to them, and I found the surface to be slightly sticky. As I crushed them and held them up to my nose, I discovered a scent that was both earthy and poignantly sweet. The aroma was quite capturing and very pleasant. Yet, as pleasurable as it was, it was at the same time quite subtle –– reminding me of the smell of rain. There was a quality to the scent that was truly unique in that, while the fragrance was not overpowering when you first encountered it, it remained on the edge of your mind long afterward, like an invisible arbor of honeysuckle vines hanging in the nether regions of your mind, coaxed by an occasional ethereal breeze — evolving pleasant thoughts and sweet memories.

"They'll all turn brown and the resin inside will harden by Samhain," Ron added, interrupting my heady thoughts. "The fragrance will also get much stronger just before they're really ready to harvest," he added, turning his head upward, measuring the enormity of the tree.

With that, Ron got up and went over to the tree and picked several of fragrant buds for himself, taking care not to tear the accompanying leaves from the weighted limb. I watched as he crushed the buds between his fingers and held them up to his nose, and noted a subtle but distinct transformation take place. He turned his head slightly, glancing off into the distance — seemingly focused on some far off place, and a faint yet discernible smile tugged at the corners of his mouth. After a long moment of silence, he began to speak, and there was something compelling, even reverent, in the timbre of his voice.

"Every time I smell these, it reminds me of the time I saw the Goddess. Did you know that these buds are related to one of the gifts given to the Christ child at his birth? I've often wondered if the wise man who brought them knew them for what they really are. In any case, these are also known as Balm of Gilead, and they are said to bring peace to all who possess them. In Magic, we know this tree as the 'Tree of Life,' and I've often wondered if it's the same tree that's mentioned in the Bible by that name. In any case, it always grows near sacred springs, and so it's definitely a tree that supports life. As you make progress in your training, you'll find that there are many myths intertwined, between the new religions and the old, and we believe that they're all connected in the past, although most of the adherents of the new religions wouldn't admit it today, or maybe they just don't know. But if you remember what I said about perception and truth, it really doesn't matter what they say, because the truth is the truth either way."

We stood together in silence for a couple of minutes as I let what Ron had taught me sink in. Then after a short pause, which I assumed was to give me time to process what he had said, he resumed our lesson.

"If you cut off a lower branch from this tree," he went on, "it will often spout like a fountain — with water you can actually drink. But I'm getting off track and that's not the real reason I brought you here today. The real reason we've come to this particular spot. . . . And to this particular tree," he said softly, "is because this is where I saw *Her*, the Goddess, herself.

"Remember during the meeting at my house when I told you about my experience with the Goddess and how she had stood by a tree down near the creek? Well this is it. This is the place I was talking about."

As he spoke, I felt chills go up and down my spine and there was a distinct change in the atmosphere. Everything around us seemed charged with static electricity, and I could sense that something really special was about to take place. As my teacher moved closer to me, I could feel the intensity of the moment building, and I wasn't sure just exactly what was going to happen next.

"Come with me," he whispered as he gestured toward a smooth sculpted boulder near the base of the tree. As I approached the tree from the east, I noticed that there were a number of cursive-like symbols carved into the rock he'd indicated, way down near the base. The carvings, which appeared quite weathered, were barely visible above the tufts of tenacious grass that spotted the edge of the sandy creek bed.

"Sit here," Ron directed, in a commanding yet gentle tone, pointing to the sloping side of the stone, which appeared to have been polished by water during some distant aeon in the past.

I sat down on the stone and eased my back into the sloping curve of the rock, finding it quite comfortable considering its hardness. Within moments I could feel my body relax as the firmness of the boulder supported each and every muscle of my body and allowed me to let all of the tension that had built over the last few minutes dissipate.

"Just close your eyes for a minute, and be really quiet," Ron suggested, "and wait to see what happens."

I followed his suggestion, gently closing my eyes and relaxing even more than before. After a minute or so, Ron added that I might want to take in a few deep breaths and just let the sound of the water fill my mind. I did as he suggested, and within minutes I found myself slipping off into a dreamy trance-like state as the tiny sounds of the forest united with the beat of my heart until the sacred rhythms joined as one and my spirit soared — freed in the moment from the weighty trappings of this world. As I made the transition, the world as I knew it gradually disappeared, leaving in its place a wonderful sense of calm. Once I had crossed over into this mystical realm, a phantom breeze rustled the now unseen leaves in the trees, and I heard a faint musical sound from far away, carried on the crest of the wind. Tiny bells, like clinking slivers of glass, played gossamer tunes in some fairie place as the scents of earth and water mixed together with mugwart and pine. Then the eucalyptus, and all the others I had yet to learn, joined in the symphony, until it came to me like a flash that I was on the edge — just a heart beat away — from the portal to the place beyond. It only lasted for an instant and then it was gone, like an elusive mirage on a hot desert plain. Was it real, or was it just a memory — awakened by the music and the smell of magic — playing tricks on my mind? I couldn't tell for sure. But either way it had a significant effect on me, and I was moved by the familiarity of the moment.

"I often come and sit against this rock when I'm feeling down or need advice," Ron shared; apparently unaware of what had transpired with me. "Ever since I saw the Goddess here, it's become my special place. I try to come here whenever I can to reconnect when I feel out of sync. And I just thought — after hearing your story about the Lady — that you might like to share it with me."

There was a wonderful moment of silence between us as his vulnerability was exposed. I looked up into his eyes, and as our eyes met, we shared one of those unique moments that seldom occur between human beings. We were each at that point in time, filled with the spirit of the Divine and, even though nothing was said, we acknowledged one another's connection. I think that it was in that special moment beneath the fragrant sacred canopy of that cottonwood that Ron transcended from the role of mentor and teacher to a higher place in my life, and became a dear and trusted friend.

I could tell by the tone of Ron's voice that it was a big sacrifice on his part to make me a part of all this.

"I can't tell you how moved I am that you shared this with me," I told him, sensing that something needed to be said. "I can tell that this is a really special place for you and the fact that you'd share it with me tells me that you have a very generous spirit. I just want to thank you for bringing me here and to let you know that I will always honor this place whenever I return." I could tell Ron was moved, and he turned his eyes away to hide the tears that were forming there. I granted him his escape and, after a moment he changed the subject, moving on to our lesson and the rapidly receding sun.

"I guess we'd better start back now," Ron ventured hesitantly. "There are still a few other things that I want to show you before we leave, and it's getting a little late."

I got up from the stone seat, sincerely understanding his hesitancy to leave. As we started slowly back up the trail toward our cars with Ron in the lead, I could see that his energy had all been spent. The day had gone too quickly for both of us, and I, for one, wished it could go on forever. As we walked along, I finally caught up with him, and we walked side by side with our foot steps matching in beat. He led me up out of the sandy creek bed and onto a recently plowed field that separated our mystical sanctuary from the housing tract just a quarter of a mile away. A short distance out, in a still sunny location, he stooped down over a low woody shrub. It had large triangular shaped leaves and very big long white flowers that looked like trumpets.

"This is thornbane," he told me. "Its common name is datura or jimson weed, but in Magic we still call it by its old name — thornbane. It's one of several related species used by our ancestors in ancient times for magical purposes. This was the plant burned by the Oracle of Delphi in ancient Greece to induce prophetic dreams, and was used throughout history to commune with the gods. It's extremely poisonous, so be sure to treat it with respect, and definitely don't put your fingers in your mouth after you've handled it. You can be poisoned just by touching it," he went on, "so try to handle it as little as possible. We use thornbane in our incense for Samhain and sometimes in our sacred oil, although we like to use another plant called bane of Soltra for that purpose — but it's often difficult to find. Bane of Soltra originally comes from Europe and is more commonly known as belladonna, but it's difficult to find in California, so we sometimes use the thornbane as a substitute. What little bane of Soltra we are able to find in our area is usually found around the old Los Angeles and Glendale areas, and is probably left over from flower gardens dating back before the turn of the century. Many of these plants originally came here from cuttings made by the first Spanish settlers. Mostly they were brought because many of the women of that time used the juice from its berries to dilate their pupils, which is why its common name is belladonna, which translates from Latin into 'beautiful Lady.' Anyway, if you ever have the opportunity to look into the eyes of a woman who's used it, you'll definitely understand why it's called that, because there's something about that particular look that is very sensual and enticing."

Figure 3: Sketch of Bane of Soltra with berries

"Anyway, thornbane has many of the same properties as bane of Soltra and so, when necessary, we use thornbane in a pinch to replace it, even though it is not exactly the same thing."

My mentor instructed me to take a leaf from the thornbane and examine it and smell it with care. It had an unpleasant fetid odor and the leaf was a sort of dirty grayish green. There were thick purple veins distributed throughout the leaf and the actual stem was tough and fibrous.

Figure 4: Dried Thornbane picked on my walk with Ron

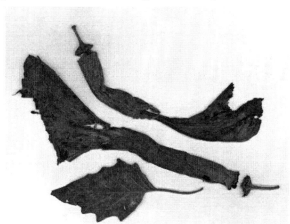

"Of course you can't taste this one," Ron reiterated, scrunching up his nose in distaste. "But if you did, you might hallucinate for days and days. On the other hand, you might just die, instead. You see, this plant is one of those whose components change daily, and it's very unpredictable when used as a medicine for other than external purposes. It is good, however, mixed with willow or wintergreen to make a salve for broken bones and to relieve severe pain. In the old times, Witches also mixed the leaf with spirits and mint to deaden toothaches, although they took a chance of being poisoned in doing so. It was also burned in the rooms where people with asthma slept, to overcome the spirits who were thought to have sucked their breath from them, although today we now know that its smoke paralyzes the part of the lungs that

72

spasm when the disease attacks, effectively stopping the spasms. Another interesting thing you might like to know is that Witches also used a ball made up of rolled up spider webs which they had their patients swallow, in order to capture the same breath-stealing spirits, the way a spider catches a fly. What's really interesting about that is that, recently, scientists have isolated a chemical in spider webs called *arachnidin* which has shown promise in treating asthma. Of course, like all other things in nature, there is much more to the story than I'm telling you right now. But, for the time being, try to remember what I've taught you about the thornbane, and the little story about the spider webs catching spirits, and we'll pick up on them again at another time."

We left the ominous thornbane behind and started back in the direction we'd come.

"In the late summer," Ron continued, as we joined the path that led to our cars, "the thornbane usually develops round spiny pods that are filled with a multitude of seeds inside. They look a lot like little chili seeds, and they're far more dangerous than the rest of the plant. But, as I've already said, there's still a lot more to learn about thornbane. So for now, just develop a healthy respect for it."

As we returned to our cars, Ron explained to me what I could expect in the future.

"We'll learn something new like this every day," he told me. "And if we can't get together on any particular day to walk around, then I'll call you on the phone and we'll just talk. It would also be a good idea to buy yourself a blank book to write down what you've learned, although for now, a spiral notebook will do just fine. When I have a chance, I'll show you an art store where you can buy a really nice hardback book that works just great, although that's not really necessary right now.

"Some covens actually create an official ritual book, which they call the *Book of Shadows*, which is later used to pass on their traditions and to formalize their practices, but our coven doesn't really do that. Instead, we keep a magical diary of sorts, which is our version of the Book of Shadows. And while we do use it to share spells and such, we don't use it to formalize our rituals. We think that keeping a series of notes about what we learn is just fine, as long as they're only used as a reference to jog our own memories about our own experiences.

"We believe that magic should only be kept in the heart and in the mind — and not in a book — because that's the old and time-tested way. Writing things down has a tendency to set them in stone for people who later read them, often closing their minds to the ever-changing world, in which the Goddess is constantly being revealed. It's important to remember that ours is a path of spiritual experience, and not one of scripture or manuscripts.

"In Magic, we draw upon the landmarks pointed out by others who've walked the way before us, and then we use those landmarks along with the wisdom our teachers have shared with us, to guide us through the experiences ourselves. It is the very process of walking the path with someone who understands what you're supposed to be looking for that leads us to our own understanding of the natural laws. By following this process, and then adding our own experiences to the story, we keep alive the mysteries for each and every new generation to come. In this way, we are ever-open to the discovery of new knowledge. So, when it comes to be your turn to pass this knowledge on, it's important that you always remember that, while you'll have your own views of what magic is, and your own experiences to share, those who follow after, will always have a different journey than yours. This is because no one who ever walks the same path in a forest will ever see exactly the same things on the trail. This is an immutable law of nature. Yet, while our experiences will always be different, what we seek will always be the same – – an understanding of the world we live in, and connection and communion with the Divine. So, even though our journeys may be different, it is still important to remember that we are all still comrades walking the same path with sincere hopes of reaching the same destination. "

When we reached our cars, Ron bid me good night and turned away from me to open his door. Then he paused for a moment, hesitating slightly, and turned back to face me once again.

"I'll leave you now with one more new thing to remember, which is the greeting of the Witches," he said. "'*Sha gadda galat,*' which in Elban means, 'may brightness greet.' It's actually short for '*sha gadda galat haji ralda,*' which translates as 'may brightness greet your spirit,' but mostly nowadays, we just say '*sha gadda galat.*' What it means to us is that we all hope that at the end of our journeys, each of us will find what we seek — the light and love of the Mother — and that we'll all return to that place of beginning, where *lazra meck* will rekindle our spirits, launching our sparks to meet somewhere in the future once again." With that he nodded and turned once again to his waiting car, opening the door, getting in, and driving off.

I stood next to my Dodge full of excitement, watching him drive away. And I found myself so literally filled with information and feelings that I was in dire need of a rest. As I drove away, my mind raced with a thousand questions brought to the surface by the events of the day. Ron had mentioned on our walk that it would take me years of study before I really would fully understand what it is to be a Witch, and I wondered to myself how I'd ever keep up, considering what I'd experienced on just my first day.

CHAPTER 5

The God, the Goddess, and the Origins of the Sacred Oil

Several weeks had passed since my first meeting with Ron. We'd made a couple of short excursions into the woods together in the mean time, and had several extended phone discussions about magic. I also spoke by phone with two of the other coven members who answered some of my questions too. In addition, I spent time familiarizing myself with the woodlands near my home.

Ron and I next met at a park near my high school and sat on the grass, side by side, leaning against a large sycamore planted there by the city. He taught me a little about the horned God who he said Witches call Cernunnos,[2] and explained that he was the male counterpart to the Lady.

"He's not Satan is he?" I asked concerned at the idea of a God with horns.

"No, of course not," he replied, somewhat annoyed, and I felt ashamed to have even voiced my doubts. "Cernunnos is associated with the Great Stags that once roamed the forests, far back in antiquity," Ron explained. "Early people saw him as the father of the herds, which they depended on for food and survival. He was considered to be the first born son of the Great Goddess, and worshiped only second to her. He was thought to be in charge of all of nature, acting as his Mother's warden over the woodlands and the forests. He was also known to be the embodiment of the primal forest itself and could take on many other forms at will. The Stag God was worshiped in the British Isles and parts of Europe long before Christianity came, and had nothing to do with evil or any of the other negative connotations associated with the Judeo-Christian demon."

---

[2] A Celtic god.

"Is Britain where our religion comes from," I asked, knowing that Stephanie and Jack were originally from there?

"No, not necessarily," Ron returned, "but it is one of the places that our religion passed through during its development. You see, our religious beliefs are very ancient, perhaps even the first in the world. I guess you'd have to define just exactly what religion is before you could make that claim for sure, but the point is this: The basic concepts, the idea that everything has life, and the worship of the seasonal cycles have all been with us since the very beginning. When the first humans wandered out into the forests, they were in awe of what they encountered there. They were driven by a lack of understanding, and a desire to know — and perhaps some degree of fear. Once they began to observe the world around them, they had to have come to the conclusion that there was something bigger and more informed than they were, running things. Witches believe that that moment, that point in time where the earliest of people first sought to understand that higher power, and how it affected the world they lived in, created the foundation for all of the faiths, but particularly for ours. Because we still worship today in much the same way as those earliest inhabitants did, we consider that point in history to be the beginning of ours."

"So where did our religion start then?" I asked.

"Well, no one knows for sure, but we do have bits and pieces of the story passed down through our legends and through walks together like this. We also have a time during each of our holidays where one of our members shares what is known as 'the song of the coven,' which serves as a time to tell the stories of our history and to talk a little about those who've walked the path before us. Witches have shared such stories since the very beginning, and we believe that there is powerful magic transferred in the process. But getting back to the source of our religion, the first people we know of, using our form of Magic, were small dark people in the very distant past. We don't know where they came from, but stories say they built their

77

houses in circles, and that they lived on the shallow water. Some say that they lived in a place called the "fen" or something like that, but no one now knows what that means or where that was located."

"As one story goes: Before the fen, the small dark people came from far, far away, crossing high mountains and large tracts of land to trade off shore. Another legend speaks of them following inland seas and rivers in boats made of reeds and skins, following the setting sun. Either way, all of the stories have a couple of things in common. They say that the people were small and dark, and, if pressed, they were particularly fierce in battle. The legends also agree that they brought with them a language of knots, which were a series of intertwining symbols, filled with magic, and that certain numbers were holy to them. Even during the earliest times, they were said to have understood the workings of the stars and to have plotted the movements of the heavens. They lived with the rhythms of the earth, and they worshiped within a circle, much the same as we do today.

"There's a place in France where there's a cave painting, which is supposed to be one of the oldest surviving examples of early human art. Within the painting there is a heard of animals and a picture of a man-stag, surrounded by a serpent forming a circle. What's particularly interesting about this is that the symbol of the rippled serpent forming a circle is very similar to the Elban rune for *na* — which if you remember from our first lesson, depicts the Goddess' womb". Ron took a folded piece of paper and a short pencil from his pants pocket and carefully drew the symbol for *na* for me so I could see what he was talking about. Then he made a rough stick figure sketch of the stag man inside a circle next to it, and I saw the resemblance.

Figure 5: The Rune for *Na*.   **Figure 6: Ron's sketch of cave drawing**

"Many people have speculated what the painting is about, but for us Witches, its meaning is crystal clear, it is symbolic of the birth of the God Cernunnos and his connection with the hunt. You haven't learned this yet, but for Witches, the art of drawing and painting — committing a desire or belief to a rendering — is the highest form of Magic, and for us it's considered sacred.   There are other symbols depicted in the cave painting that also speak directly to us.   After you've been initiated, we'll go much more into depth on that.   But for now just consider this example to be like the analogy of the apple that Jack spoke of — just the first of many layers — and a good place to start.   We'll delve deeper into the underlying layers when the time is right, but for now just remember the painting and what we've talked about.   Oh, and by the way, the Elban symbol of the birth of the God is still used by Witches today to represent our holiday called Yule," he concluded, adding that rune to the collection.

Figure 7: The Rune for the Winter Solstice.

For you see, in our religion, we believe that the Goddess gave birth to the God on the Winter Solstice. Because of this, we see the return of the sun on this day as a symbol of his birth, and its continued return every year at the Solstice as a symbol promising rebirth by the Goddess after death. Winter Solstice is at the heart of the 'Dark Time,' which is the time of the death of the earth. But at the Winter Solstice, a change takes place. After that day each year, the light returns — each day grows longer and longer, bringing back the promise of renewal in the spring. Witches see this change in the season and the movement from darkness to light, as an important sign presented to us by the gods. You see once winter takes hold, most of the animals go away, and the elderly and the frail decease. The trees lose their leaves, and times, especially for the early humans, can be especially bleak. But once the sun returns at Yule, the days grow brighter and spring eventually comes. Once that happens, nature renews itself and all is well again.

Early Witches, observing these phenomena, saw it as proof that there is life after death because they literally saw that process take place, aeon after aeon. The metaphor of the Winter Solstice was later adopted by Christianity, when Christians elected to celebrate Christ's birth during Yule. They replaced the son of the Goddess, the symbol of the new born sun, with the new born son of their God. And because they couldn't get the people of the old religion to stop celebrating the ancient holiday, they incorporated many of our rituals into their own holy celebration. That's why things like mistletoe and holly, and circular wreaths

80

and pine trees — and even the lights on those trees, are still incorporated in the celebration of Christmas.

"Are you saying that Christmas was originally a Witches' celebration?" I inquired, understandably astounded. "If that's true, why haven't I heard about it before?"

"Well, it's not the sort of thing most churches' would want known," Ron replied. "And the truth is many of them have even forgotten it. You have to remember that this all happened a very long time ago, and that the victors usually write the history. The Catholic Church, which had a unique propensity for documenting such things, has kept wonderful records from those times. Just go to the library and look it up in their religious encyclopedia for priests. You'll find all kinds of connections between the old religion and Christianity with just a little research."

"I'll do that," I returned. "It's just hard to believe: Christmas — a Witches celebration?"

Actually, Easter is one of our holidays too," Ron continued.

"You're kidding."

"No, I'm not," Ron returned. "Did you ever wonder what the word Easter means or where it comes from?"

"Not really," I responded. "What *does* it mean?"

"It comes from Eostre, one of the old names of the Goddess when she was worshiped for fertility and the resurrection of spring," Ron revealed. "The rabbits at Easter are one of her symbols and eggs, with runes drawn upon them, are another. The name is also related to the source of the words estrus and estrogen, which pertain to fertility and the continually renewing female cycle. Anyway, you'll learn more about these holidays when the time comes to actually celebrate them. All I'm trying to do for now is to give you a little background to start with. Once you've been initiated, you'll be fully accepted into the coven, and then we'll be able to spend more time on these subjects."

"Just what is the initiation," I asked, eager to know more.

"Well," Ron started, "the initiation serves several purposes. First, it's a goal for you to work toward, which allows the coven to access your sincerity and willingness to learn and also, to some degree, your compatibility. Second, the process involved in getting to the initiation — all this training you're receiving — prepares you to comprehend what our religion is really about. In that respect, it's a little like bible school for Christians, or studying for the *Bar Mitzvah* as Jew. Its primary purpose, though, is to serve as a rite of passage. Witches believe it's very important to acknowledge the changes and the important times in people's lives, much the same as they acknowledge the changes in the seasons. In fact, we see the cycles in the lives of human beings as being directly parallel to the cycles of the earth. That observation will become more and more apparent to you as we celebrate the holidays together, and you begin to see the connection between the two."

As we talked on, the subject gradually changed to the Goddess. Ron reiterated to me that in the most ancient of times, she was known as the Goddess of the animals.

"She often took the form of a beautiful woman dressed in the rich and earthy colors of the deep forest and was frequently seen walking in the company of deer. It was also said that she wore a pendant around her neck made from a piece of stag's horn, inscribed with the Elban symbol for the number nine, like this." Ron drew an illustration of the stag horn pendant with the Elban symbols and showed it to me. The stories go on to say that the pendant was hollow and that it was there that she kept the sacred oil.

Figure 8: The Stag Horn Pendant

"Why is the oil so important?" I asked.

"Well, part of the reason has to do with the cottonwood being the tree of life as we discussed earlier. But the main reason is because our legends say that Arida, during her walks in the forest, would anoint injured animals with the oil, and that once they were touched, they were instantly cured. It is even said that some animals, which had actually died, were returned back to life after being touched. Because of the special qualities that were attributed to the oil, we believe it has the ability to give life to our magical tools in much the same way that it renews the lives of the animals when touched by the Goddess. We also believe that, in anointing ourselves, the oil strengthens our connection with the Goddess, too. Actually, it's not such a strange idea if you think about it. In fact, many people in today's religions use oil to anoint their sick or to sanctify people making special religious transitions. Jesus was said to have anointed people with oil. I don't know why people in the other religions do it, and most likely they don't know either. But I suspect that their reasons have something to do with what we're talking about now."

"That's amazing," I responded. "There are so many things I've just never thought about before. It never crossed my mind to ask the ministers at the churches I've been to why they use oil. I wonder if they even know."

"It's not all that important to know why *they* use it," Ron interrupted. "What is important however is knowing why *we* use it."

Just as Ron finished his sentence, a medium sized multicolored ball rolled between our feet. As I looked up, a small blonde-haired, brown-eyed girl ran up to retrieve it. I noted that there was a group of about 7 or 8 other children waiting further down the park for her to return, so that they could continue their play. I reached over and propelled the ball back toward her with my hand, making it skip across the low cut grass like a stone skips across the water when it's thrown just right. Her face broke into a radiant smile as she picked it up, looking at me, then she turned and ran back toward her waiting friends to resume her play. As she moved away, her long golden tresses fluttered in the wind, and I was reminded of my experience with the Lady, and the way her hair had appeared to become everything that existed.

"I have a couple of questions about the Goddess, if that's all right," I queried, returning my focus to Ron.

"Sure," my teacher responded.

"Well, I know you said that her name is Arida, but you also mentioned that her name was pronounced Aridana or Arydanan a long time ago. Also, Stephanie said that Arida is the Mother of the Moon, and that we call her by a number of different names in our rituals. If her name is really Arydana, or something else, why do we call her Arida? And if she's the Goddess of the forest, what's her connection with the moon?"

"Those are great questions," Ron answered. "First, the reason we call her Arida, is because that's the first name that our coven knew her by. What I was taught, when I first became a Witch, is that her name originally was in Elban and that it was made up of three different words: *ari*, *da*, and *na*. As you already know, *na* means the womb or the beginning and, in some cases, it means water. *Ari*, means mother or, in some cases, it means to shine or to glisten. And *da*, while it has a large number of meanings, is similar to the word 'of,' as in a drop *of* rain. So, the name Aridana or Arydanan translates into something like 'the shining mother of beginning,' or 'the shining mother of the womb.'

"Over time, the name has gradually changed and Aridana has been shortened to Arida, which still basically means 'Shining Mother.' Because the Moon shines with a unique glistening light, Arida is also known as the Mother of the Moon. It isn't clear anymore if she was considered by some to be the Goddess of the Moon initially, or if her name gradually associated her with the moon because of its suggestion of glistening light. In any case, it really doesn't matter anymore because nowadays we see the moon more as a focal point to connect with her in our rituals, rather

84

than a physical manifestation of her being. As far as the other names people have given to her, there are many that have been used over time. But all of them refer to her as the Creatrix or the beginning, and from our perspective while the names are different, they all refer to the same Goddess."

"I see," I said.

"Of course there's a lot more I could tell you about her but it's best not to cram too much into one day. I think we've gone over enough for now, so let's just consider this a good place to stop."

"Okay," I responded, actually glad to call an end to our discussion for the day. With what I had learned from Ron on our first big trip into the forest, and then the couple of subsequent minor excursions we made after, and the things he had taught me over the phone, I was falling behind on getting all the information put down in my notebook. As we got up and walked casually across the park, it struck me that even in the middle of the city; there were still places that one could connect with nature if one chose. I mentioned this to Ron and he responded by telling me that even a tree in someone's front yard, or a few tufts of grass would do to lift the human spirit.

"Look at the Japanese," Ron said. "They create tiny gardens or miniature trees as small as the palm of your hand, just to find a place of tranquility. It doesn't take much, just a willingness to make the connection, and that's already instilled in us when we first come into the world."

We returned to our cars and said our goodbyes, and I drove home once again in good spirits. As soon as I arrived, I immediately went to my room to try to put down what I'd been taught. I wrote diligently in the small spiral notebook I'd bought from the local drugstore, and looked forward to the time when I would be able to purchase a blank book from the art store. I did what I could to try to capture all the information I was taking in. But there was so much that it was nearly impossible to record it all. Ron had suggested that I make simple notes for now, and then write down a more detailed version later, when I had more time.

85

I found myself filled with an overwhelming desire to learn everything I could. I was literally driven to absorb it all.

It was fascinating to me that there is so much to see and learn right in front of us, but because we're all so busy with day-to-day life, most of us just walk right by it. My decision to finally stop and see, and smell and taste, and literally bathe myself in the mysteries of the natural world affected me profoundly. I found myself laughing at little things and smiling all the time, and I especially felt connected. It's difficult to describe, but it was as though I was filled up with some wonderful intoxicating energy, until I was near the point of bursting, and that the only way I could let some of the pressure off was to radiate joy. I tried to put my finger on exactly what it was out of all my experiences that made me so happy, and then I came to the answer — I was a Witch!

❧∞☙

After several more meetings in the creek bed where Ron and I first began, we eventually made a trip to a completely different place. It was a beautiful summer's day, and I could hardly wait to get out into the country again. This time we drove in my car up to Placerita Canyon, which was just past the town of Newhall. There was another stream there surrounded by rolling hills with giant trees all around.

As we arrived at our destination, which was along the side of a winding country road, we searched for a place to park. Finally, Ron, who had been in the area before, suggested a narrow graveled shoulder just ahead. I pulled over in the place he indicated and brought the car to a stop next to two large green steel posts which were connected together by a heavy steel chain. The posts and chain served as a gate to a fire road that led to the meandering stream below.

We got out of the car and walked down the steep dirt track that dipped down into the canyon bottom with Ron leading the way.

"Those are oaks," Ron said, pointing to a large grove by the stream as we approached the bottom of the road. I looked up at the hundreds of massive trees decorating the mountainous landscape, and looked over at Ron, raising an eyebrow and answered sardonically.

"I know *that*. When I was in the Indian Guides as a kid, we learned how to make flour from their acorns. It was a lot of work and, in the end, the stuff tasted terrible. Our camp leader told us it would have been much better if we'd washed the flour a few times with water first because that would take the bitterness out. Anyway, I already know what oak trees are."

"Knowing the name or even some of the characteristics of a tree is only the beginning," Ron responded, ignoring my sarcastic mood. "Take these trees right here in front of us. There's a lot more here than meets the eye. So if you're ready, I'd like to teach you something that you don't know. What do you think?"

"That sounds just fine to me," I answered. "Whadaya want me to do."

"Well, for a start, try walking around the area and see if you can feel the essence of the trees. In fact, why don't you start over there — by that big one with the broken branch?"

I looked at him askance, not sure what he was getting at.

"Just walk around among them, and see what happens," he went on, motioning me into the grove.

Reluctantly, I wandered into the oaks, trying to get a sense of what my teacher was talking about. I didn't feel anything, and I didn't see anything unusual, so I wasn't sure what the point was. After a few minutes of walking around, I returned to where Ron was standing, not quite sure what to do next.

"What do you mean by the essence of the trees?" I asked.

"These trees are living breathing things just like you and me," he responded. "Like us, they also have their ways of communicating with one another, and they can communicate with you too if they choose. It isn't easy to understand them because they speak a different language than we do. But, if you make an effort, over time you will see just what I mean. Ten years from now, you'll walk into this grove and find yourself among friends instead of just a stand of oaks. Just clear your mind of all those thoughts racing through there and relax. Now I want you to walk back through the trees one more time until you find one that you like and just say hello."

I didn't move. I understood what it was Ron wanted from me, but I was a little too embarrassed at the idea of trying to talk to a tree with him watching to actually do it. First of all, I didn't really believe that trees could think, and, secondly, I was absolutely sure that they couldn't understand a conversation.

"Go ahead, take a chance," he prompted me.

I wandered around for a while moving in and out of the stand of giant oaks, looking at one after the other. The foliage on some of them was greener than on others, and several trees had entirely different shaped leaves — which was something I had never noticed about oaks before. All of them had the same coarse bark though, which reminded me a little of an alligator's hide, kind of lumpy and divided into sections. I finally paused in front of a particularly interesting one with gargantuan roots — fully exposed by erosion — thrusting up through the fertile black soil, like gigantic serpents entwined in an embrace. The massive tree had a large triangular hollow space at its base, shaped somewhat like a flame traveling up the trunk. It appeared to have been caused long ago by a lightning strike, or perhaps a fire. I knew this because the inside of the hollow was black and charred, even though the opening to the recess was covered by some kind of smooth inner bark which appeared to have been created to protect the tree. The smooth skin completely sealed over the edges of wound, covering up any signs of fire on the outside.

"Hello," I said, feeling a little stupid. The tree didn't answer back. I could just imagine some of my friends seeing me now. I would definitely never live this one down. I could just see it all now, all the members of the track team standing around in a huddle, and one of them saying, "Yeah, there was Pat, standing out in the woods, talking to a tree. No, I'm not kidding — *he was talking to a friggin' tree!*" Suddenly anxious and embarrassed, I looked to my right — and then my left, just to make sure there weren't any other people around. Once I was sure that we were alone, I turned back toward Ron, shrugged my shoulders, and gave him a chagrined look.

"Tell it that you want to be friends," Ron called out from where he stood. "Be sincere."

"Yeah, right," I thought to myself, "I don't see you out here trying to talk to a tree."

"Don't worry if it doesn't answer you back," Ron called out, trying to keep his voice down. "The main thing is to take the first step."

Feeling even more ridiculous than before, I told the tree that I really wanted to be friends. I tried really hard to concentrate on that thought, but it was a little difficult to be serious when you're talking to a tree. I waited, but no response.

"Nothing's happening."

"Touch the tree. Put both your hands on it and just let it feel your sincerity." I thought about that for a moment. What if he was right? What if this tree *could* feel my thoughts? If I were a tree, I sure wouldn't want to be friends with me after what I was thinking.

I decided to give in. Just the thought that there was a possibility that the tree might have feelings had a profound effect on me. I'm not sure just exactly why I changed my mind, but I decided to just go for it.

I walked forward and put both hands' palms open on the trunk. Then I closed my eyes and just let myself relax. I could feel the rough bark of the tree as tiny ants began to crawl over the back of my hand where I had interrupted their trail. I could also smell the scent of the oak which I'd never paid attention to before. It was sweet, woody, and old. I thought to myself, "I really like this tree. It has character." The wind came up gently, and crisp dry leaves — still clinging to their branches, even though last year's fall was long gone — rustled among the newer dark green leaves of summer. There was something in the rustling of the leaves. Something I couldn't quite put my finger on, a feeling, an intuition, a unique flavor of the moment that gave me a tremendous sense of peace. I don't know if the tree acknowledged me or not, but there was a definite change in me after that.

I opened my eyes slowly and backed away from the tree. I felt dreamy — sort of disconnected from the rest of the world, but at the same time, pleasurably connected to the moment. You know that feeling. It's the one you get right after a nice daydream, when you haven't quite returned to reality, but the dream is still on the fringe of your imagination. I smiled secretly to myself and felt a wave of happiness wash over me. This experience, this silly little encounter with a tree, had brought about a change in my perception of things. I can't say that I was fully convinced trees could talk, but I can say that I had a real sense that the possibilities presented to us by the Gods, if we choose to accept them, could be undeniably awesome. I looked once more at the towering timeworn guardian of the forest, with its twisted roots and blatant scar, and nodded my head in acknowledgment — toward my new found friend.

Ron walked across the small clearing that separated us and spoke to me in a hushed voice.

"Here, put this stone there by the tree as a symbol of your commitment. In Magic, it's always important to take some action to commemorate a transition in our lives." He handed me a small smooth round stone he'd picked up from the creek. I started to place it at the base of the trunk and then hesitated. I don't know why, but I picked up another sharp stone lying on the ground and scribed the letter "P" for my name on it. Then I laid it on the ground and walked away.

"You're learning," Ron said somewhat surprised. "What made you think to do that?"

"I don't know. It just seemed like the right thing to do."

"It was," he returned, throwing me a surprised look.

Ron turned toward a small clearing off to the west.

"Why don't we walk over that way," he suggested, nodding his head toward the direction he was indicating. I agreed, and we both started moving toward a grassy place where the sun shone through a canopy created by the giant trees, and Ron paused for a moment.

"In Magic," he said, "the oak is very important, because, symbolically and energetically, it represents the attributes of the God. In ritual, we often use the bark from the tree to create special incenses when we want to invoke his presence. We also use the tree as a marker and guardian to watch over magical items whose purpose has been fulfilled, like melted candles or broken magical tools. We bury these things at the base of an oak and ask its help in keeping our things safe. We believe that, by doing so, their Magic is honored, rather than just being thrown away. It's always important to remember that all items used in magic have a life of their own, so you want to make sure that you treat them accordingly. And, if someone in the coven dies, you should always bury their magical tools under an oak, to honor and acknowledge the lives of both the tools and the person. By the way, the Elban term for an oak tree is *aesma*, which means, the *guardian* or *the protector*. Also, if you decide to bury your things under an oak, it's always best to do it under one that you've developed a friendship with — like the one you met today. If that's not possible, in a pinch, you can use a tree you don't know, which we've all done from time to time, but it's always better, magically, for the tree to be a friend."

I considered Ron's lesson about the guardian and found the idea of having a friend who would protect the things that I held most dear to be very appealing.

CHAPTER 6

Symbols, Sabbats, and Getting My Feet Wet

One day when we were out on one of our outings, a pair of military jets passed by, leaving a parallel trail of billowing smoke behind as they sped across the morning sky. As the roar of the airborne fighters faded in the distance, I thought about the idea of the "guardian" and asked, "What do you think about the war protests they've been having about the war in Vietnam?" Do you think it's our country's job to defend other nations and to decide who's right and who's wrong over there?"

"Well, war is a complicated issue," Ron answered, motioning me to sit down on a fallen tree trunk and then joining me there. "I have my own ideas about it, but we also have some guidelines offered by the Goddess to consider."

"What do you mean by that?" I asked.

"Well, you know how I've taught you that nature is like a guidebook, created to help us understand what the Goddess wants from us?"

"Yeah."

"If you look at nature as a whole, you'll see that for the most part only people join together as a group to attack their own species. Other animals occasionally fight one another over food or territory or mates, but they generally don't band together to destroy each other. Witches believe that each different form of life has its own unique gifts given by the Goddess and that one of the gifts given to human beings is a greater freedom to determine our own destiny, which is why we believe that the Mother left us so many clues within the Creation in the first place. So, the real question here is: How are the actions we're taking as human beings, whether they be as individuals or as nations, lining up with that Divine guidebook? We Witches have learned through the study of nature that, whatever we do, we must first and foremost be in balance with the rest of Creation. For if we move in some different direction, our

92

actions will tip the scales too much to one side and the end result will be devastating for all.

"What do you mean when you say that the end result will be devastating?" I asked.

"Well, let me give you an example. In Australia, ranchers wanted to get rid of the animals that attacked their sheep, so they killed an overwhelming number of them. The end result was that the number of rabbits in that part of the country increased a hundredfold. This was because the natural balance of things had been broken when the ranchers intervened. The resulting increased rabbit population devoured the area's crops and also much of the local vegetation, resulting in severe food shortages for both the ranchers and the animals that normally share the rabbits' grazing areas. It also led to a loss of irreplaceable topsoil when the rainy season came, throwing off all sorts of other natural cycles. The point I'm trying to make here is that we can't just inadvertently upset the balance of nature because, if we do, the chances are pretty good that it will have very big consequences that people often do not foresee. Since we human beings seem to have been given the capacity to shape our lives and the world that we live in to a great degree, we need to be especially tuned in to the possible consequences of the actions we take. But I'm going on and on here, and we really need to get back to the lesson I had planned for today."

"But you haven't really answer my question," I said.

"When you learn more about the natural laws, you'll see that I have." We left the grassy area and wandered back among the other oaks that grew in the grove.

As we walked along, Ron constantly scanned the branches above, seeming to be looking for something in particular. Eventually, he stopped and pointed up to a clump of light green foliage, high up in one of the tree's branches. Once I became aware of it, I realized it was not part of the tree itself, but rather something growing on it.

"That's sacred mistletoe," Ron explained. "Only mistletoe that grows on an oak is considered sacred," he went on. "Witches use the sacred mistletoe in Yule rituals on the Winter Solstice."

"What do we do with it?" I asked.

"Well, mistletoe represents the Spirit of Mankind, or what some people might call our 'souls' being carried through death back to the Goddess. You see, when early humans first noticed the mistletoe, it seemed to grow without any sustenance from the earth. Because of this, they thought that it was made up of spirit like *lazra meck,* instead of form, like everything else. When they found it growing on an oak tree, the mythic symbol for the God, they were sure that it contained the spiritual essence of us all. That's why, at Yule, we each tie a piece of sacred mistletoe to an evergreen tree with red ribbon to symbolize our spirits being carried through the 'Dark Times.' You see, for us, life and death are only intervals in our continued existence. We have observed over thousands of years that the earth goes through cycles that appear parallel to our lives, and so we see nature's cycles as metaphors set forth by the Gods to help us understand what we can expect. When the sun returns at Yule, we see that its light brings rebirth to the earth, after everything has died during winter, and so we equate that first new light with *lazra meck,* which as you already know is the original light of spirit created by the Mother in the beginning. In Elban, *lazra meck,* actually means *the light that illuminates even in darkness,* which is why we believe it begins to renew the earth even though the winter's chill still has a hold at the Solstice.

"On Yule, we place our sacred mistletoe on an evergreen tree so that the Goddess won't forget to include us when her light renews the rest of nature."

"But why do we use the evergreen tree," I asked. "Why not an oak or a willow, since they're both connected to her?"

"Because evergreens are the only trees that stay green during the winter," he replied. "For us, they stand as a symbol of life being sustained through the 'Dark Times' even as everything else around is dying. We believe the Goddess left it green as a promise to us that there's always a future ahead and that there's always life after the Dark Times. As Witches, we see it particularly as a promise that there is life after death. Perhaps after knowing this, you can better understand why we perform the ritual of putting the mistletoe on an evergreen at Yule. For us, the act of doing so symbolizes our desire to have our spirits be carried on and our hope to be remembered by the Creatrix, as she continues to spin and weave and to lay out the fabric of the universe."

"Okay, I get that part, but why do we use the red ribbons, do they have some special meaning too?"

"Yes, they do. They symbolize the Goddess's fertility, and mistletoe is also a symbol of fertility. In fact, we have a special dance we all perform at Yule which we call the mistletoe dance. Stephanie will probably be the one to teach you that, but basically, everyone stands in a circle, alternating men and women, and then the men step together and slap hands. Then everyone sort of does a dance step, something like this."

I watched as Ron took a few steps back, and did a simple little dance in front of me that reminded me a little of the hokey pokey. I started to laugh because the truth was it looked kind of silly to me, and Ron immediately composed himself, saying, "Of course it looks much better when the women are doing their part too. Oh, I almost forgot, when we do the dance, there's also one coven member who stands in the middle all alone, who doesn't dance at all. That person just stands there until the whole dance is finished, and then when everyone else goes home, the person in the middle stays and sleeps in the forest all night. Then, the next day tells everyone in the coven about the dreams they had there. Generally speaking, it's a sort of divination, and the dance plays an important part in creating the space for the divination to take place. There's also a part during the dance, where if a man and woman stop during a particular step under the mistletoe that is hanging in an oak tree, they have to kiss. I believe that part of the dance is where the custom of hanging mistletoe above your door at Christmas comes from. You know the part where you kiss a girl under the mistletoe?"

"Yeah," I responded, although I never knew it had anything to do with Witches. But when I thought about it, I didn't know what it would have to do with Christmas either.

"There are also a number of medicinal uses for mistletoe," Ron continued. "But I think we'll go over them later. I think we've talked enough about plants for the moment. How about you?"

"I agree," I responded, wondering how I'd ever keep in my head all I'd learned already 'til I got home to write it down.

"Let's take a walk along the creek for a while and have a little talk about some of the other aspects of Magic," Ron suggested.

"Okay," I returned, following his example as he started walking along the well defined trail that led upstream. We walked along for a short while in silence, just enjoying the bright sun and splendid day. Then my mentor took a quick turn to the right toward the water, which was only a few feet away, and he walked down the rocky bank. We came to a flat rock that hung over the creek just a few inches above the water. Ron motioned me to sit down, and then he unlaced his boots, slipped them off, and sat next to me, putting his feet into the water.

"I love to sit here like this," he said. "Why don't you try it? The water's a little cold, but it feels really good after a day of walking around in the hills."

I took off my tennis shoes and socks and put my feet into the water too. He was right; it was cold. Even so, it felt refreshing, and in a couple of minutes I was digging my toes down into the sandy bottom stirring mud up from below as the water negotiated its way around my feet.

"You know," Ron started, "water plays a very important part in magic. Besides being sacred when it comes from a spring, it's also one of the four elements that make up everything there is. You see, as Witches, we believe that everything is created from the four elements, which are fire, water, earth and air. It's our belief that these elements,

96

combined with the spark of creation brought about by the Gods, create all things in life and are the building blocks of the universe, including Magic. Later in your training, I'll teach you more about our creation story which will better explain all of this, but for now, just understand that the four elements play an important role in our beliefs."

Moving to the bank side of the rock, Ron picked up a dried twig from a small cache of driftwood and drew a five pointed star in the dirt with the fifth point up.

"You see these four points of this star I've drawn?" he asked, touching each of the points, except the one at the top, with the slender stick.

"They represent the four elements. And the top point here," he said, moving the stick to the remaining one, "represents the gods. The overall figure, or pentagram as we call it, symbolizes an equal connection and balance between all five.

Figure 9: The Pentagram

"See how all the lines are the same lengths? In magic, this balance is very important. All things in nature are in sync with one another. That doesn't mean that nothing opposes anything else, rather it means that everything is in balance. For example, if you collect the dead wood in a forest to build a fire to keep yourself warm, several things happen. First, the tree lives and dies and completes its cycle. Next, after its dead, it serves still another purpose — keeping you warm. Even after that, the ashes become fertilizer for new plants and trees, and the cycle goes on. Both you and the tree are part of that cycle. All that is left to do as a Witch is to honor the tree for its contribution. It's only when we cut live trees in great excess that the balance is lost, and the cycle gets broken. Then the trees don't have a chance to complete their cycle and things start to go wrong. You see, if we cut down all the trees, then there wouldn't be anymore oxygen for us to breathe and we'd all die. Witches understand these relationships, and we honor them by the way we try to live. Even so, even Witches cut live trees sometimes. But if we do, then we try to plant another tree to take its place. This kind of action is what I mean when I talk about living in balance. For us, planting a new tree to replace one that we've had to cut down is also Magic."

I liked the idea of replacing trees that were cut down. There seemed to be a lot of destruction going on right now where I lived, and it was sad to me that nobody seemed to care. The whole idea of trying to live in balance with nature appealed to me and I told Ron so.

Next, my teacher used the stick to scribe a circle around the pentagram.

"When you see this symbol," he said, "it represents balance of the four elements and God, contained within a defined space — a circle. This is our symbol for Magic, itself, which we call a pentacle."

Figure 10: The Pentacle, the Symbol of Magic

"Stephanie already explained a little bit about what Magic is, but from what you're teaching me it sounds to me like there's a lot more to it than just that. Just what do *you* mean when you refer to the word Magic?"

"That's not an easy question," he replied. "I actually think that Magic is a little different for each of us, yet it always has something in common too. For me, it is the law of nature that makes something happen when, for all other reasonable purposes, you wouldn't expect it to. It is something like a miracle you know, a time that you desire something and then you get it without any reasonable explanation, except that God is on your side. We believe that if you live in accordance with the natural laws and honor the gods, your right desires will be met.

"So is that what a spell is?" I asked.

"Sort of," he answered. "A spell is like a very sincere and directed prayer. Basically, you get everything lined up to bring about your desire and then you ask the Gods to add their special spark to make what you want come about."

"I noticed that you and the rest of the coven continue to use words like God, the Divine, and the Goddess a lot, I replied. "Nicky already explained some of it to me before when we met at your home, but it's still a little confusing. Are they all the same, or just how does all that work — at least as far a Witches are concerned I mean?

"Well," Ron returned, "we see all visions of God as being just different aspects of the Goddess. We believe that in the beginning everything was created by a force that was female in nature. The reason we think that is because over thousands of years of observations, Witches have seen that it is always the female of the species that actually gives birth. Since everything else in the universe seems to have distinct repetitive patterns and cycles, and since the laws of nature are very consistent, it seems unlikely to us that the Creator would be any different. Even so, we actually think of the Goddess as being much bigger than that and able to take any form she wishes. We believe that She always presents herself to people in a manner that they are most ready to receive at the time, considering their culture and their specific physical circumstances.

"Let's take the Stag God, Cernunnos for example. The Goddess made herself known to the early hunters in that form, because She knew that the hunters saw the herds as their primary means of survival, and that they already revered the lead stag because of its prowess, and because it was the one that protected the herds and impregnated the females. Consequently, a stag god was a perfect choice for her to assume at that time, because it fulfilled the needs of the people of that particular culture, and fit within their understanding of the universe.

"We see all the other visions of the Divine in a similar light," Ron continued. "Whether it was Jesus or Buddha, to us, they were all timely and met the current needs and concerns of the people of their time. The bottom line for us is that there is a Creator and that most people seek connection with that force. One other thing to consider is that if you step back from the fray, and consider all the different versions of the Divine since the beginning of time, you will see that many involve similar stories and often have reoccurring themes. The names change, and some of their attributes may fluctuate, but the basics continue on. That's why we see a clear connection between ourselves and many of the themes presented in the mainstream religions of today."

"What do you mean by that," I asked, intrigued by his statement and particularly by the subject at hand.

"Take Christianity for example. The Christian story speaks of God having a son, who is born of an earthly mother on the Winter Solstice, and who takes earthly form and brings spiritual light to the earth, ending eternal darkness, and offering redemption and life after death to those who believe. Our faith teaches that the Goddess had a son, who took earthly form and was born on the Winter Solstice. He brings with him the light that renews the world after the darkness, which carries with it the promise of life after death. Don't you see the similarity in that?"

"Yeah, I do."

"There are similar legends in other religions too. We believe that each generation tells the story and then adds their particular spin on it to match the times. It's funny, but everyone seems to want to claim God for themselves. Witches just want to be close to her in whatever form she takes. There's nothing wrong with different religions imagining God in their own way, the only thing that's not okay from our perspective is to deny others their own way of imagining or experiencing God.

We continued our conversation, discussing several different concepts of God, and then returned to the subject of spells.

"The simplest spells," Ron continued, "involve using simple objects to represent our desires in a manner that keeps our primary goal in mind. Let me give you an example. Let's say you want to help someone who's sick to get better. You could use a candle to represent the illness the person has and take some specific action with it to commemorate your prayer and direct your focus on the problem at hand. The most common way to do that is to have the candle represent the illness and then light it. As it burns, you make a simple request before the gods something like this:

> Gracious Goddess, as this candle burns down, let
> the power of the illness diminish in strength.
> When the candle is entirely gone, let the illness
> also be gone.

This general process represents the basics involved in creating a spell. As with everything else, there's a lot more to it than that, but that's the basic idea. Magic is really very practical. If you want to grow crops, you don't just say a few magic words, and poof, there's a field of corn. You begin by learning about the soil and the climate. Then you learn about corn. Once you've accomplished that, you plant the seeds and water it. Finally, you cast a spell to the Gods to bring about a good crop. The Magic isn't only in the prayer, it's the whole process. This might all sound a little silly since most everyone knows the procedure for planting corn, but a few hundred years ago, planting corn was truly a magical act. The reason it's not considered magic anymore is because everyone has the knowledge now to do it. Witches don't consider the act of planting corn to be any less magical now, just because more people know how to do it. Instead, we just see that there are a lot more practicing Witches today than there were a few hundred years ago. Granted, they don't call themselves Witches now. Maybe they consider themselves scientists and teachers and doctors, but they're fledgling Witches by our accounts.   And there's still a great deal more in our traditions that science and philosophy has yet to discover and explain.   You mark my words; ideas that have been a part of our beliefs for thousands of years will become reality for others in our lifetime."

"What do you mean by that," I asked, not quite sure what he was getting at.

"Well, take the power of a crystal, for example.   Witches have used them to store, direct and transmit energy for thousands of years.   We've also used the energy stored in them as a source of power and to communicate on a spiritual level with each other and the gods.   All these things are considered simple knowledge by even the most beginning novice in Magic.   Yet it is only in this century that the concept of the radio originally created through the power and transmitting ability of the crystal, has been put to common use in society.   There are people right now in the space industry who are working to unlock the potential of the crystal in areas of advanced communications and as a power source, who believe that it may well revolutionize the world.   Personally, I believe that one day, not only will crystals power our ordinary communications, but I believe that there will soon be technology that allows ordinary people, using the power locked within the crystal, to be able to do as Witches have done throughout our history — communicate with others across the world instantaneously. I even think that the time will come when someone will merely think about what they want communicated, and the power of the crystal will transmit it for them.   If society ever gets to any of these points, it will finally achieve what Witches have known all along — that the crystal contains special power, placed within it at the moment of creation, and that the force that brought that about instilled in the crystal the potential to tap the power of the universe.   The point I'm trying to make is that Magic has been there all along.   Just because certain members of society rediscover it later and put a different name on it, or refine it, doesn't change the fact that it was magical in the first place.   A few of the special intuitions practiced and passed down by

Witches may be off, but for the most part, we've been way ahead of our time all along.

"I don't mean to get off track," Ron explained — realizing that he was moving to a much bigger subject than what a spell was, "but in order to understand what a spell is and how it works, you must first learn to look at it from a Witch's perspective. As far as spells go, even those of us who use them don't fully understand the full significance of all the steps we take to bring them about. But I can tell you this: They work! Perhaps there are still some hidden truths within the ritual that we haven't yet discovered, or perhaps there are hidden truths that we have discovered, but long ago forgotten. One way or the other, the truths are there."

After a while, we took our feet out of the creek. No one in particular suggested that we do so; rather it was just one of those natural acts that took place spontaneously.

"We should start back," Ron said. So we both got up and put on our shoes, which was a slow task because our feet were nearly paralyzed from long exposure to the penetrating cold of the water. Then reluctantly I followed Ron back to the car, wrestling with all we'd spoken of and trying desperately to keep it all in my mind. As we walked along, Ron paused by a plant that grew on the upper bank of the stream. It had a tall round stalk about three feet high with large leaves that were slightly toothed at the base and smaller leaves that looked more and more like the willow as they progressed up the stalk. The tops were a bright shiny green, and the undersides were also powdery like the willow. Once again Ron had me pick a leaf and smell and taste it. This particular plant had a very distinct odor. It was pungent, yet pleasant, and it smelled very familiar. The scent reminded me of previous trips to streams and swampy areas.

"This is mugwart," Ron instructed. "Mugwart gets its name from ancient times when Witches believed that a piece of the leaf rubbed inside a cup would ward — or 'wart' — off poison. There many kings and queens during the middle ages that wouldn't drink from a cup or 'mug,'

103

unless it was first treated with the plant. Modern medicine stopped using it for that purpose long ago, writing it off as superstition, but Witches still use it today to counteract certain poisonous metals. We've actually found that, while it seems to have little or no effect on most poisons, it does seem to counteract lead and mercury. Personally, I find that particularly interesting because we now know that arsenic, which is a form of lead, was the primary poison used to assassinate royalty during the Middle Ages.

Anyway, that's not what we do with it now. Instead, its primary use for us is to stimulate visions or, if you will, to see things. You know, like the future. We sleep with it in our pillows so that we'll have prophetic dreams, and we throw leaves of it into still water and then use the water like a crystal ball to see the 'unseen.' Mugwart, we believe, allows us to actually see *lazra meck* and consequently the things that are illuminated by it. Witches believe that this unique light isn't limited to the here and now. Instead we believe that it's capable of moving between multiple worlds, and that it is neither limited by time nor by space. Because of this, it can illuminate events not only in the present, but also in the past or in the future. So we use mugwart in conjunction with our divinations.

"What do I have to do for initiation?" I asked.

"Well, you'll need to learn a lot more along the lines we've already been following and you'll also have to learn the basics about the elements and the elementals, including their connection to the creation of the universe. You will also have to have a much wider understanding of the magical plants and herbs that we use to create the sacred oil and our special incenses and a strong understanding of why they're considered magical in the first place. Mostly, we'll just continue to spend a lot of time out in the forests and hills together, observing nature, and learning the natural laws and discussing the spiritual metaphors presented there. We'll talk about the God and Goddess and how we human beings fit in the scheme of things, and we'll also talk a lot about why we do what we do and where we come from. The idea is to give you a strong foundation to build on.

"It's easy to go through the motions of casting spells and making magic circles. In fact, pretty much anyone can learn the necessary words and follow directions. But Magic doesn't come from reciting secret phrases or following some series of intricate instructions. It is a unique physical and spiritual experience that takes place when you combine your personal understanding of the laws of nature and your friendship with its inhabitants, and then use that base and your connection with the Gods to bring about your right desires. And it's very important for you to have that base before you begin to participate in the rituals of the coven. If you didn't learn all this beforehand, you'd probably never really get it. Or, at best, you'd only get the first and most basic level, which is fun, but doesn't really connect you in a deep way.

"It's important to keep in mind that one of the primary directives of Witches is to be someone who looks beyond what is obvious to everyone else. Think of it in terms of learning to drive a car. Someone *could* just give you the keys, and, if you spent enough time observing other people driving, you might actually be able to do it on your own without any prior training or knowledge of how a car functions. The problem with this is that you can get into trouble with that kind of training. It works fine on a basic level, such as driving around the streets and highways and starting and stopping. But you run into trouble when your car goes into a skid on an icy highway, or you blow out a front tire going 70 miles per hour, or even worse, your brakes go out on a long down hill curving mountain road with cliffs on the sides. These are situations that any trained driver has been taught to handle in advance, but self taught drivers would be literally flying by the seat of their pants. That's why you have to go through all the training before you can participate in the rituals. We want to be sure that you have the training necessary *before* you start out on the road.

"If there were one thing that I could tell you that would be the most important advice I personally could give you, it would be to understand where things come from and why we do them. There is great history behind all this. When we speak of walking the path that those before us have walked, we aren't just saying words; we are literally referring to our connection to each and every person that has made this journey before us. There are centuries of questions and observations, successes and failures, that have packed this earth beneath our feet. This is holy dust you see flying around, when the wind stirs the dirt in our path, as you and I walk together. Remember this each and every time you take a walk in some secluded glade. Remember it when you bend to harvest the mugwart or when you reach to pick the fragrant buds of the cottonwood. And remember it when you work your way carefully through the nettles along the creek to cut a wand from the willow for the first time, for each of these acts has been performed before, thousands and thousands of times – – and there's Magic in that."

I left the grove that day feeling more confident in my ability to understand and more capable of remembering what I'd learned. I was beginning to see that learning magic was something I could do. Every step seemed to be designed to support the one that followed it so that, once you got started, each new piece fell into place comfortably and made sense. There was something very calming about it all — the stories, the connection with nature, the feeling of closeness to God — and particularly the reassuring sense that I was a unique and important part of it all. I felt sure that the connections I was making and the lessons I was learning would be valuable tools in the future, and that they would somehow come into play as I sought ways in the years to come to honor and serve the Lady.

CHAPTER 7

Myths, History, and the Winds of Change

I finally bought a blank book from the art store Ron had pointed out to me. It was a black and had a hard cover and several hundred pages of blank high-quality paper inside. It was actually designed to be a portfolio for artists, where they could make sketches and record ideas for future projects. On the front cover, I painted a picture of a pentagram the way Ron had illustrated it in the sand for me the day I made friends with the oak, and on the very first page I composed my first written spell. No one told me what to write or how to write it. Instead, I just opened up my heart and asked for help from the Lady. Once I got started, I ended up writing a nice little poem that seemed just right for the purpose.

By light of moon, by darkest night, protect this book from enemies' sight.

For love of the Goddess, and Cernunnos' might, this book of Witchcraft is mine by rite.

To use its powers, I shall read, and within its pages, my mind shall feed.

Let the Magic found there, help me a lot, and, at the end of my days, *sha gadda galat.*

When I'd finished the poem, I felt confident that my spell would work.

Gradually over time, I transferred the notations from my spiral notebook and tried to record everything I could remember about my lessons with Ron. I also added notes regarding my discussions with the other coven members and made sketches of the various plants I'd come to know. Overall, recording this information proved to be a monumental task, so I had to make a decision to write only the high points of my lessons and experiences or to give up the entire project all together. As I progressed, I developed a unique set of abbreviated symbols for myself that I hoped would jog my memory later when I had time to write more.

I also made a firm commitment to myself to continue to make what notes I could in my spiral notebook and then, later, when things were more settled down, to create a much more organized and complete book in the future. In the back of my new book, where I'd started sketching the flora I was learning, I began to press actual samples of the plants themselves, and then lay the dried herbs between the unused pages as a record of my progress. All in all, the book grew in both content and thickness and, within a very short while, I was already dreaming of starting a bigger one.

But, as Ron had pointed out, the book itself became more of a creative art work than an actual guide to knowledge because; as I progressed along in my studies, never once did I use it to actually review anything. Instead, the forests and the fields became my guide book with the landmarks of the terrain serving as anchors for the knowledge I'd accumulated. And each and every plant, rock, and tree I passed sprang forth as if in poetic verse, reinforcing the lessons I'd learned. And I was reminded daily, as I traversed back and fourth through forest and glen, that the path I walked was the Sacred Path, and that the journey I was on, led straight to understanding the Divine!

❧ ᘓᘓ ☙

As the year progressed, Ron and I got together more and more often, and I found myself learning at a faster and faster rate. By mid-September, I knew most of the local birds by sight and could greet them properly in Elban. I'd also learned most of the magical salutations for the plants and wildlife in the area and could address the creatures of the forest easily as I ventured out more and more on my own. Although to some this may have all sounded a little silly, I was dead serious regarding these communications with the world of nature around me. By this point in time, I was developing a special sense of kinship with the plants and animals around me, and I knew in my heart that they in turn were responsive to me. There wasn't any direct communication, no "Hello Pat, how are you?" or anything like that. Instead, what I felt was a pleasurable sense of security, much like you would feel upon entering your own home. You know, that sense of belonging, safety and familiarity that comes when you walk through your own front door. Yes, that is what it was like. Nature, itself, had become my home.

I had mastered each of the four directions and was confident on how to locate them. I also learned that the direction the sun travels is called *deosil*, and that we always walked *deosil* or, as people sometimes call it, sunwise or clockwise, when creating our magic circle.

"We begin in the east," Ron had explained one day, as he and I walked the hill tops in Sylmar, looking for a particular plant that was indigenous to the area. "For us, the east represents the direction of the first light and serves as a metaphor for the beginning or the place of creation. From there, we proceed around the circle in a *deosil* direction, acknowledging each of the directions as we pass. When we complete the circle, we return once again to the east to signify our return to the beginning after we've completed the circle of life."

"Why do we stop to acknowledge each of the directions?" I asked.

"There are a number of reasons," Ron responded, "but the primary one is to reenact creation itself and to acknowledge the parts that each of the four elements played in that."

"What do you mean by that," I asked.

"Well, the story of creation is somewhat complex from our perspective, but I'll give you what we'd consider to be the 'first layer,' so that you can get the gist of it. Later, as you learn more, we'll fit all the pieces together and then you'll have a more detailed explanation. But for now, I'll just share the story as we tell it in ritual, and I think you'll see the beauty of it in its simplicity and be able to really grasp the Magic of it all.

"Basically," he continued as we walked along, "Witches believe that in the beginning there was nothingness and that nothingness came together to become the Goddess.

Once the Goddess was, she screamed a primal scream that turned into the first light which, as you know, we call *lazra meck*. When the scream turned into light, it didn't want to leave the Goddess, so it began to travel *deosil* in a circle around her. The point where it made the turn and the circle first began, became the direction of the east, or as we call it, the place of beginning. The reason we consider it to be the place of beginning is because *lazra meck* is the light of spirit, and without spirit, there can be no beginning. Because light is a form of fire, and fire to us represents purity, the east also became the place of fire.

"Next, the light continued around the circle until it reached the south. There it began to solidify and take form and so it became the place of potential, which we represent by the element of earth. As the light continued, now having potential and form, it came to the west, where it transitioned from the nothingness of preexistence and was birthed to become life. So we consider the west to be the place of water and to represent the primordial cauldron of creation, which is the Goddess's physical womb.

"Finally, the light, now having potential and form and being birthed into actual existence, came to the north, where the Goddess bestowed upon it the last gift that was necessary for it to become life as we know it — air. And so all life was created by making the transition from spirit into form and then through the process of birth to the first breath, until the light, full of the creation and having completed the first sacred circle, returned to the east, and finally, returned to the Goddess in the center, who became the beginning and ending of all things. And, from that first circle, began the cyclic order of things, which has continued to this very day.

"That is why we worship in a circle and acknowledge each of the four directions for the part they played in the creation, and that's also why the Goddess is seen to be in the center of the circle and within each of us, rather than outside. Do you remember when we discussed the pentagram over in Placerita Canyon and I told you that four of the points of the star represented the four elements?"

"Yeah!"

"Well, the circle is just like the pentagram. The four directions represent the four elements, and the center — or the sacred space within — represents the essence of the Divine."

"That's cool," I said, understanding the correlation between the two. "So the pentagram and the circle are really like the same symbol."

"That's correct," he confirmed. "In fact, it's that way intentionally."

"What do you mean by that?"

"Remember we talked about how Magic is discovered in layers?" he went on. "Well, the correlation between the circle and the pentagram is a great example of the hidden layers you'll discover within magic as we go on. This is no accident. There are actually a number of other similarities between the pentagram and the circle to be found, but you'll have to discover them for yourself because that's our process. But those discoveries are only the beginning. Far beyond those are even deeper connections that unlock the secret of life itself."

"How will I know where to look for these things?" I asked. "And even more important, how will I know if I'm on the right track?"

"Trust me, they will come to you when the time is right," he answered. "When you think you have the answers, let me know, and we'll sit down and talk. For now, just know that the combination of these deeper connections, once they're fully understood, contain answers that scientists will probably spend centuries decoding even though the answers are right there in front of them. Many such answers are woven within our myths, symbols, rituals, and practices just as is so with the circle and the pentagram. Remember the crystal? And some have to do with healing. For example, Witches have a saying:

Make your tea from the rod of gold,
and say goodbye to a nasty cold.
Make your tea from the bark of a willow,
and leave your fever upon the pillow.

111

"Today, such sayings are treated as 'old wives' tales' and are often written off by science as invalid. But these sayings are often later found to be true. If you drink a tea made from goldenrod, you will be much less likely to get a cold. We know this even though science hasn't yet 'discovered' it. And the part about the willow, as you already know, has already been verified by science. People think that all of these bits of archaic wisdom, because they were developed by what we would now consider to be uneducated peoples, are false, but the truth is that many of these myths are based on generations of observation and practice. There are many more. You'll see."

"I'll be open to these things; I promise. And thanks for telling me the story of creation, and explaining about the directions."

"We're not done yet," he responded. "The story I told you gives you the spiritual reasons we do ritual the way we do, but there are also physical reasons in nature for our choices that also play a part in the puzzle. The east, if you recall, is fire because it represents the light of spirit, but it is also the place where the sun rises and provides us with the light and heat that supports life as we know it. And the south, which represents the direction of potential and fertility and the element of earth, is also recognized as such because the soil on most southern exposures is warmer and more fertile and supports a wider variety of life than that of all the other directions."

"Why is that," I asked, not understanding just what my teacher was saying.

"Well, for example, the south side of a hill receives the most sunlight and so more plants grow there. This in turn creates compost, leaves, and other organic materials which support even more plants. Because the south side of the hill has more vegetation, there are more animals there. It's also generally warmer there than the other directions, so it's a more comfortable place to be. Just take a look around you, you'll find more insects, animals and people in the southern locations of an area than anywhere else. Consequently, the south, not only symbolizes, but *is* the place of the highest degree of fertility and the greatest potential for life.

My mind raced back to the lesson where Ron first taught me how to find the directions. I remembered the ant hill and how the ants built it with a larger southern exposure in order to stay warm during the winter time. Once again, the more I learned, the more the puzzle pieces fell gently into place, and I felt even more secure, knowing everything around me is so connected.

"The west represents the element of water," Ron interrupted, bringing me back to the conversation at hand. "The sea, in all its glory, was to the west of the people who first defined these concepts. Also, water, particularly the ocean, has been referred to as the cauldron of creation by Witches as far back as our oral history can trace. I'm not sure exactly why they called it that, other than that for them the sea, I guess, must have provided most everything they needed to survive. You know, like salt and fish, and a means of travel. I've often wondered if they're actually referring to the ocean when the world was first created, but then who would have been around then to have seen that?"

Focusing on Ron's question, I visualized a primordial sea surrounded by mists in the beginning of time — churning and boiling, driven by storms and volcanoes in the dawn of creation. "Maybe they're right," I thought to myself, wondering what sort of cauldron the sea might have been in the very beginning.

"The north," Ron continued, "is the direction of air. Of course that one's pretty obvious, because most of the strongest wind currents that generate the most pronounced storms originate from the north. Myths of the power of the north wind can be found throughout the world, and its awesome presence has been repeated over and over again in ancient legends and popular folk tales.

"There are also other reasons why the directions are represented by the elements in this way. You wait and see, all of this will come together over time, especially after you're initiated and start to participate in the rituals.

113

"By the way, there's something else," he continued, lowering his voice and moving closer — implying that this was special information. "Each of the elements, has tiny beings that live within them. . . ." He paused for a moment letting that idea sink in, before continuing with his lesson.

"Tiny beings," I thought to myself — not really believing the idea. If there were tiny beings everywhere, then why hadn't I ever seen them?

"Okay," I responded, trying to act as though his disclosure was normal. But the truth was, I was feeling somewhat bewildered. On one hand, I was delightfully overwhelmed by all of the fantastic things I was learning, and on the other, there were some things that just seemed too far out to accept. In any case, I decided to just go with the flow and see what happened, so I gave my mentor all of my attention.

"The elementals, as we call them," Ron continued, gesturing with his right hand in a circular motion that encompassed the surrounding landscape, "are the spiritual essence of the particular element they live in. You can befriend them just like the trees and the other inhabitants of the forest, and they — like the rest of nature — can help you feel at home in the world we live in and will assist you along the way as you make your journey."

As my teacher spoke, something in his statement struck me and opened a new level of understanding for me. I realized in the moment that making friends with nature was much like making friends in society. The more friends and acquaintances you make, the more secure and happy you feel on a day to day basis. And just like society, the better connected you are, the more chance you have of finding happiness in the world.

As I reviewed my progress with Ron, I came to the conclusion that this process proved to be absolutely true for me. Each day as my learning progressed, I felt more and more secure in my environment. I was rapidly developing a new type of appreciation for the world, and I felt more and more connected as my understanding grew. The thing that was really special about this transition was that I felt closer and closer to the Mother of Creation. I could see her beauty in everything around me, and spiritually I was on the top of the world. I was just beginning to understand what the Witches meant when they said that the Lady was part of everything — for she left a small piece of herself within each and every thing she created. And if you look hard enough, you can see her beauty there, shining through from below the surface. From the pulsing veins that carried the sap through the translucent leaves of early spring, to the vastness of the deep blue velvet sky just before dawn — she was there.

"After you are initiated, you'll learn all about the elemental beings," Ron continued. "The coven will teach you how to make a spiritual transition called *chanala ralda* that will allow you to actually experience what it's like to be one of the elementals. When the time is right, sometime after initiation, you'll actually participate in a series of sacred ceremonies where you will physically and spiritually become an integral part of each of the four elements. If all goes well, you'll experience exactly what it feels like to *be* water, earth, fire and air."

"Just what does *chanala ralda* mean?" I asked.

"Literally speaking, it means to be *in the spirit* or to become the spirit. But in plain terms, it simply means to become intimately connected with the spirit of creation or to allow oneself to be filled with it. Remember the other day when you were describing to me how you're beginning to feel more in touch with nature every time you walk in the forest, and how at times you find yourself at peace when you're alone in some secluded place and you feel like you belong there?"

"Yeah."

"Well, you've reached a point where you feel like you're a part of everything around you rather than being separate from it. The only difference between *that* feeling and *chanala ralda* is that you don't just feel like a part of the forest, you actually *become* the forest. This process is important to complete because transitioning from our separateness into our oneness with everything is the first

115

step in creating a sacred space and communing with the Gods."

The thought of participating in such a ceremony was so exciting to me that I wanted to do it right then. There were so many wonders I'd already experienced, and I could just imagine what there was in store for me in the future — as a Witch.

Ron and I continued to study together, and I learned a few more words in Elban as we went along. Mostly, they were the magical words used by the coven to speak to the elements and the other forces of nature during rituals, and I practiced them whenever I could. Phrases like *"nak lazos neck luna,"* by light of moon, and *"ma bacha chook,"* the Gods are present, helped me to gradually learn to put together more complex sentences.

"Sometimes we use mystical symbols and alphabets from other ancient languages to express ideas in Elban," Ron told me one day. "There are very few of the original symbols from the Elban language left," he went on, "because most of the written language has been lost over time and no longer exists. As a result of this, our ancestors began to substitute letters from other archaic languages to spell out Elban words."

"Why did they do that?" I asked.

"When we first began to write Elban phrases in the Arabic alphabet, people sometimes got words confused with similar English ones. Over time, we discovered that by writing in alphabets that no longer have any particular meaning to us, we are forced to *think* in Elban rather than in our native tongue. To Witches, the underlying symbolisms are the most important part of any language rather than the specific words themselves. This method of writing works for us because it falls in line with our belief that magic is presented to us in layers with the real magic concealed slightly below the surface. We've found that by teaching Elban as a written and spoken language that stands alone, students find it easier to grasp the Elban concepts and remember the words much better than through any other method."[3]

"I noticed that there are a lot of symbols in our religion," I remarked, recollecting the images carved on the stone near the Goddess tree, and the various symbols drawn on candles that I'd seen as we'd progressed along with my studies. "What do all those pictures and stuff mean?"

"They have lots of different meanings," Ron responded, smiling at the way I posed the question. "Symbolism plays a very important part in Magic. We often use single symbols or as we call them, *runes*, to represent an entire magical idea. Sometimes symbols lose their original meaning over time as they're adopted by successive generations. Yet they often still carry a part of their original message at a subliminal level, which is not even noticed by the people using them. In Magic, we believe that it is the subliminal message, combined with the additional messages later attached to them that make them so powerful.

"A good example illustrating what I mean would be the cross in Christianity. Here, let me show you what I'm talking about," he said, taking a small notebook out of his satchel, and opening it to a blank page. He drew a simple Christian cross on the page and then tapped it with his pencil as he explained.

"Many today think of this particular symbol as a representation of Christ and his sacrifice for humanity. They also see that sacrifice as a promise of life after death and an assent into heaven. In addition, some also see the cross as a symbol of light overcoming the darkness. These ideas are actually new messages attached to earlier representations of the cross, which already had many of the same metaphors connected to the cross long before Jesus was born."

"Like what kind of meanings?" I asked.

---

[3] In this book, however, I am using Arabic letters to spell the Elban words phonetically, for purposes of pronunciation.

"Well, the symbol of the cross is very ancient," Ron answered seriously. "Some of the earliest representations exist in rock carvings originating from the early Paleolithic era, where its original meaning is still uncertain, although some archeologists speculate — because it was always depicted in the sky — that it probably symbolized either the sun or the moon. Then during the earliest civilizations, the symbol surfaced again, and it looked something like this," he went on, drawing a cross much like a plus sign. "In this case we know that it was used as the symbol for the sun, because there is archeological evidence to support that. We also know that, at that time, the sun was worshiped as a God or sometimes as a Goddess and that its light was considered holy. In addition, there is also evidence from that time, that the symbol was used to attract the blessings of the Gods. Later, it became the symbol of the sun's return at the Winter Solstice, and it was seen as an early metaphor depicting the seasonal change that gave hope after the Dark Times. As we've already discussed, early observations of the sun's return on the Solstice helped to lay the foundation for the idea that there is life after death because the earth itself appears to die during the winter, and then comes back to life when the sun returns. In response to that, ancestors on our path built rock cairns, with an elongated cross shaped tunnel inside of them with an altar at the intersection of the cross, which became illuminated by the sun on the Solstice, creating a direct connection with the rebirth of the sun and life after the death of the world. What is even more interesting is that when the first cathedrals were built in Europe, they exactly replicated these cuneiform cross shaped tunnels and chambers, and made the altar in the intersection of the cross into an altar for Christ.

"The first cross I drew continued to be used in our practices to represent the four elements and the four directions equally balanced, with the center of the figure representing the Gods, or metaphorically, the origin of creation, which then connects it to the sacred circle and to the pentagram as well. Once you know these things, you can see how powerful and magical the symbol of the cross actually is.

"You don't have to be a genius to see that all of the early symbolisms attributed to the cross are still represented in Christianity today. The Christian cross still represents God, although the sun God has been replaced by Jesus. The icon also stands as a symbol of the promise of life after death, or in the particular case of Christianity, salvation through Christ, similar to the way the newly risen sun for us is depicted as the 'Lord of Light,' who through his divine connection resurrects the earth after the winter and is the promise of continued renewal. Then, lastly, there is contained within its symbolism the idea that Christ is the light, and that he will overcome darkness for us, as the light of the Solstice did when it entered the cuneiform chambers in the dawn of history. And he also connects us with the Divine, and through his light, we are said to be blessed. You can even see the idea of the elements and the Gods connected and in balance. Because in Christianity when you connect with Christ and go to heaven, everything earthly and divine finally joins and becomes perfect and in balance."

11: The Crosses drawn by Ron, depicting the progression of the sacred symbol throughout History

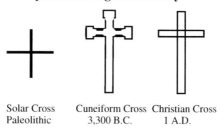

Solar Cross   Cuneiform Cross Christian Cross
Paleolithic   3,300 B.C.   1 A.D.

I was absolutely fascinated with Ron's explanation. It became obvious to me that there was truth in what he said. What I liked most about our discussion was that, while he showed me how Christianity subsumed symbolism from preceding beliefs, he did not devalue Christians or their use of our ideas. In fact, other than criticizing them for

119

demonizing us and trying to make everyone else out as evil, Witches seemed to see the new religion as an extension of their own, and were always hopeful that the two religions might come together in peace to explore their earlier connections.

Ron and I spent quite a bit more time talking about symbols, metaphors, and hidden meanings. He alluded to the fact that there are many other symbols used in religion and society that have spiritual connections to our beliefs also. He suggested that I spend some of my time looking for them, but only hinted at how I might do that.

Each time the two of us got together, I learned more and more. There was an incredible amount to study, and I fell into a pattern of staying up late at night trying to get it all down. It was interesting to me how much easier it was to digest my lessons and put them into perspective now that I had been studying for a while, than it had been when I first started. Ron had told me that my capacity to comprehend would continue to improve daily, and that the study of Magic would open doors in my brain, that would develop whole new ways of thinking. Ron was right.

CHAPTER 8

Michael, K.D., and Ireland

Sometime in early October, after several months of instruction, the coven met to review my progress. It was really great seeing them all together, and I felt much more connected with them after studying so much with Ron. I hadn't really spoken much with any of them in all that time, and now that I knew so much more, we had a great deal more in common. We met at Ron's house in the early evening and Jack, Stephanie and the others asked me many questions about what I had learned. It wasn't as if they grilled me for answers or anything. Instead, they just started a conversation about Magic, and I joined comfortably in.

We talked about the history of our coven and Stephanie spoke a little about how she first got involved.

"I was always drawn to the woods," Stephanie told me. "It didn't matter where I moved to — and I moved a lot as a kid — I always found some secluded place to spend my extra time. My dad was in the Foreign Service and we lived in several countries by the time I was in my teens. I actually first met Michael — my High Priest — in France, when my father was stationed there and Michael was there on holiday. I met him, entirely by accident, or perhaps it was fate. It's hard to say, but my life definitely took a change in course after that day. It was during the summer and the weather was particularly lovely at the time, so I would get up early and walk around. That particular morning, I took a walk down by the river near our house, and he just happened to be there standing on my favorite bridge. We struck up a conversation about the river and how peaceful it was to stand by it, and things just went from there. I was only thirteen at the time, and not particularly prone to speaking with strangers, but for whatever reason, I ended up speaking with this one. He was quite a bit older than I was, and I found myself

121

thoroughly engaged with him. Anyway, we talked about nature and how there was something very relaxing about standing by the river, or walking in the woods, and during the course of the conversation, he revealed to me that he was a Witch. It may sound kind of funny now, but I wasn't really surprised at all at the time. I wasn't exactly sure just what a Witch was — other than the typical old hag in a black pointed hat stirring a cauldron, which it was obvious he was not — but after he explained the word's true meaning to me, I felt we had a lot of the same interests, especially around nature.

"He gave me his address in England, and suggested we might write once in a while. Then, after a few niceties and words of parting, he left. I wrote to him a time or two after that, and I think he may have answered me back once or twice, but nothing of any real importance happened until about two years later.

"When I was fifteen, my dad was called back to England, and we moved to Chelsea, which was the same place Michael lived. I wrote to him almost immediately, and he came over to see me. He asked if I might be interested in joining his coven and without really giving it a lot of thought, I told him I would like to. By the way, that was also where I first met Jack — in the coven I mean.

"There were eight of us in the group, and we met fairly regularly. Michael was the High Priest and in charge of the coven, and a woman named Celia was the High Priestess. I didn't get to know Celia very well because she left the coven a couple of months after I joined, but I became close friends with the other members. Jack, and I, and a guy named Hadsley were new to magic, but the others had been working with Michael for six or seven years. We did rituals for all the holidays, and Jack and I worked a lot together on our own. Over time, I fell in love with Jack, and as you can see we've been together ever since. I don't think my parents particularly liked him, but we managed to stay together anyway. The coven in Chelsea was great fun, but looking back, we weren't anywhere near as serious about Magic and

122

learning as we became when we moved to Ireland three years later.

"Michael was originally initiated in Ireland, which was where his family was from. He had been in contact over the prior few years with his original High Priestess, a woman named K.D., and decided to move back there. After much discussion, Jack and I decided to go with him.

"We all moved to Ireland just after my eighteenth birthday. And I finally met K.D. a couple of weeks after we arrived. I liked her immediately. She was in her mid-sixties, with long gray hair, and she was slightly overweight. She had a very friendly way about her and got along well with everyone. K.D. had a unique low voice, which was almost a whisper, and a heavy Irish brogue. When you were engaged in a conversation with her, it made you naturally lean forward when she spoke — which gave the impression that everything she said was important.

"The other two members of the coven were men about Michael's age. Their names were Tim and Larin, and I got along with them right away too. Tim was tall and slender with short dark hair and a great personality. Larin was also tall, although not quite as tall as Tim. He was also more the quiet type and could sometimes be a little moody.

"I liked everyone I met and we all worked very well together as a coven. K.D. led the rituals and taught us all about Magic, and Michael served as High Priest. We spent a lot of time walking the land near K.D.'s home, and we worked very deep magic together.

"K.D. had a great deal more knowledge about Magic than Michael did. I don't know if he just hadn't taken it seriously before, or if, perhaps, she didn't teach it all to him when he was with her the first time for some reason. In any case, it was quite a change for Jack and me, and Michael too, compared to what we were used to in the Chelsea coven.

"During our first few months together, I learned that Michael's High Priest, whose name was Thomas, had been married to K.D. for almost forty years, and that the two of them had practiced Magic together for most of that time. I also found out that Thomas had passed away about five years before, and that K.D. had never quite gotten over it. Michael told me that Thomas was liked by everyone in the area, and that he was also a very skilled woodcarver.

"We all worked together and practiced Magic for about a year, then, K.D. became seriously ill. At the time, no one could seem to figure out exactly what was wrong with her, but her health generally had been going downhill since before I'd met her. Because of her illness, she had to stay in bed a lot. She also had a problem with her feet swelling, which she said was very painful, and her ability to walk in the woods was greatly reduced. She became so frail, that, after much discussion with me and the others, she decided to start preparing me to act as Priestess in her absence. She and I worked together every day. When she couldn't make it out to walk the forest with me, I sat by her bed and we talked for hours on end.

"Finally, about seven months later I was initiated as High Priestess by Michael, with K.D.'s blessing — and the coven began to take a new direction. At first, I didn't feel qualified to lead the coven. I didn't have anywhere near as much knowledge or experience as K.D., and I was very self conscious about that. But the coven needed a Priestess. I began to lead all the rituals and started spending a lot more time by myself in the woods and walking the moors. Over the next few months, with help and support from K.D., I learned at a very quick rate and began to have incredible mystical experiences on my own. Eventually, I reached a point where I really did feel qualified to be the Priestess, which made it so much easier for me to fill the position.

"I really think the Goddess was guiding my path because things that were mysteries to the other members of the coven began to become very clear to me. During the next couple of years, I spent a lot of time working deeply on the 'Golden Key,' an ancient mythical coven key that reveals not only secrets hidden within our rituals, but more importantly, information that points us to wisdom that unlocks the very foundation of the universe. Once I started to better understand that path, I began to experience the many layers of Magic in the rituals which were not so obvious to me when I first started.

"Around 1959, Jack talked to me about moving to the United States. We were having a hard time getting by on the money we made and good paying jobs were pretty limited in Ireland. Jack had lived in the U.S. before, for a couple of years, back when he was going to school, and he was sure that if we moved, he would make a much better living. He also had several friends who had invited us to stay with them while we got ourselves established. It wasn't an easy decision to make, especially because K.D. was so ill and the coven was very important to us, but after a lot of discussion, we just knew it was what we had to do. Of course K.D., Michael, Tim, and Larin hated to see us go, and we too were sad to go, but they were still supportive of our decision.

"Once the decision was made, things moved along fairly quickly. K.D. and the others decided to help us form a new coven in the states, and they gave us several of the coven's most prized possessions to get us started. There was a handmade book whose outside cover was made from the bark of a poplar tree stitched together with red wool yarn, which contained notes on some of our rituals and spells, and was filled with runes used in magic. K.D. also gave us a share of the dried herbs and incenses made by our coven to use until we could harvest our own once we settled in the U.S. There were other things — a quartz crystal that belonged to Thomas, and a set of simple hemlock pan pipes, which made the most wonderful sound in the world, and that we often used in ritual. But the most special of all was a container of our original thick fragrant Sacred Oil, in a beautiful old formulary bottle, which was simple but elegant — and had been in our coven for a very very long time. We all made a vow to try to keep in touch, and then Jack and I set sail for America."

"Did you meet any other Witches when you got here?" I asked.

"No, we didn't." Stephanie answered. "There weren't really any others around — at least none we have ever heard of."

"Are there other Witches around now?" I asked.

"There aren't any that we know of, but there are a few people around the L.A. area that practice ceremonial magic."

"What's that?" I asked.

"Well, basically, it's magic that involves a bunch of complicated rituals where you command various spirits and sometimes even angels and such. It's really more complicated than that, but I guess, for the time being, it would be easier to explain the primary difference between the ceremonial people and us, than to try to teach you what they do. The people who study and practice ceremonial magic learn secret names of the spirits and such. They believe that, once you have that knowledge, you can supposedly control the spirits and make them do your bidding. Witches, on the other hand, make friends with the spirits of nature and then ask their help as friends to achieve Witches' goals. And sometimes the spirits of nature ask for our help too. So it's more of a cooperative relationship. We actually think it's wrong to try to force the elementals and the spirits of nature to do anything."

"How come you know that there are these ceremonial people around, but not whether there are other Witches?"

"Well, there are a few books around on ceremonial magic and several of them say right in them that there are ceremonial magicians in our area. In some social circles, it is actually in vogue to belong to a secret lodge or society. I guess it's been that way here since the 1920's. Covens, on the other hand, have to be very careful about having any contact with the outside world. People seem to be a lot more afraid of Witches than ceremonial magicians. I'm not sure why that is, but it was the same in Europe before we left. Mostly, it's the churches that have kept the prejudice alive. Jack and I think that it's because their beliefs often cause them to personify evil — an enemy to save people from. In any case, there's a great deal of prejudice here and you do have to be very careful about who you talk to and what you say."

"It's not just us either," Ron added. "They treat the Jews the same. Did you know that there've been people beaten up just for going to temple, and that there have even been people killed right here in the U.S. just for being Jewish. In fact, my parents' temple has to have guards with football helmets and baseball bats every time we have a service, just to protect the congregation."

"Well, I have heard some of that," I responded, "But not everyone is like that."

"You're right," Stephanie agreed. "There are a lot of people trying to break down some of the old religious prejudices, but I think it will be a long time before we'll really be safe. In any case, we could all be in serious danger from some of the church people in our area, so it's really important that you maintain the secrecy of our coven. When you're initiated, you'll have to take an oath to protect the other coveners and to promise not to let other people know our names or where we live. That's the only way we can be safe."

"Yeah," James joined in. "I was beaten up really badly in Canada because I told a Christian friend that I was a Witch. He went and told his parents, and a bunch of people from their church came over and confronted me. When I admitted that it was true, several of the men started hitting me. After awhile, the women joined in too, kicking me and spitting on me. It was so bad that I lost consciousness and, when I woke up, I had to be taken to the hospital. After I got out, I started getting death threats from some of those people, and I ended up having to move. That's when I came here. I still have this scar on my cheek, see? And I have trouble seeing with my right eye because of that whole thing."

I considered his story. While I believed James about the beating, I found it hard to believe that Christians would beat us up or threaten us. My own family was Christian, and I was sure they wouldn't act like that. Even so, I assured everyone that I wouldn't talk about being a Witch with anyone. And I agreed to keep everything about the coven a secret.

Everyone paused for a moment, seemingly in acknowledgment of the gravity of the subject.

"I'm interested in knowing more about my initiation," I said, breaking the silence.

"We can't go into too much detail about that right now," Jack answered, "because most of the things you'll need to know about initiation will be taught to you when the time is more appropriate. There's actually a whole process involved in learning about your initiation and answering your questions about it, which we wouldn't want to compromise by revealing now. But there are some things we can discuss. For example, your initiation will involve bringing together all of the things that you're learning now and being able to incorporate them into a keen understanding of Magic itself. It will also involve a rite of passage where you will experience a spiritual transition and, when you're finished, you will in essence start out with a new beginning."

He went on to explain that each covener, after their own initiation, takes on a special magical name to use within the coven, and that everyone would disclose their secret coven names to me when my initiation was completed. Stephanie also joined in the conversation and told me that, as a coven member, I would be able to draw on the power and support of each of the others in the group by just calling upon their magical names in times of need.

"We'll also consider you to be like a member of our family," Jack interrupted, "once you've passed initiation. And there won't be any secrets between us after that."

"When *will* I be initiated?" I asked anxiously.

"We considered the possibility of initiating you at the end of October on Samhain, which is only a few weeks away," Ron answered. "But then we decided it was better to have you wait until the first of February.

"Why do I have to wait so long?" I asked. I've learned everything I'm supposed to haven't I? Why can't I just do it at Samhain?"

128

Stephanie interrupted.

"Imbolc, which as you know, is what we call the second of February, marks the time that life returns to all the plants that have gone dormant during the winter. Witches consider this day to be the time of new beginnings. Your initiation ceremony commemorates your new beginning as a Witch, and it's appropriate that we celebrate that new beginning at the right time in the cycle of things. Besides, Samhain is the most powerful holiday we celebrate. It is dedicated to honoring our ancestors and exploring the mysteries of death. While you have learned a great deal so far, you haven't been prepared spiritually yet to experience that celebration. Even if you could learn everything that was required in time, which would be nearly impossible, it would still be the wrong time in the cycle of things to be initiated."

I was very disappointed to learn that I would have to wait so long, and I told them so. Jack spoke up in support of what Stephanie had said and reinforced her position.

"Our whole belief is based on understanding the natural laws. That's why it's so important to learn to follow nature's cycles. One of the problems with our society today is that we live way out of sync with our world. We do the wrong things at the wrong times, and we don't think about the consequences. Look at all the trees we're cutting down around the world. Those trees serve a purpose in the cycle of things. If you cut down all the trees, there won't be any air to breathe — and everyone will die. Witches aren't against cutting trees exactly; we're just against cutting them randomly without first learning how they fit in the cycle of things. When we cut a tree to use for making something, we plant a new one. We've learned that that's what nature does when left on its own.

"The cycles and interdependencies we see all around us aren't just some coincidence; they were created that way by the Gods. If we want to honor our Creators then we need to honor what She's created. That's why the most powerful Magic is the Magic that's done at the right time in the cycle for the particular type of result you desire. For example, we know that the early spring is the best time to plant most seeds. If we plant them earlier than that, they'll just die from the frost. On the other hand, if they're planted too late in the year, the plants will grow, but they'll never reach their full potential to provide a harvest. Magic is like that. If you want to reap the harvest of the fulfillment of your potential, you must learn to cast your spells at the right time. Your initiation will probably be one of the biggest steps that you'll take in your life and, as such, Imbolc is the right time to take that step."

"Okay," I replied reluctantly. "I guess I'll just wait."

I felt very disappointed and somewhat rejected. I wanted to be initiated right away. But I had learned enough by then to understand the reasoning behind their decision. They all seemed to feel it was very important for me to do things the right way at the right time, and it was my experience, at least during my tutelage with Ron, that there was a great deal of wisdom in their teachings. I wanted very much to be like them, and if that required waiting longer for my initiation, then I would wait.

About this time, Stephanie announced to everyone that she, personally, would teach me for awhile. I'm not sure, but I thought I saw a look of surprise in Ron's eyes. There was an uncomfortable moment of silence where everyone in the room looked back and forth at each other, and then everything seemed to return to normal. I had the sense that something unusual had happened, but I wasn't exactly sure what it was. I later learned that Stephanie always directed someone else to teach newcomers, and that I was the first of our coven to be instructed by her personally at this early stage.

"I'll call you next week, and we'll get together and talk," Stephanie said.

I was a little nervous because she always seemed to be at a higher level than everyone else. There was something a little unsettling about the idea of being alone with her in the woods. After all, she was a High Priestess. I considered what it would be like to walk through the hills with her, the way I had been doing with Ron, and I got butterflies in my stomach just thinking about it. But I agreed to meet with her, and then the course of the conversation turned to other things.

We all talked about music, the draft, the war in Vietnam — and how builders were gradually tearing down the sacred places where the coven did ritual and collected herbs. There was a lot happening in our country, and, for that matter, there was a lot happening in the world. We talked about the protesters who were marching in the streets, saying that it is wrong to kill people in other countries and that the whole idea of war itself is wrong.

"We've *got* to find ways to change the way everyone thinks," Stephanie said.

"And to make everyone in the whole world think about how they can learn to love each other, rather than kill each other," Jack added.

"Well, we can't solve the problems of the world," Karen joined in, "unless we start in our own backyard. I mean look at the racial problems we've got and the riots."

"Everyone keeps talking about the generation gap," Ron chimed in adding his two cents, and this is it."

"You're right," I agreed. "And things can't continue the way they are now or we'll just destroy ourselves." Everyone nodded in agreement.

As we talked, I realized that these were really times of change. There was a big gap between the ideas that our parents were raised with and our own. To us, it seemed like the whole world was in turmoil — and it was. Everyone in the room felt a change on the wind and we were both anxious and excited about it. On the one hand, people talked a lot about peace and love and ending war and prejudice, and we were hopeful for the future, and on the other hand, we all knew that, any day now, some anxious person under tremendous pressure in some country, maybe even our own, might push a button and end the world.

Finally, someone pointed out that it was getting really late, so we decided to call it a night. I drove home that evening with mixed feeling stirring around in my head. I reached over and turned my car radio on, just as a Dylan

131

song was playing. I tapped my fingers on the wheel of my Dodge and kept time with the music. Then, absentmindedly, I nodded my head in agreement, as the singer repeated his prophetic message for the last time: "The times, they are a-changing." He was right: they were.

CHAPTER 9

Wise Woman of the Forrest

A week after my meeting with the coven, I got a call from Stephanie. She suggested that we meet in the evening down by the stream where Ron and I first started working together. I drove to the now familiar place and met her where the pavement ended in a little *cul-de-sac* on the edge of the wilderness area. Once we met up, we started together down the narrow dirt trail that led to the creek. It was already nearing dusk, and I had never been down there at night before.

Stephanie led the way into the forest and, as soon as we entered the trees, her way of moving changed. The change was very subtle, but quite apparent to me. It's difficult for me to describe exactly, but, basically, all her movements became very sensuous. She seemed to literally glide through the trees, and I could hardly take my eyes off of her. When she spoke, it was almost as if time had slowed down. The effect was very much like being slightly intoxicated with the end result being that she had my full and complete attention every single moment we spent together. I followed her down the embankment and onto the sand along the edge of the water. When she reached the bend in the creek, she turned slowly and looked directly into my eyes. It was just twilight and only a few stars shown overhead. I could see the outline of her long hair, dark against the shadowed background of the trees.

"Patrick," she whispered.

"Yes," I answered feeling a little shy from her glance.

"There's magic here tonight — can you feel it?"

I nodded my head, afraid to speak. I wasn't sure just exactly what would come next. She raised her hands toward the sky, palms outward and fingers slightly separated.

"*Alock ma shum neck meck,*"[4] she chanted.

---

[4] From the depths of darkness

133

Through the shadows, I saw the edges of her hair begin to flutter and curl as a gust of wind worked its way up the sandy draw. I could feel the coolness of the moisture laden air softly brush against the skin on my face, and I could smell the strong pungent sweet combination of sage, pine, mugwart and willow, especially the willow, on the face of the wind.

As she continued the unfamiliar chant, I felt the forest close in around us — not in a frightening way — but rather as though everything green and growing had just moved in a little closer, in a circle, seeking to separate us from the mundane world. I didn't understand the words she spoke, as they were none that Ron had taught me in the course of our lessons, but it was obvious to me that she was creating some kind of a sacred space in Elban. The wind continued to blow until she finished her incantation, then as abruptly as it had began — it stopped.

I stood mesmerized, not sure what to do. It was obvious to me in that particular moment, that Stephanie, my High Priestess, had actually made the wind blow at her command. I had never seen anything like it before. And until you do, you will never be able to fully appreciate the sense of wonder that surrounded me at that moment. This was Magic. *I'm talking Real Magic.*

When she finished her incantation, she beckoned me to come and stand before her. I walked over hesitantly, still in awe of what I had just seen. For a moment, she seemed to dominate the landscape, and then a smile blossomed on her face. There was a mischievous look in her eyes and she actually laughed. "Pretty heavy stuff, huh?"

"Yeah," I replied.

Her smile had driven away the unsettled feeling I had had, and she motioned me to sit down in the sand. Next, she followed suit, sitting next to me on my right, and she turned her head toward me as she began to speak.

"It's all real you know. You just have to get connected to the right channel." Stephanie was always saying clever little things like that. I didn't get it at the time because I didn't know about channeling, and so I assumed she was making a comparison with TV, which actually she was. But at the same time, she was also referring to channeling in a spiritual sense. Stephanie was like that, very smart, very wise, but with a great sense of humor. Everyone liked her — and so did I.

"I figured I should show you some Magic, before we start talking about it," she said. "There is a great deal of work required to get to the point where you can work with the forces of nature like that. I also thought we should start off our lesson in a sacred space, so I've created a simple circle for us. If you don't mind, I thought maybe you could ask the Goddess to join us here tonight."

"I'm not sure just exactly how to do that the right way," I replied.

"I wouldn't worry too much about that," she said. "I can feel her presence in you every time I see you. Just stand in the middle of our circle here and ask her to be with us while I teach you."

I rose from the ground reverently and looked upward directly overhead for a moment — taking in the millions of stars that had blossomed since we'd first started into the canyon. I raised my hands toward the sky, as I'd seen Stephanie do just minutes before, when she'd created the holy space we now stood within. I paused for a moment and cleared my mind, and then I opened my heart to the Lady.

"Gracious Lady, Mother of all, come be with us here in our circle." I said. "Help me to learn and to understand about your ways and be here with Stephanie, too."

I turned my head toward my Priestess to see if what I'd said was good enough.

"That was perfect," she said, giving me a beaming smile that raised my level of confidence tenfold.

"Now, let's get started. You've learned a lot about the plants and trees and the other inhabitants of the woods, and that's good. In fact, there's still a great deal more to learn about that. But there are other things that are also important to know, too. So I'm going to begin by teaching you about the seasons and helping you to understand more

135

about our sacred holidays. I'll also share with you what we call the 'song of the coven,' which is the oral story of our history. Even I don't know everything there is to know about our history, but I will share with you what I do know. And, over time, if it works the same for you as it did for me, other pieces of the puzzle will fall into place in their own in good time. So, let's begin first with where our coven comes from and how our religion got started, okay?"

"Okay," I answered.

"Now I know that Ron touched on this a little with you already," she started, but I'm still going to start from the beginning so we don't miss anything, all right?"

"Yeah," I responded, "that's just fine."

"Thousands and thousands of years ago, probably when human beings were still living in caves, they were fearful of everything they saw in the world. They had no concept of God and they had no idea why things that affected them happened — one way or the other. Over time, they began to notice that there are certain cycles within nature, itself, that repeat themselves over and over again as the years pass by. There are night and day, the rising and setting of the sun and moon. And there are the seasons of the year: summer, winter, spring and fall. Along with the seasons, there are also the migrations and behavior patterns of the animals, and the agricultural cycles, which governed the lives of the plants and trees.

"As the people watched these cycles over time, they observed that when the solar cycle reaches the winter, everything grows cold and the days grow short. They also noted that the animals go away, and all the trees and plants die. In addition, they also saw that their own people, particularly those who were sick or elderly, also passed away during this time.

"Imagine for a moment living in those harsh times and being out in the forest like we are here tonight — just before the beginning of winter. Imagine how frightening it must have been, huddling together against the cooling tides, knowing that some unseen force was creeping through the

136

dark forests and desolate moors looking for someone to satisfy its gruesome hunger."

As she spoke, a cold damp mist began to settle in the basin formed by the banks of the creek. It worked its way up from the bend down wind, and seemed to move toward us in a wispy animated way. I'd never noticed before, but the fog seemed to materialize right out of the sand. Slender tendrils winding up from beneath rocks and decayed wood joined force, forming a living, moving mass. It was like some creature from the grave, half in that world and half in this, advanced slowly toward us. Stephanie lowered her voice almost to a whisper, staring trance-like at the progressing mist.

"Can you feel the chill?" She asked.

I actually felt my skin begin crawl when she asked the question, and I moved a little closer to her as my eyes kept track of the advancing mist. Chills went up and down my spine, and I felt a twinge of fear take hold just below my throat, where it joined my shoulders and chest. Just at that moment, the wind came up — not a great wind, but enough to send the mist spiraling in small swirling funnels, which rose up above the ground like specters still moving toward us.

"And *we* know it's just mist, condensation — fog," she went on, "but those people back then, they didn't know that."

As she spoke, I could understand exactly what she meant by that statement. There was something very eerie about being out in the dark on a cold October night in the woods.

"They could feel the awesome power of winter coming on," she whispered. "And while they didn't understand it all, you could be sure that they believed there was something that governed those forces. It's our belief that it was times and experiences like these that first brought people to seek out what we now refer to as God. There's something comforting about knowing that we are not alone in all of this, and that there is something bigger and more powerful to appeal to in times of fear and unknowing. And

137

so those early people began to worship that bigger thing, that force that reigned supreme over all the natural forces they encountered. The force that had created all we see around us. And because everything else they observed in nature — all living and breathing things, came from the female of the species, they worshiped that being as the Creatrix, the primordial cauldron of creation, and as Goddess — the Mother of all things. In fact, one of the early names for the Goddess in Elban is 'Shee' which means 'beginning' or 'creation.'

"Anyway, because the beginning of the winter was the time people contemplated death, it became a holy time to acknowledge those mysteries that relate to death and dying and to celebrate those who've already passed on. Also because it was the first time people really thought about creation and the Mother Goddess, it is also associated with *wada na*,' which is Elban for 'the pathway to and from the cauldron,' or in today's terms 'the womb.' As Witches, we believe that we return to the place of beginning, the womb of the Goddess, at the moment of death, there to be re-birthed when the time in the cycle of things is right. This idea came from thousands of years of observation of the natural seasonal cycles of the earth. We have observed that everything around us dies or retreats in the winter, but comes back to life again in the spring. The holy time when this cycle of darkness first begins, that time when everything returns to the womb to be rebirthed again, eventually became known as Sow-en, which is spelled S-a-m-h-a-i-n, and is celebrated on October 31st.

"Samhain is considered to be the first and last day of our year, much like New Year's Eve is for our current society, and so we celebrate a part of it like that. Like our ancestors, we believe Samhain to be the time when the two worlds of existence, the universe we live in (the world) and the place where the Gods and those who've passed away live (the womb), come together for a short time. And so we also use this time to study about the world beyond, so we'll be prepared for that journey, when our own time comes."

In the course of our conversation, Stephanie also taught me that over time, some of the Witches beliefs and practices had spilled over into other cultural and religious holidays. She pointed out that Halloween and the Hispanic celebration of the Day of the Dead were but a few of the cultural and religious celebrations that grew out of early magical tradition that took place at the beginning of the Dark Times.

"On Samhain, we hold a special feast in honor of those that have passed over," Stephanie continued. "We invite them to return to our world for just this one night. We all bring pictures and heirlooms associated with those we've lost, and we share them with the other members of our coven so that those who were important to us in life are not forgotten when they make the transition on to death. During the feast, we share stories of their lives and express our grief at their parting. We also hold a special ceremony called, 'caile' nai marigwyn, na neg maru,' where everyone joins in a divination during which we ask the assistance of our departed loved ones to foresee the events of the coming year.

On a typical Samhain, we get together, during the early part of the day, and go out into the forest to gather the plants and herbs we use to create the sacred oil of the coven. Everything is ritualistically harvested, and the herb lore associated with the season is passed on to those who are new to our way. These ingredients, harvested at this sacred time, will be combined with sacred oil from past generations and a new oil will be made. This tradition continues year after year, so that a little of what is old is always present with what is new. In this way, we maintain a connection with those who've walked this path before us, and those who'll follow after. And, in doing so, we keep alive the heart and spirit of all those who tell the story. That's why we use the oil to consecrate all of our magical tools, and to create a magical bond between ourselves and the other members of our coven. When you're finally initiated, a bottle of the same oil will be the first gift you'll receive from us. You should treasure it and use it sparingly, for it's the most precious of all our possessions."

As Stephanie told the story of the sacred oil, Ron's constant repetition about looking for that which is unseen returned to mind. When I was first told about the oil, I understood that it played an important part in the Witches' beliefs. But I could see now that I had only been seeing the first layer. It never occurred to me that there was a connection between the oil from those who walked the path before and those who walked it now. Through Stephanie's instruction, I now realized that when we spoke of connection to those who walked before us, we were speaking also in the literal sense, not only in the metaphorical sense I had imagined. The sacred oil actually carried a *real* connection between Witches in the past and Witches today. All the energy, the harvesting of the herbs, the knowledge of nature, belief in the God and the Goddess, the magical tradition, it was all there hidden within the oil.

As Stephanie and I sat close together in the misty river basin that night, I could smell the scent of the sacred oil she always wore. The smell was sweet and earthy and yet subtle, and while it was created from many of the plants right here in this clearing, its unique fragrance reached and held a place in the mind and spirit that was not touched by anything else here in this forest or of this earth. That scent, connected with what I had learned in the preceding few moments, sealed in my memory the mystical journey I had taken since the day I chose to become a Witch. And from that moment 'til this, I am still moved in a very special and spiritual way, every time I experience the aroma of that magical liquid.

"Getting back to the 'Dark Times,'" Stephanie went on. "Our ancestors noted that that time of the year came as the sun moved toward its lowest point in the sky. They also observed that once the sun passes that lowest point toward the end of December, and begins to return again, its light increases. When that happens, all the plants and trees that have died and the animals that have retreated or hibernated, return to life once again. Once that transition takes place, the earth is returned once more to the beauty and majesty it held when it was first created.

"Because of this, the next sacred point in the cycle of the seasons that we celebrate after Samhain is the turning point that takes place somewhere between the twenty-first and the twenty-third of December. We call this sacred holiday "Yule" and it takes place on the day of the Winter Solstice, which can vary from year to year depending on the movement of the sun and its relationship to our calendar."

"I know about Yule," I said. "Ron taught me about it before, during our lessons together."

"That was good," Stephanie returned. "And I'm well aware of what you and Ron have already discussed, but there are additional things that you need to understand. Yule, as you already know, represents for us the time of promise and lays for us the foundation of our belief in life after death. I believe you also know that early Christians later chose to celebrate the same holy day, as the day of the birth of their Savior. But what you are not aware of is that, in Christ's time, the Solstice actually fell on what would now be December 25th, and that it is only because of the gradual shifting of the universe over the last couple of thousand years and its relationship to our calendar, that the Solstice and Christ's birthday are now celebrated on different days.

"Another thing that you don't know is that there was a lot of controversy in the early Christian church as to when it was that Christ was actually born. There is significant documentation that the early church — seeking to unify various opposing Christian factions and their differing accounts of that event — held special meetings to settle their differences and to decide when it was that they should acknowledge that event. Eventually, after much discussion, they finally decided to place Christ's birthday on the Solstice because, for them, the birth of Christ represented many of the same metaphors already attributed and celebrated at that particular time of year. That is why, as Ron taught you earlier, Christian ideals like the promise of life after death, and Christ's holy light washing away all

141

sin from those who are touched by it, fall right in line with previous aspects of ours and other pre-Christian beliefs.

"There are actually even more connections between Christmas and Yule than I'm telling you about now," she replied. "In fact, after you're initiated, you'll actually participate with us in the Yule celebrations, and then you'll get to see, first hand, that there are many other similarities between the two.

"And speaking of celebrations, what other holidays do you know about? Did Ron explain Imbolc or any of the other Sabbats to you?"

"Yes," I answered, "he did tell me a little about Imbolc, like the fact that it's the time the sap returns to the trees, and how the herd animals make milk. He also told me a little about Eostre, but I don't know exactly what we do on either of them or exactly what we're celebrating."

"Well," Stephanie started, "after Yule comes our next Sabbat which is Imbolc as Ron already told you. It's also known as Brigit, and it honors the quickening of spring and the return of sap to the willows as you pointed out. We honor the Goddess in the guise of Brigit or Brighid on this Sabbat, and share tales with each other of smith craft, law, and childbirth. We also drink warm Ewes milk, and use the same, mixed with a few drops of our own blood, to do divination. But most importantly, this is the time that new members cut their Magic wands and also the time at which we hold our initiations into the coven, which we'll discuss in more depth with you later.

"Aren't ewes' sheep," I asked, repulsed at the idea of drinking milk from a sheep?

"Yes they are," Stephanie answered, smiling at the look on my face. "In ancient times, it was common for those on our path to drink the milk from sheep. In fact, the word Imbolc literally means, 'in milk.' This refers to the birth of the lambs after the Dark Time and to the bonus of fresh milk after the winter.

"What other holidays do we celebrate," I asked.

"Well, after Imbolc, comes Eostre, which is the time of the resurrection of spring, and the celebration of the Spring

Equinox. This is also the proper time for planting seeds — both literally and metaphorically.

"After Eostre, comes Beltane which is celebrated on the first of May. Beltane is the time we celebrate fertility and dance the May Pole. After that, we celebrate Midsummer, which is the Summer Solstice, and honor the marriage of the God and the Goddess. Then on August 1st, we celebrate Lammas which celebrates the first of our three sacred harvests. Following that, comes the Fall Equinox, which is the second harvest, and lastly, we finish up the year with the celebration of Samhain, which is the third and final harvest and the beginning of the next year. The eight Sabbats make up what we call the wheel of the year, and each has a special drink and incense associated with it, that relate specifically to the season and the magical purpose at hand."

By this time in our conversation, Stephanie and I were entirely surrounded by the mist, and the rest of the forest had all but disappeared.

"There's something else I want to teach you though," Stephanie intimated, lowering her voice even more, as though what she had to disclose was a great secret. Her surreptitious manner, combined with the loss of perspective originally offered by the now hidden woods, prompted me to move even closer to her in the swirling fog. "You see how the mist has obscured our view and made it difficult for us to see even those things that we know for sure to be there?"

"Yeah," I answered.

"Well, Magic is often like that. As you've been told before, there are some things that are unseen, even though they are right there in front of us. And tonight. . . . Well, tonight, I want to introduce you to one of the most significant of all of those hidden secrets."

"What is it?" I asked, intrigued.

"Well, I'm not going to go into a lot of detail about it right now, because we have to wait until after you pass your initiation before I can tell you everything. But I do want you to know that it exists so that you'll be able to think about it ahead of time."

"Okay," I returned, now even more anxious to know what she was talking about. "What is it?"

"The Golden Key," she responded in a whisper.

There was a moment of silence in which the surrounding stillness prevailed as we huddled together in the misty haven. As we sat there, I recalled that she had mentioned the Golden Key earlier, back during our meeting at Ron's house, when she spoke about the coven in Ireland, but she hadn't really said anything about it then. After about a minute of silence, in which I was dying to ask her what the Golden Key was, she finally resumed her talk.

"The Golden Key is actually both a process and a mystical key, which opens not only the secrets of Magic, but also unlocks the very origins of the universe and the secret of life, itself. It is both simple, and at the same time extremely complex, and is, by far, one of the greatest mysteries of all."

"So tell me what it is," I pleaded, anxious to know the secret.

"Ah,' as Shakespeare would say, 'there's the rub.' I can't tell you the secret because it's something that you have to discover for yourself."

"I don't understand," I queried, somewhat frustrated by the riddle she presented. "If you can't tell me, how am I ever going to discover it?"

"By going through the process." she returned.

"But what is the process?" I asked.

"Now we're getting somewhere," she replied, smiling. "The process begins with a riddle. Just solve the riddle, and you'll have the answer to the key. So, here's the riddle: 'Thrice three, the Golden Key.'"

I sat dumbfounded with no clue as to what the riddle meant. "Thrice three, the Golden Key," I repeated to myself.

I know it's frustrating at first, but every member of the coven has solved it, and so will you. You must be patient and ask questions. But let me give you a place to start. What do you think thrice three, the Golden Key means?" I paused for a minute and then said, "Well, let's see. The word thrice sort of means three right?"

144

"Yes."

"So, thrice three, huh? Does it mean three hundred and thirty three?

"You're close, but that's not quite it," Stephanie answered patiently.

"Does it mean three times three?" I asked, determined to get it right.

"Yes, that's it," Stephanie answered smiling.

"So three times three *is* the Golden Key?" I asked.

"Yes and no," Stephanie answered. It's not just discovering that three times three is the Golden Key. That's just the first step in a long and complex process. It's actually the whole path of experiential learning connected to the riddle that will eventually lead to the Key you're searching for."

"So, I'm looking for the path that leads to the Key?

"Yes."

"But the Key to what?"

"Take a look around you, just what is it that you see?"

I glanced around as she requested and noticed that the fog had begun to lift a little. Not all the way, but just enough to expose the shadowy shapes of the forest beyond — between wispy gossamer tendrils.

"I don't know if I get it," I returned, not sure if the retreating fog and the exposed forest were a part of the Priestess' lesson.

"Don't worry," she responded compassionately. "This is just the first step, and there will be much more later. For now, all I want you to do is to think about the saying, and to decide just what you think it might mean. And while you're doing that, just remember that the riddle is very much like the fog that surrounds us now. When you pass initiation, either Ron or I will give you more clues, but for now, what you've learned here is all that you need to know."

The creek bed was getting very chilly now, and I was shivering because it didn't occur to me to bring a jacket. Stephanie suggested that we continue our lesson on another day, when we both had more time and it was a little warmer. I still wanted more, but the cold won out, so I

145

nodded my head in agreement and Stephanie stood up. She raised her hands toward the night sky like she had when she first created our circle and began a simple invocation.

"Arida, Mighty Mother of us all — we thank you for allowing us this special time together, and we ask that you let your wisdom be upon us as we make our journey throughout this life. Also, please help Patrick in his search for knowledge, and open the door for him into the mysteries of the Golden Key, when the time is right. We also would like to give thanks to the elementals and to all the spirits of nature who've joined with us here this night, and to thank you all for your participation and friendship as we seek to unravel your mysteries. *Sha gadda galat, sha ma na gadaf gadou. Dukaat!*" [5]

Shortly after the closing of the circle, the closeness of the forest subtly retreated, and the mist gradually began to subside. It didn't leave entirely, but it did settle somewhat closer to the ground, leaving the creek bed more defined, and the way home more visibly exposed.

Stephanie turned to me and held out her hand, framed by the shadowy shapes of the surrounding wilderness, and I reached up taking it gently, as she gracefully helped me up from the ground.

"I like you Patrick," she said quietly, with a real sense of warmth conveyed in her tone. "I see something special in you that I sometimes find within myself," she continued, her smile illuminated by the starry sky. "Not everyone is like that, but when I meet someone who is, I always know it. I think you and I will become very close — and there aren't too many people in my life that I could say that about."

I was too embarrassed to respond, so I just nodded my head, and we started walking together down the misty

---

[5] A complex greeting with multiple meanings which goes something like this: May brightness greet your spirit, and may the water forever flow to meet your thirst. And by your will and connection to her may you be a sacred vessel for her magic. May you also be as a circle — never beginning and never ending — but rather continuing as spirit ... Forever! It is so.

ravine back toward the pathway to our cars. As Stephanie led the way, I marveled once again how gracefully she moved through the misty causeway, much like a ballerina gliding across an unseen dance floor — and I thought about how something in her earthly elegance reminded me very much of my vision of the Lady at Easter, as she moved down the narrow streets when I sought to catch her. The difference, if it were indeed the Lady I saw within her, was that this time she'd offered me her hand like she had in the tunnel at the beginning — not to take me to the world beyond — but instead, to join her walking the pathway of Magic together. And instead of me running after her, always trying to catch up, she was guiding me gently and patiently, every step of the way.

CHAPTER 10

The Sanctuary

About a week after our trip to the creek, Stephanie took me out for another lesson. We left my house in the earlier morning and drove west to the neighboring city of Chatsworth. After driving for a short time, Stephanie stopped along one of the main streets crossing the northwestern end of the San Fernando Valley, and pulled off to the side of the road. The area was composed of what appeared to be a strip of vacant lots that stood between several housing tracts at each end of the strip. The strip of vacant lots was lined on the side bordering the road with large trees and overgrown brush. The general appearance of the area was, for the most part, run down, and it appeared to be used by some people as a dump site.

"Why are we stopping here," I asked, seeing nothing of particular interest along the well traveled and generally indistinguishable road.

"There's something special I want to show you," she returned, prompting me to exit the car.

Once we stood on the roadway, she reached out and took my hand and led me to a runoff ditch along the side of the highway. The ditch was marked by a bent steel post with what appeared to be a county mile marker, printed in black, affixed to it. As we made our way down into the narrow gap, the ditch took a sharp turn to the left and dropped substantially down into an even deeper gully, which flowed into a four-foot diameter corrugated steel drain pipe about twenty feet below. There was just the slightest hint of water trickling into the pipe from our end, but its source was not discernible from our point of view.

We made our way down the slope past a discarded mattress spring and an old rusted washing machine, and, with Stephanie leading; we entered the pipe, clearing spider webs before us as we proceeded into the uninviting darkness. The inside of the pipe was stuffy and damp and

148

smelled of foul water and decaying vegetation as we made our way forward. I couldn't, for the life of me imagine why we were descending into this foul place. After a short distance, the tunnel turned, and I saw a circle of light ahead as we neared the end of the rank passage. When we reached the end, Stephanie, who was leading, stepped out into the light and then offered me her hand once again. When I exited the pipe, I was taken back and totally amazed by what I saw.

In front of me was a large estate, filled with exotic grounds and tropical birds. There were palm trees and waterfalls amid winding well manicured pathways made of stone. There were also large ponds, filled with lilies and other water plants, and I could see bright orange and black fish swimming lazily among the shallow pools. The whole scene was tied together with half a dozen arched bridges crossing the rock waterways that connected the pools and cascading waterfalls.

"What is this place," I asked excitedly

"Shhh, this is private property, and we're not supposed to be here."

"I'm sorry, I whispered, looking around to see if anyone heard me.

"It's okay," Stephanie said, "I just like to take a look around first before we get too loud, just to be sure that there isn't anyone else around.

"So, whose place is this?"

"It belongs to a man from India," Stephanie went on. "See all the statues?"

I looked around the property and noticed that there were a number of stone statues with scary or unusual faces, and several with dozens of arms brandishing swords and other odd things.

"Here, come with me," she whispered, taking my hand and pulling me behind her down a stone path. We crossed a small bridge and the path split, with one division veering left through a stone archway covered with ivy. I followed Stephanie through the opening with my heart pounding at the possibility of being discovered, and found myself before a fifteen foot tall female statue carved out of sandstone. The statue wore an intricate headdress and had its arms outstretched, palms up toward the sky. At the midpoint of the statue, built into the protruding belly where the navel would have been, was a large concave bowl, holding a coiled spiral of smoking incense. The smoke from the incense rose up through some internal channel within the sculpture, and exited through dozens of small holes in the outstretched hands.

"Isn't she beautiful," Stephanie said, as we watched the tendrils of scented smoke weave together and then work their way up into the hibiscus, maples, and palms above, almost like some magical force, seeking to touch every leaf and surface as it made its way into the sky.

"Each time I come here, I'm reminded of the Goddess," she went on, gesturing to the whole scene around us. "It's as though she's just standing in the middle of everything with pure energy radiating from the palms of her hands, and that the energy is turning into all of the wonderful and beautiful things around us."

I looked at the statue and the lovely garden that we stood in, and I could see that Stephanie was right. It was just like she'd said.

"Anyway," Stephanie continued, "I thought that this would be a nice place to sit and talk about Magic, while, at the same time, introducing you to another of the special places that we've found over the last few years."

"But what about the people that own this place?" I asked, concerned about getting into trouble. "What if they come?"

"Don't worry about that, there's never been anyone here during the daytime so far. I just like to check each time I come to be sure. Actually, the house that this all connects to, which is where the people live, is way on the other side of that stone wall over there." I looked at the massive river rock wall nearly a quarter of a mile away and felt somewhat more secur when I saw that there was a large wooden gate separating the house side of the estate from the garden area where we now stood.

Stephanie motioned me to sit down on a concrete bench near the base of the statue, and then she joined me there as she began her lesson.

"I want to talk a little more about Magic and some of the ways that we use it in actual practice," she began.

"Okay," I responded, giving the Priestess my full attention.

"In Magic, we use spells to focus our intentions and to create physical connections with events that we would like to see come about. Now, as you can imagine, there will often be times when what we human beings want might not necessarily be what is best. In fact, in some cases, when we're angry or hurt, we might even wish harm on someone else. Do you understand what I mean?

"Yeah."

"That is why it's so important to understand the interconnectedness of everything, so that we don't misuse what we know, when our feelings get out of whack. I'm sure that you've heard at one time or another that Witches use spells to turn people into toads, or to make them sick, right?"

"Yes."

"But how often have you heard of them working Magic to heal someone, or to help a mother deliver a child into the world?"

"Well, I haven't really."

"Why do you think that is? Do you think it's because it never happens, or do you think that it's because certain groups of people prejudice the stories, so that only the parts they want heard come out?"

"Probably the latter."

"You're right. That's why it's always been interesting to me that, while the Bible is full of people praying to God to help them kill their enemies, no one ever talks about that as being evil magic. Yet, if a Witch were to do the same thing, it would be construed in the most heinous way. Even so, I think that you can see from my example that there's a flip side to every coin. But that's not the point I really wanted to make.

151

"What I really want to get across is that we are *all* human, and that the gods have given *all of us* access to substantial power, whether we're Christian, Jew, or Witch. That power is neither good nor bad in itself, but instead can be used for either purpose — whether it be the chemicals within the earth that can be used to make medicines or to poison one another, or whether it is a spiritual force that can be used to heal people or to win a war against them.

"As Witches, we have a responsibility to live in harmony with the world, rather than against it, and so we have to work extra hard to consider our actions before we take them. We believe that what we put out in the world either contributes to that harmony, or takes away from it, and that there is no such thing as middle ground — and so, ultimately, we believe that if we do something against that natural balance, disrupting the harmony created by the Goddess, that the weight of that power gradually shifts against us.

"Now, don't get me wrong. We don't believe that every little mistake we make, condemns us for eternity, but we do believe that there is a cumulative effect, and that the magnitude of our deeds has a direct impact on the degree of imbalance we suffer ourselves."

"So, what you're saying is that we shouldn't work negative Magic, right?"

"Yes, generally, but, more importantly, what I'm saying is something far bigger than that, and that is that all of us — Witches, Christians, and others — should spend a lot more time defining what positive and negative *really* are, rather than categorizing them by our own self-serving standards. If we can learn to do that, then our prayers and our spells will be much more in line with what the Gods want from us, rather than in opposition, and that's a very important thing — because, ultimately, when people are kneeling in prayer, or when they're working a spell toward some specific end, there won't be someone else overseeing them to be sure that their request is right.

"So how *do* I learn how to make good decisions about the right and wrong ways to use Magic?"

152

"By studying what the Gods have provided for us here and by realizing that we're all just a part of something much bigger. And that single purpose is what the coven is all about."

Stephanie and I continued our talk for a time and then gradually fell silent, mesmerized by the beauty of the sanctuary. While I sat and contemplated the things we had discussed, my Priestess got up quietly and walked down by the water lost in her own thoughts.

When Stephanie returned, we started back up the path across the garden. We entered the dreary pipe and worked our way back through the darkness to the road ahead. When we exited the tunnel, I looked around me, taking in the rusted washing machine, the mattress and the other discarded trash, which greeted anyone who might consider venturing into the shaft, and I came to a significant understanding of my Priestess's earlier lesson regarding the Golden Key.

During that lesson, she had pointed out that when you first looked at the Key, it appeared to be something quite different from what it actually was, and that the part hidden from view, once you got past the exterior, was really the thing that was most important to discover. And, as I looked back at the dismal tunnel behind us, I realized that the tunnel itself stood as a metaphor for the whole concept that Stephanie was trying to teach. At first look, it appeared as an uninviting filthy place, with nothing to offer and nothing to see, and so a person looking at it from that perspective would never even imagine venturing into it. But if instead, the person was someone spurred on by the principles that Stephanie had laid out to me to help me discover the Golden Key, he or she might very well have pressed beyond that dismal facade, and discovered the beauty and serenity hidden there. And so I made a commitment to myself to really think about the riddle Stephanie had given me, and to press beyond those things that I considered to be given. As we returned to the mundane world of cars and houses and men, I felt sure, that the discovery awaiting me, should I fulfill my new commitment, would be well worth the task.

Over the course of the next three months, Stephanie and I got together on a regular basis. I worked diligently to try to assimilate all that she was sharing with me. I also wrote down all I could in my magical book, but it became obvious to me that I would never be able to record even a small portion of what I was learning.

We met often, and regularly took long walks outside, particularly in the woods or canyons surrounding our area. My admiration for her grew, and we became great friends, talking for hours on end about ritual, the sacred holidays, and Magic. I learned more about each of the eight major holidays, including, within a rough framework, the development and purpose of each, and some of the major things that would be done during these seasonal celebrations.

Stephanie made a point of letting me know that I didn't have to remember each and every detail at this time because we would be going through the ceremonies, themselves, in the future. She went on to tell me that there was way too much to learn about the holidays in sessions like these even if we spent a month just studying each one. She also said that it would take me years of practicing Magic to understand the subtle secrets hidden within each ritual.

"You should think of the ceremonies and spells that you learn as being like the tip of an iceberg — with the largest portion hidden below the surface. The majority of the secret knowledge you will discover in Magic will be revealed to you in time, not by me, but by the Gods through your experiences. Ron and I and the others are more like a set of individual keys — each of us unique and fitting different doors — that will open your mind to particular experiences. It is not the key that holds the knowledge, but rather the pathway you walk, which is beyond the door. Even so, without the keys, the doors cannot be opened. So, there is a lesson in the metaphor itself. Sometimes even small things count. Remember that our journey is about searching for the pieces of a giant puzzle. No matter how many large pieces you find, one small seemingly insignificant piece missing leaves an incomplete picture. Give honor to all who play a part in the riddle because you never know who or what holds the final key that will unlock the universe."

I continued to study with Stephanie until just before the end of October. At that time, she announced that we would stop our lessons for a couple of weeks. She told me that she had to devote her time to the coven now, as Samhain was coming up very soon.

"Everyone has a lot they have to do to prepare," she said. "This is our highest holiday, and we will all take the day off to participate. We have herbs to harvest and supplies to get, and it takes a full day to prepare our ritual site up in the mountains. I'm sorry you can't participate, but you will be able to be with us next year." With that she ended our meeting, leaving me feeling left out, sad, and depressed.

The next two weeks were very hard for me. It was much like being left out at a Christmas party with everyone else you knew laughing and having fun, while you're locked up in some lonely room studying for a test. That was just how I felt, and it was such a contrast to the way I'd been feeling over the last few months. I knew from my conversations with Ron and Stephanie that all of the coven members were out in the woods together, searching for the necessary plants and things to make the incense for Samhain and the coven's sacred oil. I could just imagine them, holding hands in a circle, reciting their magical invocations, while Stephanie bent to cut some special plant with her little handmade knife made especially for that purpose.

On the night of Samhain, which was also Halloween, I put candy out for the kids that would come to "trick or treat" that evening. As it began to get dark, I stood outside in the cool evening, and I could hear the excited voices of small children beginning to walk the streets in their costumes. I remember wondering how all of this fit — real Witches on the mountain tops, honoring the dead and

155

laying out their ritual feasts, while at the same time, small children dressed as ghosts and skeletons ran from house to house yelling "trick or treat," collecting goodies and candy.

While I hadn't learned everything about Samhain yet, I could still feel the Magic in the air as the evening moved on toward full darkness. It was like a giant web of static electricity, exerting gradually increasing tension in the air, like a thin membrane of pure energy stretching to the limits before breaking. As I stood on the rapidly cooling street, watching the sun dip below the horizon, I could really feel the natural forces of winter waiting to flood the autumn landscape, while more and more pressure built up, behind the unseen dam. As it got darker, the wind gradually began to gust, first in small fleeting currents, and then in an ever-increasing fury, which forcefully made its way through the nooks and crannies of the neighborhood where I lived. Even more noticeably, I could hear the rising gale, high above us in the foothills to the north of where I stood, where I had my Easter vision of the Goddess and chased her through ancient cities, trying to connect.

I, if anyone, knew that there really was a doorway between the realms of life and death. And it struck me for the first time that this ancient holiday, this time when those worlds were said to meet, as children walked the streets mimicking the world beyond, and adults got together for parties and costume balls, would become for me, a very special day. I moved from the sidewalk across the small grassy median to the curb at the edge of our street, and stood under the street light located between our house and the next. Ignoring the would-be goblins and protective parents bearing flashlights to ward off the dark – – a tradition I now found odd considering that on any other night they would have been fine with the streetlights — I raised my hands to the heavens as Stephanie had taught me.

"Gracious Lady, you who stand at the threshold between this world and that which is beyond, don't ever let me forget this most sacred night. Let it always be special for me as I grow older, and let me never forget that I have been touched

156

by you." With that, I thanked the Goddess for giving me back my life, and I walked quietly back into the house, slipping early into bed, anticipating the day when I would finally be initiated.

❧ ⊙℘℘ ❧

I didn't hear from Stephanie or Ron at all until about a week after Halloween. Then on a Thursday night, just before dark, I got a call. It was Stephanie, and she informed me that I would be studying with Ron again. She said that she and I would work more together in the future, but not until after my initiation. I was a little taken back because I really wanted to learn from her, and I very much enjoyed the time we spent together, but one thing I had particularly learned about Stephanie was that, once she had made up her mind to do something a particular way, there wasn't any changing it.

Ron and I began to meet again as before. The first time we got together, he explained more about initiation.

"Now that you've gotten this far, I can finally tell you about the Magic you, yourself, have been working in this process, and how the coven helped initiate that Magic to get you started.

"We began your training in a very organized and specific way," Ron continued. "Nothing you have learned in the course of your instruction was done haphazardly or on the spur of the moment, even though it might have appeared so. In fact, each and every step so far, has been designed to impart a particular way of thinking and understanding for you, so that you would be properly prepared to take the next step when the appropriate time would come. The process of the initiation and its preparation if properly done provides the initiate with all of the steps necessary to bring about real Magic. Now that you're actually ready to finalize your journey, I'd like to explain each of the steps you've taken so far, so you'll fully understand the process you've been going through. That way, when the time comes for

157

you to pass this knowledge on to others, you'll know exactly what to do.

"First, we began by creating a desire within you. This was a very important initial step for you because, without desire, there wouldn't be any reason to need Magic in the first place. In your case, we developed the desire for you to change your life by joining our coven and learning Magic. Once you achieved that step, the next thing we needed to teach you was to have focus. Witches discovered long ago that, in order to have Magic, you must first be able to direct all your attention to the change you want to make. In your particular case, we pressed you to make a commitment to take in a tremendous amount of information in a short period of time, which forced you to focus all of your energy on the particular project at hand.

"We did this because another thing that Witches have observed is that true desire — that is, something that you critically feel you need, rather that just some frivolous want — always leads one to focus, and so, as you can see, desire and focus are intimately connected. We also believe that when we combine true desire with focus, we actually create a spiritual key that unlocks our own divine potential and that once we have connected with that potential, we can better envision the tools we'll need to accomplish tasks that lead to fulfillment of that potential.

"Understanding this important concept," he went on, "leads us to the next step in the magical process, which is gathering up the necessary tools to achieve your objective. We believe that if you collect everything you need to address the problem at hand, you will be fully prepared to take action when the time comes to accomplish your goal.

"In your case, at least regarding the pursuit of Magic, the tools needed were knowledge and understanding. If you look back, you'll see that your intense focus automatically led to gathering what you needed to accomplish your goal. So, once again, we can we can see that there is a connection between the building blocks of Magic. In this case, we can see that focus leads to gathering what is necessary to reach the goal at hand, in this case, your initiation. So, if we step back, we can see that desire leads to focus, and that focus leads to preparation. Are you following me so far?"

"Yeah," I answered, seeing the logic of it all.

"Good," he returned, resuming the lesson.

"Once you began collecting the things needed to accomplish your initiation, there were still two steps left to actually realize your goal. The first was taking action, which you already began to do when you decided to pursue your desire, and which will be completed when you actually enter the coven. And the last ingredient, which is the power of faith itself or, as we see it, the belief in Divine intervention, will be fulfilled when your goal is finally reached, and the Goddess, herself, intervenes on your behalf."

"What do you mean when you say the Goddess will intervene?" I asked.

"What I mean," he said, grinning from ear to ear, "is that there will be a moment in time and space, when you've done all that you can to make your wishes and desires come true, yet the final the outcome can still go many different ways. But through your faith in the Goddess, and your belief in a higher power, it goes your way instead.

"In the case of your initiation, there will be a point in the ceremony where you'll ask for her blessing and for a sign that she's with you as you make the transition. And when that time comes, and she gives you that sign, both the Magic and the initiation will be complete.

"So, as you can see from our talk, there are five things required to bring about your initiation, or if you will, working the Magic that leads to it. They are desire, focus, preparation, action, and faith. Each of these building blocks — if we can call them that — is represented within the symbol of the pentagram, which as you know, is the symbol of Magic."

"I thought the pentagram represented the four elements and the connection with the Gods," I interrupted.

"It does, but the pentagram like everything else in Magic has more levels of meanings than what you see at first. It isn't like some Witch just looked at the symbol somewhere back in time and said, 'What a cool symbol. Why don't we use it to represent Magic?' Instead, there was a long process of development over time that led to it. For example, did you know that the star was one of the very first symbols used to represent God in ancient times? Or that the pentagram is the only figure in the universe that contains the requirements necessary to represent the Golden Key? There are actually even connections within its construction that reveal to us the very origins of the universe and the secret of life itself. Once you've been initiated, we'll teach you all about these mysteries, and you'll begin to have more and more experiences on your own, and I think you'll be completely blown away by what you'll see there.

"Anyway, getting back to the pentagram as a symbol for the initiation: Just as the symbol represents the elements of fire, water, earth, and air, and connection with the gods, with each of them being equally balanced and connected as are the points of the pentagram, the five steps to initiation are also similarly connected and balanced. Witches try to use this simple formula, not only in pursuit of the initiation, but also in everyday life. And we believe that, if you do, you'll find that your goals are reachable.

"Just remember, though, that success is not just a personal thing but has more to do with understanding your part in the scheme of things. Don't be confused by what others consider to be success. Our primary goal as Witches is to be in harmony with nature and the Gods, not to be rich, famous, or powerful.

But don't misunderstand me; I'm not saying that there is anything wrong with pursuing these latter goals. Just don't confuse them with what the Goddess wants from and for you. Spiritual fulfillment comes not from without, but from within. An empty cup surrounded by water is still just an empty cup. No matter how many times you drink from it, you will still find yourself thirsting when you're done."

I gave great consideration to what Ron told me. Once again I was fascinated by the way everything in Magic made sense. I also could clearly see that the first rule of Magic, looking for what is unseen, applied to everything we did. Now I understood for the first time what Jack meant when he told me that it would be easy for someone who only studied what was obvious to think that he had all the information, and that he understood everything about Magic.

As both Ron and Stephanie had pointed out, each layer appears to be complete and whole unto itself and doesn't particularly lead one to search further. In fact, that's exactly how it was for me when I first began. But now that I had had some time under my belt, and began to grasp some of the knowledge concealed within what seemed to be small and simple things, I realized that it is only by walking the path with someone who has walked it before, someone who knows what we're supposed to be looking for, that we learn to look for the rest of the picture. I felt both pride and privilege to be able to make my journey with the coven, and I hoped with all my heart that I'd be able make it through my initiation and become a Witch and a teacher myself.

Our lessons continued as the weeks went by. Yet, more and more, I was encouraged to walk the woods by myself. Ron referred to it as the "weaning process" and explained that it was very important to be able to be out on my own.

"If you are to be initiated," he explained, "you've got to be capable of standing on your own. A coven is a group of equally balanced individuals, each with something unique to contribute to the whole. There is a saying that "power shared is power lost," but that only applies to an uneven exchange. In the coven, we are all capable of being alone, and it's only by our own choice that we remain together. Before you walk the path of initiation, you must be confident within yourself that you don't need us in order for you to continue on. When you are sure of that fact, just let us know, and we will prepare everything for your transition.

"In the meantime, there are a series of questions and responses that you'll have to learn as a part of the ritual to make that shift. I'll give them to you now, and I want you to spend as much time as you can learning them. As always, there's far more within them than what you'll see at first glance, but I'm confident that you'll understand their full meaning, once you've have the time to think about them. In any case, as I said before, when you know that you're ready to take this last big step, just let us know. Believe it or not, we're looking forward to finally completing your initiation as much as you are."

I took the questions and responses home with me that day, and I pondered them and practiced them day and night. I was working mostly by myself now, and my walks in the woods proved to be wonderful, peaceful, and inspiring. I discovered new mysteries there every day as something in my training opened a previously closed part of me. And, once it was opened and its new vision was revealed, hidden things became crystal clear. With each and every falling leaf, as the earth floated safe in Her womb, the Lady guided me through field and wood like a shuttle through a loom.

Then, sometime in the early part of December 1966, I called Ron to let him know that I was ready. The following day, I received phone calls from every member of the coven offering me congratulations and support. When Stephanie finally called, she told me that my initiation was set up for Imbolc, February 1st. I was so excited that I could hardly stand to wait the two months 'til the ceremony. But now that I knew that it was set, I also felt a real sense of accomplishment. Stephanie also told me that she was proud of me, and with her long awaited blessing, I felt I was on the top of the world!

Yule Passed and I was not allowed to participate in that coven's ceremony either. Even so, I didn't feel as bad as I did on Samhain, because I knew that my initiation was near, and that I would be participating in all of the Sabbats in the future. Then in January, I received a wonderful and unexpected surprise. I got a letter from the coven in Ireland who I'd never communicated with before. They welcomed me into the coven and told me that they would do a special ritual for me to commemorate my initiation. They also sent me a few leaves of Bane of Soltra from K.D.'s garden, which they said were cut from a plant that she had tended since before World War II. They said the bush had been one of her most prized possessions, and they suggested that I use little pieces to make the oil for the coven in the future. They said it would help connect me with them and with all those who had come before. They also wished me well, and said they hoped that we'd all meet some day in the future.

Figure 12: Letter from the coven in Ireland with dried Bane of Soltra

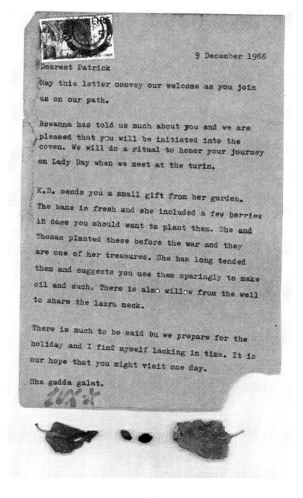

It was really quite a surprise to hear from them, as I didn't know that they even knew that I existed, but I guess Stephanie must have kept them up to date. In any case, I was exhilarated by all the attention, and I remember falling asleep that night completely exhausted with the letter tightly gripped in my hand and thinking to myself that I had finally made it.

CHAPTER 11

Initiation

By the last week in January, I was completely ready for initiation. By this statement I don't just mean that I wanted to be initiated, I mean that I was fully prepared — mentally, physically, and spiritually — to take that step. It wasn't until now, just before the event would actually take place that I really understood why it was that I had to wait so long for this special and pivotal moment. For, as the time for my initiation drew near, it became very clear to me just how little I had actually understood — just a short, yet seemingly distant, time in the past. I was thankful for the wisdom of my teachers, and for them having insisted on patience rather than speed during my training. And it was to their credit that, as I stood on the threshold of this new beginning, I was truly able to appreciate the gift being offered and the complexity and mystery of it all.

The coven chose a place for my initiation in the foothills of Saugus, which was a sparsely populated rural area five miles to the north of my home. To get there, we drove through Beal's Cut — the famous pioneer pass that joins the Los Angeles basin with the Santa Clarita Valley. The very first gold in California was discovered there beneath the "Oak of the Golden Dream," twenty years before Sutter's Mill. The place they chose had a small seep surrounded by dwarf willow trees that formed a dense circle around the spring.

To get into the area, we had to kneel down and crawl through a natural tunnel in the brush that was created by animals so they could to get to the water. Once inside the grove, there was a clearing about thirty feet in diameter with a small, clear pool of water in the eastern portion that was about three feet in diameter and that smelled slightly of sulfur. Mixed among the willows were stands of nettles and mugwart, and the scent of the mugwart dominated the area with its rich earthy smell.

The ground was slightly damp throughout the area but not muddy, and there was a large gray rock about two feet high and three feet in diameter in the northeast. The trees grew up about ten feet high in a circle, and from the center you could see only the sky directly above. After showing me the place where the initiation would be held, the coven members walked me to a place higher up in the surrounding hills — about a quarter to a half a mile away.

It was still early in the morning when we arrived at our destination. Jack instructed me to remove anything that was metal from my person, and then he presented me with a simple white cotton robe, which appeared to be made out of a sheet.

"Walk up into the trees over there," he said, pointing to a small forested area several hundred feet away, "and take off all of your clothes, including your shoes and socks. Then, put on this robe and return back to us down here with your shoes and clothes. I did as Jack instructed, following a faint game trail up and across the rocky ridge, and into the trees, in search of a place to disrobe. When I finally found what I considered a private place, I worked my way out of my current outfit and slipped carefully into my new robe — bundling the rest of my belongings as I did so. It felt odd to wear the robe with nothing else on. Because it was so light and loose fitting, I actually felt naked and slightly embarrassed to wear it. There was just the slightest hint of a breeze working its way through the trees, and the cool currents caressed my body in a sensuous way, increasing my sense of nakedness. After a fleeting moment of shyness, where I found it difficult to return before my peers, I finally started to walk back toward the waiting coven. The stones and leaves hurt my bare feet as I tried to return, so my progress was slow and difficult. Several sharp rocks left painful bruises, and twice the sharp points of dried oak leaves stabbed the bottom of my feet. About half way back to the coven, the trek had become so painful that I even considered stopping altogether rather than bruising my feet anymore. Then a powerful memory flashed across my mind.

166

My Easter vision of the Lady, standing among a crowd of villagers, surrounded by mud huts appeared before me. For a moment I was transported once again to that difficult walk where I had tried so hard to reach her across a field full of stones and thorns, and I had given up. I'd learned from that vision and others, that one must *pursue* the Divine in order to connect, and that it isn't until we make the most sincere effort, even in the face of adversity that we finally make that connection. Once I saw the similarity between my earlier vision and the path I now sought to travel, I viewed the difficult trail ahead as somewhat of a revelation rather than a hindrance, for I knew now that, whatever else happened, I had to press on — not only for my initiation, but throughout my life. And so I continued on down the arduous path to the waiting coven below and not surprisingly, like an affirmation of my decision to press on, the rocky ground became more soft and pliant as I approached my destination. When I arrived back before the waiting group, Jack reached out and took my bundle and proceeded to give me further instructions about what was expected of me.

"Make yourself comfortable here until someone comes back to summon you. It's okay if you move around a little," he continued with a gesture that took in the small plateau we stood on, "but under no circumstances should you leave this general area."

Stephanie stepped forward, nodding assent to my High Priest's instructions and added in a friendly, yet authoritative, voice: "While you're waiting Patrick, you should take the time to introduce yourself to your surroundings and to make friends with the spirits that live here. This is a very sacred place, and my guess is that you'll return here often in the future. This is also a good time to contemplate the spiritual journey you've made to get to this point and to think about all you've learned since we met."

I thanked her for her wisdom and agreed to take her advice. Then I watched somewhat anxiously as the coven members started down the winding trail towards the ritual

167

site, gradually becoming only voices and then, finally —
silence.

I looked around for the first time, really taking in the
area that surrounded me. There were a few of the ever
present oaks scattered here and there, which all seemed to
have been there for centuries, with their gnarled and
twisting branches somewhat devoid of leaves reaching for
the hazy sky. I don't know what it was about the oaks in
the area, but there weren't any little ones. In fact, there
didn't appear to be any new growth at all. Perhaps the
climate had changed or the soil had evolved to a different
structure, but it was apparent to me that there wouldn't be
any more of the treasured oaks growing here in the future.
There were also a few colorful manzanitas, and while they
were generally considered to be more of a bush than a tree,
the few that were present on the hilltop were well over ten
feet tall. I also noted that there were several smaller elders
clustered near a rocky shelf to the east at the base of the
next plateau above me, and I wondered if there might be an
intermittent seep present below the broken rock, as I then
knew that elders generally prefer more than an average
amount of water.

The plateau where I waited was on a small knoll atop a
range of rolling hills, and I could see for many miles in
several directions. The knoll and all the surrounding hills
around me were covered with sage and Yerba Santa and
chaparral, which I now easily recognized due to teachings of
my mentors. There were also occasional yuccas popping up
here and there with their grey-green spiny leaves forming
formidable tufts against possible intruders, and dozens of
other sparse, yet still present, species. Overall, the view
from the mountain was uplifting and my spirits were
souring high, as I waited for someone to come for me, and
anticipated the initiation that would follow.

The day moved on — and no one came. Around noon or
so, I walked a small circle following the tree line and
introduced myself to the surrounding flora and fauna.
Later in the day, I spent some of my time studying the tiny
foliage that grew among the rocks where I was stationed,

168

while mentally reviewing my walks with Stephanie and Ron, and all that I'd learned from them.

When the sun finally began to set in the west and wide bands of orange and magenta gradually dimmed into a solid velvety purple, I started to worry that the coven had forgotten about me, or worse, that something had happened to them. The sun continued its downward journey and darkness crept from east to west, bringing with it the small sounds of animals and insects as night solidly stepped in. Even with all of my training and although I felt intimately connected with the nature surrounding me, I began to feel somewhat uneasy on the mountain top because of the human element that was involved. As the darkness set in, I started to worry that, perhaps, they had all been arrested, or, even worse, perhaps they had run into some of the local farmers and ranchers that lived among these hills. I was also worried that someone who wasn't a member of our coven might discover *me* up on the mountain top. Jack had instructed me not to leave under any circumstances, but I began to question whether or not this was what he meant. Then, shortly after the sun disappeared below the horizon, I heard the soft sound of footsteps in the dark behind me, and I hoped it was someone from the coven.

"Are you ready to make the journey?" Ron's welcome voice asked from the darkness, somewhere in the trees above and to the left of me. I turned toward the sound and responded to the query, which I recognized as the beginning of the ritual colloquy I'd been practicing for weeks.

"I am ready and prepared," I returned, recalling an earlier lesson by Stephanie where she'd gone into a very detailed explanation regarding this ritual play on words.

"The questions and responses are a very important part of the ritual," she had said. "Each line moves you through the transition from beginner to initiate and commemorates the steps you've taken to join the coven. Don't just repeat the words when the time comes to recite them. Instead, really take them to heart and consider what they mean. Remember, this initiation isn't just about you. It's actually a huge commitment for all of us."

169

Ron stepped out from behind a tree and came up to me. He took out a blindfold and tied it gently over my eyes. Once the blindfold was securely in place, and he was certain that I could not see, he resumed the poetic dialogue, pacing his words slowly and carefully as though each held a special meaning and he wanted to be sure that nothing was missed.

"The way is long and the path is difficult to follow in the darkness."

I considered the weight of his words and responded sincerely, allowing the full meaning of his observation to penetrate to the core of my being before doing so. I responded in kind with a sincerity matching my mentor as I answered my teacher's challenge.

"I am blind and cannot see the path before me, yet I am still ready to make the journey, for the Goddess is with me — and her light will illuminate my way."

I couldn't see, but I could literally feel Ron smile at my response. I knew he was proud of my accomplishments and his voice was filled with emotion as he placed the next obstacle in my way.

"Your path may be illuminated, but there are many twists and turns in the course of your journey. Even in the light it is easy to get lost in the forest."

"I have befriended all of nature and one cannot be lost when in the company of friends," I returned, confident that I was now ready to walk the path of initiation.

"Then take my hand and I will be your guide, and we will make the journey together," Ron concluded. "For the path you seek is not new to me and I can help you on your way."

With that, Ron gave me a gentle nudge on my back, and I stumbled slightly forward in the darkness, unable to see the trail before me because of the blindfold. I could tell by the slope of the ground that we were heading gradually down the hill, and I could feel the coolness of the night earth on my feet as he guided me gently in the direction of the sacred grove — and what I knew would be a new beginning. I was without fear this time — quite different than my first encounter with coven, which seemed like ages ago.

I felt a unique familiarity with my surroundings, even though I'd never been on this particular hill before today. The blindfold actually heightened my senses, and I could hear the familiar sound of the breeze rattling small leaves nearby. I made the proper greeting to the sage as I passed, recognizing its pungent minty odor, as my leg brushed against its branches. Then on the right, just a little farther down the path, I nodded to several crows calling from high above, probably perched in an oak. I knew from my lessons with Stephanie that crows seldom ever call out from low brush or small trees, as they like to be sure they're safe before alerting would-be predators of their presence. And I also knew, after months of traversing the local hills that only the oaks up here were large enough for crows to feel secure in. *"Sha ma na gadaf gadou,"* I said in Elban, nodding to the unseen oak as I passed by. I knew that my greeting, "may the water forever flow," would be received in friendship, and I opened my mind in anticipation of the receptive response. The tree's subtle reply touched me like an elusive daydream, filling me with a peaceful serenity — as the gap between the guardian and myself bridged for a ephemeral moment and our spirits connected in friendship. I thanked the tree for its welcome support. Then Ron, sensing I was ready to proceed, resumed the journey toward the hallowed grove and the waiting mystery beyond.

As we continued forward, there was a very special sensation present. Transversing the pathway to the grove, I couldn't see what was before me because of the ritual veil, but I could tell from the smells and sounds in the vicinity who and what was near. I remembered thinking that perhaps this journey was yet another layer in the mystery of *lazra meck*, the light that illuminates even in darkness — for while I was blindfolded and couldn't see in the normal sense, I was still able to perceive clearly what was most important for me to know on this particular spiritual quest. The multilayered nature of this magical tradition never ceased to amaze me. Even the simplest of things, like Ron having me smell the plants and trees on our first lesson, were so intimately connected to the process. And once again I could feel the pieces of the puzzle falling neatly into place as I took this final step toward becoming a Witch.

As I continued on my journey, my new found special sense revealed to me that I was surrounded by friends. So I let myself move forward through the darkness toward my destination in total trust, guided by my knowledge, guarded by my friends, and accompanied by the spirit of Lady.

My excitement grew as I neared the grove. There was a surrealistic quality to my whole experience that is somewhat hard to describe. Imagine being blindfolded and unable to see, and then walking through an unknown forest guided only by your imagination. While it is true that Ron was with me to keep me from falling or from walking into a tree, my perception of things and my relationship to my surroundings was derived purely on my own. I recognized familiar sounds and smells, and plants and animals literally sprang up before me in my mind's eye, but their colors and qualities were highly exaggerated in much the same way that we see things in dreams. When a coyote howled somewhere far off in the east, I envisioned a pack of ragged and slinking canines, in constant motion, meandering through the brush — searching for food. I was even able to see small rocks tumble down the steep hillside, dislodged by the beasts' spreading paws, as they sought surer footing among the manzanita and greasewood. When I first approached the area where the ritual was to be held, and smelled the willows and mugwart, a circular grove of tangled trees immediately appeared on the fringes of my mind. I could see the slender branches woven tightly together, shimmering as the light of a thousand stars caught the opposing colors of their narrow leaves.

The path grew damper, and I could feel an increasing amount of give to the soil between my toes, as it changed from the hard dusty clay of the mountainside to the dark loamy soil of the grove. Ron applied slight pressure to my right shoulder and turned me slightly, and he informed me that we were nearing the radiant ring of waiting willows and the sacred spring within. He guided me carefully to the entrance where the living tunnel made up of a thousand fragrant spiraling tendrils interlocked and became the gateway to the other side. Once I was positioned safely within the entrance to the passage, he informed me that I would have to proceed from that point alone.

"This journey," he whispered so close that I could feel his breath move the hair on the back of my neck, "is one that you'll have to make on your own — for only one person at a time can make the transition through *wa da na*, the pathway of the womb. And it is only through this very personal transition that one can return to the source and be reconnected to the Mother and the beginning."

I recalled the first time that Ron had told me about the transition from the mundane world to an experience of the Divine. We had stood together on the top of a pine-filled peak at night, looking at the stars and feeling the chill of winter moving in. The landscape below was surreal with fog collecting in the canyons and valleys far below. And far off in the distance, barely visible beyond a second range of mountains, spread the lights of the great city of Los Angeles, which gradually faded into the low hovering clouds along the coast as it moved away from us, finally disappearing into the blackness of Infinite Pacific Ocean.

"God is not off in some distant place like some believe," Ron began. "Instead, God is right here with us, here and now. She's all around us in the trees and the streams and the sky, and even dwells inside of each of us — hidden deep within our spirit. That's the reason Witches walk the paths through the forests and learn about the plants and the animals and each other there. It's also the reason we move through rituals and dance to exhaustion beneath the brightness of the full and fertile moon — high on the tops of towering mountains like this one, or why we sit with our feet buried in the sand along distant shores like those below, seeking spiritual communion. For knowing God comes not from reading books or listening to sermons, or even by going through the motions of our own sacred rituals, but rather through personal experience at the

173

moment of ecstasy, when the rhythm of the dance blends with the hidden wisdom of the circle, and the magnificence and the beauty of all that surrounds us comes together in a swirling star-filled sweet scented spiral of trees and rocks and people and thoughts, spinning and spinning and spinning until our spirit soars into the oneness of everything that is. And it's at that special moment, when everything comes together, and you're touched by the Creatrix within you, that we truly remember how we all fit and where we come from. For it is only at that moment, when we find ourselves divinely filled with joy from that connection, that each of us truly experiences God."

I had felt a jolt of realization shoot through my body as I recalled the spinning tunnel of light filled with color and everything that was. I had remembered how that vortex lifted me into the presence of God and the feeling of absolute oneness and connection I felt as I experienced Her awesome presence. In his description of how to connect with the Divine, Ron had unknowingly actually made the connection so for me, and I was grateful to him for that. It was odd to me how even though I'd actually stood before Her, and held Her hand, I could still forget Her presence at times. And in coming to that realization, I had a profound insight into the nature of God and our relationship with Her. I knew, in that moment, that we must always pursue connection with the Creator, even though we may have done so in the past many times before. And I began to recognize that it isn't knowing God that is really important, but rather our ongoing pursuit to remain connected to Her that really counts. Having previously come to the conclusion that the Goddess could feel pain, I began to comprehend for the first time that She might also require love just like the rest of us.

I recalled once again that special moment when her hand touched mine as I floated alone in the infinite blackness of space, and I remembered how everything, and I mean everything, seemed to become complete at that precise moment. And, looking back, I believe that that moment — that instant in time when she and I touched and the circle was complete — was as much a moment of completion for Her, as it was for me.

There was a pause for a moment, as Ron and I had stood there together, each caught up in the powerful inspiration brought about by my mentor's explanation. As had often happened before, Ron seemed surprised by the effect of his words on me — and himself.

"Sometimes the Goddess just seems to takes over," he said with a somewhat embarrassed laugh. "I just wanted to convey that it is only through our direct and personal experience with nature and ourselves that we can really know and experience the Divine. And that very soon now, when you travel through the living entrance to the circle within, you yourself will have made the mystical journey of *wa da na.* When that time comes, you will in a sense be personally returned to the womb where you began, and find yourself nourished by the Mother there and presented with her mysteries. Afterward you'll return to the mundane world through the pathway once again. But this time, unlike your first journey at birth, you'll remember everything you found within her sacredness and you'll see the world in a clear and pristine new way," Ron had said.

As I bowed my head and began to feel my way through the tunnel of initiation, it was in fact very much like the spiraling vortex between heaven and earth that I experienced when I first met with the Lady. The tunnel seemed to go on forever, with a pulsing rhythmic sound engulfing me as I made my way forward. When I reached what later seemed to be the mid-point of the passage, the pulsing beat became more clear — evolving into a melodious Elban chant that signaled that I was close to my final destination. At the end of the transitory passage, a familiar voice greeted me, and a strong yet gentle hand joined with mine.

"Patrick, you have walked the ancient path of initiation and your long journey is almost at an end," Karen's voice proclaimed as she helped raise me from the ground and stabilize me on my feet. "Yet the end of every journey is only the beginning of another, and the beginning of each

175

new journey always marks the end of the one before it — for all things created by the Gods are a circle and a circle goes on forever. So, Patrick, are you ready now to leave behind your old journey and start out on a new one?"

"Yes," I replied.

"And are you also ready to enter into the realm of the Gods?"

"Yes I am," I returned.

"Then let the journey begin," she announced, taking my hand and leading me determinedly forward into the future.

As we began to move, I could sense the pale flickering light from glowing candles, which created an eerie display of light and shadow within the confines of the fabric of my blindfold. I could also smell the sweet heavy scent of incense — mixed with the scent of the mugwart and the willow — transported by delicate gusts on the edge of the ever-present wind. As Karen guided me in a *deosil* direction around what I knew must be the circumference of the coven's circle, I could smell the sensual aroma of the sacred oil emanating from her. She moved me around the perimeter of the unseen circle, staying very close to me, using the weight of her body to guide me this way and that. After awhile, we came to an abrupt stop, and Karen repositioned her hands on my shoulders and turned me sharply toward what I imagined must be the center of the large periphery I had been circling.

"Stop!" another familiar voice commanded. Nicky's words challenged me from the darkness.

"Who goes there?" she demanded."

"Patrick," I responded, knowing from my training that this was the proper answer. There was a short pause and some shuffling of feet behind Nicky's voice, and I had the sense that the whole coven stood behind my interrogator, awaiting my response to the question that I knew would come next.

"And why, Patrick, do you walk the pathway outside our circle, and what do you hope to attain by doing so?"

I'd spent nearly the whole last month considering this and several other questions that the coven had asked me to contemplate in preparation for this important occasion. I paused for a few moments, reflecting on the time since I'd been touched by the Lady and the sequence of events that had followed after. I'd memorized the customary response to the question being posed and could easily recite it, but I knew in my heart that there was more. My mind wandered back to a walk several months ago with Stephanie, where she'd showed me a tiny rivulet of water that transversed back and forth down a steep hillside from above the area where she and Jack lived. The watercourse was dwarfish, not much more than a thread, and originated somewhere in the heavy brush above it.

"Why do you think the water chooses the course it takes," my Priestess had asked as we walked along the steep path that traced the boarders of the silvery thread.

"Because water always travels to the lowest place," I answered, confident that my understanding of the laws of nature would impress my teacher.

Stephanie paused, shaking her head slightly, and just a ghost of a smile crept forward from the corners of her mouth. I'd seen that particular smile before, and I knew from past experience that her question held some important lesson, concealed below the surface of the seemingly benign inquiry.

"What you've just said is true," Stephanie continued. "But if you look at this particular tributary, even though the hillside's very steep, you'll see that rather than heading straight down the mountain it chooses a much longer journey. See how it works its way substantially back and forth across the hill before reaching the bottom. In doing so, it provides nourishment for a far wider variety of life by extending its journey rather than by limiting it."

I looked at the stream on the mountainside and saw that what Stephanie said was true. It *didn't* trickle straight down the slanting bank as it could have done, considering the steep angle. Instead, it had created a series of switch-backs as it worked its way down the slope, distributing water back and forth across a large expanse of land.

177

"This is how it should be for us also," Stephanie continued. "People often limit their lives to a small simple journey, rather that taking a chance to see what the world really has to offer them — and what they have to offer the world. Sometimes this is brought about by chance, but more often it is brought about by fear. Fear of the unknown, fear of failure — fear of discovering the truth. When you're faced with the decision whether or not to expand your capacity to know, you should always move toward it. For it is this action — the conscientious decision to achieve your Goddess-given potential — that will allow you to contribute to the world we live in, rather than take away from it. So, when you look at the stream working its way down the mountain, the question you really have to ask yourself is this: Does the stream choose its own course or is there something guiding it? And more importantly, should we as human beings deny the desires of the Divine, in order to feel more secure in our own existence?

"I walk this path because it is the path that I choose to walk," I responded to Nicky — choosing my words carefully as the vision of Stephanie and the tiny stream faded. "And what I seek is my own destiny — for it's only by choice that we can truly follow the love of the Lady. It was She who set me on this course by holding my hand and giving me the choice between life and death. And it was I who decided to choose life. Now She's placed another choice before me: Whether to walk a simple journey with the security that that choice offers, or to reach out to discover my full potential. So, on this day, I choose to walk the path of the Witch. And it is my hope that, in so doing, my passing will contribute more to the world in which I live, than I will take away from it."

Nicky acknowledged my answer, although I could tell by her hesitation, that she was taken back by my unorthodox response. I heard a chuckle in the background and recognized Stephanie's voice as she whispered, "See, I told you," then silence.

Nicky continued on with the welcome of the east, and I listened intently to the words she spoke.

"I am *aesma* of the east," she said. "And it is here that all things must begin. For it was in the east that the first sound became the light of spirit, and it was out of the east that *lazra meck* was born. And so it is I who bestow upon you the first gift of the Goddess, *djinn ralda*, the spirit of the element of fire, and present you with the purity it carries within it — that your journey may begin as new and that all that is undesirable from your past be left behind."

The inside of my blindfold began to glow with an undulating pulse, as light struggled to penetrate the folds of the scarf that covered my eyes. The scent of hot melting wax mixed with the occasional smoky aroma of a burning wick as the light became brighter. The glow finally settled, low and near my left hip, remaining there for several seconds. Then the glow moved — rising above my head, hovering there also for a few moments. Eventually the candle lowered, resting finally at my right hip. As the light, moving *deosil*, completed its path and formed the sacred symbol for fire before me, Nicky in her capacity as *aesma* of the East continued my purification.

"As I bathe you with its holy light, let *lazra meck* purify you and animate your spirit. And as you walk the path of the Witch, let the illumination of that spirit light your way."

Just then, the motion she'd made, made me recall one of Ron's earlier lessons where he'd taught me that the triangle was the symbol of fire and hence the symbol of purity and beginning.

"The triangle," he'd explained, "is the building block of the universe, and so it represents purity and is a symbol of the beginning."

"Why do you say it's the building block of the universe?" I asked, not sure exactly what he meant by his statement.

"As you study more, you'll understand how they came to that conclusion. But, for now, just know that the reason we chose it to represent fire was not by chance, but instead, was brought about by thousands of years of observations, which led Witches to a keen and unique understanding of the workings of the universe. It was also these same observations that led Witches to discover the secret of the Golden Key and a number of other mysteries."

Karen placed her hands on my shoulders once again and quietly instructed me to move on to the next cardinal point in the circle, which was the south. When we reached our destination, I was challenged a second time, only this time it was by James.

"Stop, who goes there?" James challenged.

"Patrick," I answered.

"And why, Patrick, do you walk the pathway outside our circle, and what do you hope to attain by doing so?"

"I desire entry into your circle and to be initiated as a Witch.

"Why should I allow you to pass the gates of the south?" He asked.

"Because I have been purified by fire and my spirit is illuminated by the light of the Goddess."

"I am *aesma* of the south," he said. "And while it is true that one must be pure and filled with spirit to enter the circle, one must also have form and be fertile in order to receive that which is attainable within. The south is the place where spirit first turned into form, and existence was created. Without physical existence, spirit has no meaning, for it is only through experience that the Divine potential within us can be realized. And so it was in the south that *goba* was born — the solidity of existence. And it is through this transition that I am able to bestow upon you the second gift of the Goddess, *goba ralda*, the spirit of the element of earth."

With that, I heard a scraping sound, like something dry being mixed in a bowl, and then I felt the sprinkling of earth from above my head, falling on my shoulders and down through the neck of my robe. I could smell the pleasing earthy fragrance of fresh fertile dirt reminiscent of the black fertile soil one finds in a forest river basin, and I shuddered in a kind of spiritual ecstasy as the cool moist loam touched my naked body finding its way through the neckline of the sheer cottony habit and settling on the warm skin below. And I was transported back to a walk

180

with Ron months before along a winding trail in the Saugus foothills. We had stopped to rest under a choke cherry tree and had just sat down on the earthy mound beneath it. The wild cherries were colorful and ripe, and there were a few fallen fruits here and there, lying on the ground in front of us.

"These cherries are a good example of how the element of earth plays an important part in the scheme of things," Ron began, reaching down and picking up one of the maroon skinned fruit between his fingers. He broke the skin with his thumbnail, exposing a giant seed, which took up the majority of the inside of the fruit, leaving only the tiniest bit of meat between the skin and the pit. "This fruit, as you can see, is really just a seed, and, like all seeds, it is very much like spirit was in the beginning before it took physical form. While spirit, like this seed, contained the knowledge of everything it could become, also like this seed, without the nourishment and sustenance of fertile physical existence, it had nothing to feed or grow on to reach that potential.

"If you watch this tree over time, you will see that some of these cherries never fall and that instead they just hang on the branch until they become dried out empty shells. Others, however, drop to the ground, surrounding themselves with the fertile earth, and in doing so they sprout and grow, becoming beautiful trees, which again bear fruit. There's a lesson for us in all of this: The Goddess isn't a crutch for us to hang on to and to expect everything from. If we live our lives that way, like the cherries that stay on the tree, we will eventually just shrivel up and die without offering anything of ourselves. It's important to remember that the world we live in is like the fertile ground beneath the tree, and the people, places and things within it, which have been specifically chosen for us by the Goddess, have the potential to nourish and enrich us just like the soil does the seed, if we choose it, so that we, then, have something to offer in return.

"The Goddess is the one who gets us started in life and instills within each of us the potential to carry on Her sacred purpose. When we ground ourselves in this way, by participating in the sacred cycle, we help Her creation to bloom and grow, so that Her beauty, just like the beauty of the tree, can continue on forever. We are free to seek our own journey, still carrying within us Her spark of divinity, while hopefully, never forgetting the tree and that we are its fruit. Our life here on earth is a gift and this is sacred ground which should be cared for to the fullest, for without this, our journey is meaningless and the creation itself is undone."

"Let your new existence be formalized and your full potential be realized as you enter the realm of the Gods and begin your journey as a Witch," James said, bringing me back to the moment.

When the earth had settled and the *aesma* of the south became silent, Karen started me once again on my journey around the perimeter of the circle. This time, we moved toward the west, and I anticipated the challenge from the *aesma* there.

"Stop, who goes there?" R.J called out, as I came to a stop before him.

"Patrick," I returned.

"And why, Patrick, do you walk the pathway outside our circle, and what do you hope to attain by doing so?"

"I desire entry into your circle and to be initiated as a Witch."

"Why should I allow you to pass the gates of the west?" he inquired, sounding quite serious in his response.

"Because I have been purified by fire and my spirit is illuminated by the light of the Goddess," I returned. "I have also been endowed with the element of earth, which has allowed me to experience existence, and, with that new existence, my being is fertile ground for the potential offered to me by the Gods."

"I am *aesma* of the west," he countered, in a soft, yet vibrant, voice. "And while it's true that one must be pure and filled with spirit in order to enter the circle, and that one must also have form and be fertile in order to receive that which is attainable within, it is only through birth that

182

one can make the transition from one world to another. And so it was in the west where form first made the journey through *wa da na* — the pathway of the womb — and was transformed into life. And it is through that transition that I am able to bestow upon you the third gift of the Goddess, *neck na ralda*, the spirit of the element of water — which is the primordial cauldron of conception."

With the completion of his words there was a period of silence once again, which was broken by the faint sound of trickling liquid — much like the ripple of a euphonious eddy in an otherwise unobtrusive stream. In my blindness, I visualized water taken from one of the sacred wells — cold crisp and pure, filled with millennia of memories gleaned from its long circular journey — being poured into a chalice. I imagined its course through sky and earth and ground, and visualized its meanderings deep within the bowels of the earth — through caverns and fissures — gradually working its way to the surface in some sacred place.

Momentarily, I felt the cool trickle of the hallowed liquid seeking refuge in my wind blown hair. Gradually, it continued down hill, tracing the curve of my neck and chest and bringing a shudder of exhilaration as it worked its way down my body seeking the waiting ground below. I was reminded of an afternoon earlier in the summer when Stephanie and I went down to Bow Creek to have a lesson. We sat together along the edge of the stream watching the water racing through a deep slender trough filled with a million bubbles, and I mentioned how nice it would be to just lay down in the cool water and relax on such a warm summery day. Stephanie's lips curled sweetly into a knowing smile, and she agreed, nodding her head slightly, sending nut brown curls shimmering in the radiant beams of sunlight that filtered their way through the canopy of oak and eucalyptus high above.

"There's no higher aspiration than to immerse ourselves within the elements of nature, and to find that special niche, where we can be both the recipient and the conduit of the life's blood of the Gods, she answered." She went on to tell me that it wouldn't be long before I would participate in *chanala ralda,* the ceremony dedicated to joining oneself to the elemental spirits, and that I would know what it was like to actually become that churning stream.

I'd never thought of being in the water in that way before, and the words she'd said really struck me in a poignant way. Nothing I'd ever done before I decided to become a Witch had prepared me for the relationship I was now developing with nature. Everything I touched and saw and smelled had new and deeper meanings now. And the changes in the way I looked at things, like lying in a cool mountain stream, gave me a childlike sense of wonder that lightened my spirit and added an extra degree of happiness to thc way I perceived the world as a whole.

The last of the water traveled down my body and the *aesma* of the west touched me gently on the forehead.

"Now that you have experienced birth, you are ready to enter into the world beyond the womb," R.J. said. "There are many mysteries there, but like the world you now leave, there are also many distractions that lead away from the truth. Never forget that you have been touched by the spirit of water and birthed by the Mother, for there is no connection stronger than that of a mother and her child. Keep strong that connection and remember it always, for, if you do, like a mother to a child — She will always be there to pick you up if you should trip and fall."

When the *aesma* completed his say, Karen tapped me gently on the shoulder and whispered that it was time to move on. We worked our way slowly continuing in a *deosil* direction around the next quarter of the circle until we reached the north where I was challenged again.

This time the challenge was thrown out by Eldon who stood as the *aesma* of the north.

"Stop, who goes there?"

"Patrick," I answered confidently, now familiar with the overall process.

"And why, Patrick, do you walk the pathway outside our circle, and what do you hope to attain by doing so?"

"I desire to enter your circle and to be initiated there as a Witch.

"Why should I allow you to pass the gates of the north?" He inquired.

"I have been purified by fire and my spirit is illuminated by the light of the Goddess," I returned. "I have also been blessed with the element of earth which has allowed me to experience existence and, with that new existence, my being is fertile ground for the potential offered to me by the Gods. And lastly, I have been birthed anew through the element of water and, through that transition, I am now new to the world — and a child of the one who created it."

"It *is* true," he said, "that one must be purified and filled with spirit in order to enter within the circle. It is also true that you have to have form and be of fertile mind in order to receive that which is offered within. And without the experience of transition, from one world to another, the full meaning of the holidays would be lost in the everyday motions of the rituals rather than the underlying Magic contained within them. All of these are worthy comrades on the pathway you have chosen to follow and worthy allies to say the least. Yet by themselves they are not complete. For it is not until each living thing takes its own first breath that it is truly alive as an independent spirit and able to have its own personal relationship with the Gods. And so this is the gift I offer you last, the gift of *pa ralda* — the spirit of the element of air."

And with that statement, I heard a sharp intake of breath and then a slow unhurried exhale, as I felt the movement of air ruffle the cloth that covered my face.

As the unseen currents passed across my face, I drifted back to an earlier lesson with Ron.

We were walking on a trail in Placerita Canyon together near the area where I first made friends with the oak tree. We were in another heavy grove of trees above the canyon floor, when a heavy gust of wind whistled through the trees. The wind reminded me of my first lesson with Stephanie and I asked Ron about it.

"When I went out the first time with Stephanie, she made the wind blow," I stated, looking up into the giant trees as they shuddered, responding to the wind.

"I'm not surprised," Ron responded. "Witches consider a rise in the intensity of the wind to be a sign of magical energy. In fact, we have a old saying, 'The wind at night is power,' which is pretty much why we mostly hold our rituals at night. We also consider the wind that comes up during the day to be powerful; too, especially if it comes up in response to Magic that we're working. Remember that wind is just another form of the element of air and that, as such, it carries with it the breath of life. But it also plays an important part in physically shaping the world we live in by affecting everything with which it comes in contact.

"What do you mean by that?" I asked.

"If you watch closely, you'll see that while the air itself is invisible, everything touched by its presence, as it journeys across the land, is moved in some noticeable way. There isn't a rock, or tree, or pond, or, for that matter, any living or breathing thing in the world that doesn't acknowledge its presence in one way or another. We, too, have a divine characteristic like that. When the air focuses itself into a great wind, it has tremendous power to move and shape the world around it. When it presents itself as a gentle breeze, it plays music in the trees and adds a sense of tranquility to our spirits. So like it is with the air, what we do in our time here moves and shapes the world around us also — even when we don't realize it or mean for it to. It is important to know and remember this, and become conscious of the part that we play, so that we play it with intention and with love of the Goddess in mind, rather than just inadvertently in a self-centered way.

When the *aesma* of the north was finished, Karen started me moving around the circle again. We still traveled in a sunwise direction and after a moment or so, we returned to the east where we'd first begun.

As we came to a halt, I was greeted by a different voice this time, rather than that of the *aesma* of the east.

Instead of Nicky, my High Priestess, Stephanie, addressed me as I approached.

"Patrick," Stephanie said quietly, "you have answered the challenges of the four directions and learned of the story of creation. You have also been given each of the gifts necessary to experience Magic and to be a Witch. Now there is but one more mystery to know — the mystery of the circle."

When she finished her statement, she carefully lifted the blindfold from my eyes and welcomed me into the sacred circle pulling me gently forward to stand before her. At the same time, Karen, her body pressed close to mine from behind, pushed me forward toward the waiting Priestess until I was fully inside the circle. Once I was actually within the sacred space, Stephanie leaned forward gracefully and kissed me softly on the lips.

"With this kiss, I welcome you to our circle and seal the bond between our coven and you. For it is only through love and trust between us that the circle can be formed and Magic revealed. So I say to each of you now as we stand openly before the Gods, let none of us break what has been forged in love. And from this day forth let each of us make our sacred pledge — to honor that which is born of this day, and to share our knowledge freely between us."

When Stephanie finished her statement, she instructed me to remain where I was until she came back. I stood in the eastern quarter of the circle near the candle that marked that quadrant, and watched as my Priestess turned toward Ron, who still stood outside our sacred space. Ron slowly approached the circle, which was marked on the ground with a white powdery chalk-like substance, from the north. Even if I hadn't know any other direction, I would have known this was north because the big dipper had just cleared the horizon and the two stars that Stephanie had taught me pointed to the north Star were clearly visible above the circle of holy trees. I could also clearly see the Andromeda cluster higher and to the northwest of the Pole Star, which shown brightly due to the absence of a moon.

As Ron approached the glowing white candle that marked the northern boundary, Stephanie began to move gracefully toward the coarsely textured granite slab in the center, which served as the coven's altar. Reaching the protruding stone, which was deeply anchored in the moist fertile soil, she extended her slender hand down carefully, amid an array of mystical paraphernalia and flickering candles, and picked up a long delicate tapered knife with strange symbols carved deeply into the blade.

The magical blade had been mentioned several times during my training, both by Ron and by Stephanie, although I really knew very little about it. What I did know was that it was used to create a sacred space and occasionally to direct energy for a specific project. I also knew that it was never used to cut anything, and that its creation involved intricate ritual and the highest workings of Magic. Jack once told me that there were many secrets contained within the blade, but he'd never gone beyond just stirring up my curiosity. I also knew from instinct, rather than instruction, that this was the very blade that was used to create the sacred circle for my initiation and, as such, I was in awe of it.

Once the blade was retrieved and safely in hand, Stephanie proceeded to walk to the northern quarter of the circle, pausing tentatively in front of my waiting guide. After a long moment of hesitation in which she whispered some unheard invocation, Stephanie raised the blade — its highly polished surface shimmering brilliantly in the reflected warm yellow glow of the altar candles — and deliberately cut an invisible doorway into the circle that set us apart from the mundane world. Ron had described this process before, so I knew that she was cutting a portal. Once the portal was opened, Ron stepped through, saying something in Elban as he crossed the threshold of our temple and greeted Stephanie with "*sha gadda galat.*"

As soon as Ron was well within the circle, Stephanie re-traced the doorway she had cut, with the shimmering blade, and I would swear that there was a faint blue white

188

light that remained stationed over the silhouette of the doorway for several minutes after it was sealed.

With that, Stephanie returned to the place where I had entered the circle and sealed that doorway also in a similar fashion. Afterwards, she returned to the altar and placed the blade back from where she had taken it. Once the knife was safely at rest, she returned to my side, and gently taking my hand, led me back to the altar she had just left. As if choreographed in advance, everyone else moved in perfect timing along with us and assembled near the center of the circle forming an arc in the southern quarter behind us, facing the altar. When everyone was in place, Stephanie reached out and took my other hand and turned to face me head on. Her face lit up into a radiant smile and she looked me in the eyes and said,

"Patrick, my magical name is Rowanna, which means child of, or heart of, the sea. I give it to you as a sign of trust between us so there will be no secrets standing in our way. And with the giving of my secret name, I also pledge before the Gods to teach you all that I know and to protect you in times of hardship and trouble."

I knew that this was an important step as a Witch. Ron had taught me that when another Witch gives you his or her secret name, you could use it to draw power away from them. I was pleased that Stephanie trusted me that much, and I also knew that it symbolized that I was now a real member of the coven.

Next, Nicky came forward and took my hand in place of Stephanie's.

"I'm called Brooke," she said, beaming as she disclosed her name. "It isn't Magic or Elban or anything," she went on, "I've just always liked the sound of it."

"Hello Brooke," I responded, returning her smile and squeezing her hand.

"I also pledge to teach you and to protect you in times of hardship and trouble," she went on. "And if anyone ever asks me to tell them who you are or to give them your name or where you live, I swear not give you up."

189

When Nicky was finished, Ron stepped forward to take her place. "Solomon is *my* name," he disclosed," after the wise man of the Hebrews." I knew that Ron's family was Jewish, so it made sense to me that he would choose a Hebrew name. He also pledged to teach me and to protect me as each of the others had. One by one, the rest of the coven stepped forward, revealing their magical identities. James was Astra because of his interest in the stars, and Karen had taken the name Chanalyn which was derived from the Elban word *chanala*, meaning connected. Jack was Rwyllin, which had something to do with a story he was told as a child, and Eldon just used his own real name, which he said already held power for him. R.J. was Merlanthis, after the Arthurian magician Merlin, who he held was an ancestor of his, and Derek, was Bentwix, who he explained was one of three magical associates of the Lady of Soltra, an Elban mythical sorceress.

As I looked around me, the stars and the candlelight revealed a small intimate group of men and women, brought together through a time honored tradition. We stood cradled within a shimmering circle of candlelight, filled with the fragrant smoke of eons of herbal knowledge, and there was a particular sense of ecstatic tension and sensuality between the participants as they moved about in their flowing robes stopping occasionally to look up at the radiant star in the east, which Stephanie informed us, was really the planet Jupiter. For me, there was something provocative and delicious about the scent of their heavy robes, a combination of incense and wood smoke, intermixed with the sweet earthy aroma of our sacred oil, which was especially comforting and filled me with a sense of security that I had never experienced before.

All of these scents were delicately balanced with the fragrance of trees, damp wool, and years walking in the woodlands — all trapped within the fibers which joined together to create a unique scent that took me to another place beyond this world. There was a sense of oldness about it, a flavor of antiquity, like entering an old attic, or opening a long stored steamer trunk. If you've ever experienced that, you know the feeling I'm speaking of. That sense of mystery and history, lovingly folded in carefully placed quilts and old clothes, set aside by the packer — who saw within them, potential for those loved ones who would follow in the future.

But there was also a deeper more powerful image brought about by this earthy scent as I stood for the first time in a magical circle, here at my initiation. The pleasant, yet compelling, aroma also evoked powerful visions of ancient ceremonies and hooded figures, venturing out into the elements in search of wisdom. I could easily imagine men and women reenacting this sacred dance, this spiritual journey, millennia before we stood here today. My own personal journey and the transition I'd made to arrive here and now in this sacred space, made it easy to visualize acolytes walking narrow pathways through the forests at a time when none of the knowledge we now take for granted was commonly known. Having walked their path myself, I now I felt connected to them and could see for the very first time that the journey we in modern times take to achieve knowledge falls short. For as good as it is, our education in schools and universities, and even the instruction we get in our homes, leaves out the most important components of human understanding — the wisdom and mystery of it all. For no matter how much we learn, there is always that which is unseen, and it is the unseen — that which is holy — that drives the spirit of humanity. Somewhere, somehow, sometime in the ancient past, we separated intellect from the sacred, and we have become divided as human beings. But my journey, my walking of this archaic way of knowing, my initiation, literally and figuratively, restored what was divided in me, and it is a wonderful feeling to be made whole again.

As I stood in the starlight, surrounded by others who had made the same journey before me, I found myself touched in the most intimate and personal way. And, as I stood there filled to the point of bursting with the spirit of it all, I turned my gaze skyward and thanked the Lady for allowing me a second chance. I knew now that She isn't just up there lost in some far off untouchable place that I would have to wait until death to reach, but, instead, that She is a part of me personally, and that Her infiniteness is just as it had been when She'd held my hand — flowing, expanding, and becoming everything that is. She is the trees and the mountains and all of nature. She is also the stars and the sky and the universe beyond, and so I celebrated that night, Her greatest gift — the deep feeling wisdom of what it is truly like to be alive!

Stephanie returned reverently to the altar and retrieved a small glass vial of amber colored liquid. It was thick and rich with a slightly reddish cast which appeared to be illuminated from within, like a beautifully cut topaz. She raised it up before the starlit sky, and as the heavenly light struck it, the curve of the vial joined the holy liquid within, forming a lens, which bent and condensed the light of all the heavens above into a single and brilliant star which shown in the center of the liquid.

"This is a container of our sacred oil," she said. "It was created by our coven from the magical plants and herbs that have been used for centuries for that purpose. In every drop, there is also oil from the coven we originated from, and the one before that, and the one before that, and on and on 'til some time and place lost in antiquity that no one remembers. For us, it represents our connection to those who knew and understood the mysteries that came before us. It is the life and blood of the coven, and it should be treated accordingly. Never use it in a manner that would dishonor our traditions, and use it sparingly, as it is valuable and irreplaceable."

With that, she opened the vial and placed one small drop of the fragrant liquid on the end of her middle finger. She called me forward and I stood before her, as she transferred the shining drop to the center of my forehead and drew a pentagram there. As the magical oil touched my skin, I felt exhilaration and reverence pulse through my entire body.

"With this oil, I consecrate thee, and proclaim you a member of this coven," she said, carefully replacing the cap on the vial, and handing it carefully to me.

"And with this consecration, I give you the gift of the sacred oil, as a sign of our bond, and as a token of your connection to all those who've walked the path before." Then turning to my coven mates who stood close behind me, she continued with her proclamation.

"Let each of us honor and support Patrick now and in the future, and let all of us welcome him into our family and into our coven. *Dukaat!*" Then everyone repeated, "*Dukaat!*"

In that moment, when the coven members chanted *dukaat* in unison, I felt something mystical and magical join with me, and I knew that my time had come. And as the last echo of my confirmation reverberated off the canyon walls far below, a huge owl took flight, signaling to me that the Lady gave her blessing and confirmed my transition. It was as though all of my training, my new relationship with nature, and the kinship I felt with those who had sought this path before me, had all come together in a unique and liberating connection and that I had finally become a part of them. "This is it," I said to myself, "I've finally made it, *I'm in the coven!*"

It had been a long journey from that morning on my 65 Triumph to this and the acceptance of my peers, and the magical sensation that accompanied it has remained with me from that day to this. I can say without hesitation that it has been by far the most significant means of support for my spirit — through times of conflict and calm, and times of prosperity and loss, for over thirty-nine years.

Once the excitement settled down, we all sat in a circle within our circle and began to talk. I had many questions about Magic and being a Witch, and the coveners answered each I asked without hesitation. They pointed out, as Stephanie had earlier in my training, that my initiation was exactly what the word denoted, a new beginning, and that it was not the be all and end all of Magic. They also pointed out that many of my questions would take years of study to answer completely, but at the same time they made it abundantly clear that they would provide any information they could to satisfy my initial need to know.

I learned that the circle we now sat in was created using a complex ritual, which I had not been able to participate in because I was not yet initiated. I also learned that we would cast another circle soon, to consecrate my magic wand, once I cut a branch from the sacred willow tree. Jack told me that traditionally the wand was cut today on Imbolc, but that they didn't want to break the journey of my initiation to do that just yet.

"I'll take you out in the next day or so," Stephanie joined in, "and help you select the proper tree to harvest. I know a great place for that above Balboa Boulevard. In the mean time, you should give some thought to choosing a magical name for yourself to use with the coven and for when you're working Magic.

It can be anything you choose, but it should have spiritual meaning to you when you use it," Stephanie explained. "Some people take the names of others they admire or persons in history that have inspired them in a spiritual way. Others make up a name that is entirely of their own creation, to represent some particular desire or path they choose to follow as they learn. Either way, the choice is yours, and you will know when you discover the one that's right for you."

"When we cast the next circle," Jack chimed in, "you'll be involved in every step of its creation. Ron will explain everything we do in advance, so you will understand exactly what's going on, and he'll answer whatever questions you might have. He'll also teach you more about the Spring Equinox, which is our next holiday, so you can take a part in that ritual when the time comes up. The Equinox is on the twenty-first of March this time, although the date can vary a day or so from year to year.

"Why is that?" I asked.

"Well, it varies because the Equinoxes and the Solstices are based on the movements of the sun," he returned, "and the days on our calendar don't exactly match those cycles.

Because of this, from time to time, the actual dates of the Solstices or Equinoxes can vary."

"Gradually, over the coming year, you'll learn more about all of the holidays and eventually begin to pattern your life around them. Each of these times have many different levels of Magic represented within them, and I think you'll really enjoy the discovery of the mysteries hidden there."

"Besides that," Ron added, "you'll also make each of your magical tools. We'll start with the wand, soon and later this year you'll make your blade."

"Now that's a big undertaking." R.J. piped in.

Ron continued. "There are several others to be made too. Each of the magical tools are in themselves a substantial undertaking and will, with their creation, open new doorways to understanding for you. I know you've heard this many times before, but it can't be said enough times. Everything in Magic is interconnected. Each and every implement, every ritual, the plants, the symbols — even this conversation — are brought about to lead you to some specific understanding or conclusion. So, pay close attention, for there's still a lot more to learn.

Now that you've been initiated, you've finally finished this one journey, but like most journeys in life, once you have ventured beyond your realm of understanding, you can never return to where you began — for one open door always leads to another and everything is changed once you've taken a step forward. Even so, you should never fear the journey, for the odyssey of life is the Gods' first gift to us, and the dance that ensues — if you just join in — will bring many occasions of joy and fulfillment in the future."

I was very excited about that future, and I could hardly wait for Stephanie to take me out to make my wand. I was also looking forward to learning how to create a magic circle and all of the other things that Ron had alluded to. As we talked further, we returned to the subject of my secret name, and the other members gave me a number of suggestions to consider. Most of them were mystically based and some were names used by famous wise men or warriors. Stephanie suggested a couple of Elban names to think about and Jack brought up that I might take on the name of an ancestor. No one pushed me to take any particular suggestion one way or the other; rather, they used their examples to illustrate the idea of what I should be looking for. Their suggestions were actually quite helpful, and an idea began to emerge in my mind as to how I would arrive at my own choice for a magical name. Derek had disclosed to me that he had originally chosen the name Merlin, and then later had an inspiration during a coven ritual where he received a message to change his name slightly by adding a few extra syllables to the original. After hearing that, I decided that I would do a ritual on my own, where I would ask the Lady herself to inspire me. I made a vow to return to the site of my initiation to do so as soon as possible, and I felt sure that she would help me.

After awhile, Jack changed the direction of the conversation and talked a little about the casting and closing of the circle.

"Whether we're beginning or ending a circle," Jack explained, "we always travel *deosil*, acknowledging each of the four directions in the order that things were created. We follow this pattern, even when we're ending our circle because, in doing so, we recognize that the creation can never be undone, and that, while we may choose at some times to acknowledge its existence in a formal way, and at other times to return to more mundane tasks, its presence, in either case, still continues forever.

"You might be might be interested to know," Stephanie joined in, adding to the conversation, "that we acknowledge the creation in more ways than one when we make our circle. For example, we always begin with an Elban invocation that describes the absence of light and the swirling mists, condensing to become the cauldron of creation from which everything is born. Many Witches speculate that when those primal mists first condensed, they not only became the stars and the planets and the universe, but they also became the sea, which in some ways is a womb in itself. There are also other components within the rituals that repeat these themes, but I think we should wait until you help create the circle yourself before we go too far into those. The important thing to remember for now is that just as the casting of the circle is a reenactment of the creation, so is the initiation. And that, like the circle, once it's cast, your new beginning, just like the creation, cannot be undone."

"Normally," Jack took over, "after we have thanked all of the elements and the Gods for participating in our ritual, we end the circle and return to our mundane lives. But tonight we're going to do something different. We are going to leave the circle open — and let it dissipate with the dawn. We'll still thank the elements for being present, and give thanks to the Gods too, but this time we will ask them to remain with us 'til the dawn rather than leave.

When Jack finished his explanation, Stephanie rose and went to the altar. She picked up her knife and made her way around the perimeter, acknowledging each of the elements and their corresponding directions as Jack had just explained. Then she asked the elementals and the Gods to remain with us 'til the dawn, and we all joined in a final *"dukaat"* as the ritual was completed. Once the ceremony was finished, Stephanie turned to the rest of us and said,

"The circle remains unbroken and will disappear with the dawn, but for now, we're all still within its sacred space. So, let's all just sit back and relax, and enjoy the beautiful night sky — and acknowledge the wonder of it all."

We all lay back on the damp ground and stared up into the blackness of space and the billions of stars scattered throughout it. Somehow during the course of the ritual, time had slipped skillfully away unnoticed, and Jupiter had transversed most of the way across the velvety sky following its divinely inspired cycle. It felt good to me to see how even the gibbous giant far out in space fit within our story of creation by following the simple yet ever present laws of Magic, as it confirmed once again that the circle, never beginning and never ending — symbolizes the Divine order of the universe. And the luminous globe — now hanging over the shadowy mountains far off in the west — also verified for me that all I had learned in preparing for my initiation, the laws, the metaphors and the sacredness of it all, was true.

As we lay there beneath the night sky, we discussed the same things people have talked about, when lying underneath a similar star filled realm, since the beginning of time — the creation of the universe and the unfathomability of it all. In the distance, coyotes sang and an occasional owl called out, adding music and harmony to the already haunting beauty of the painting that the *Mother* had rendered. And, as if that weren't enough, she then threw in a brief display of subtle blue-white lightning off to the west, even though there wasn't even the slightest hint of rain, just to remind us of the power underlying it all.

At some point far into the night, we all succumbed to sleep although I had no memory of the transition actually taking place. I awoke with a start some time later, noticing that all of the candles had burned out, save one. I raised myself up from the soft ground and watched as the last glowing sentinel sputtered and flickered in its final attempt to remain aglow, then gradually succumbed also to the darkness and dampness of the all-consuming night. I looked towards the east just as the abundant crescent of the currently waxing moon was beginning to rise above the horizon as it started its upward journey in what must have been the precursor of the pending dawn. Its rising silvery crescent had not yet reached such a height as to illuminate the clearing where we lay, and I could just make out the other coveners who were still fast asleep in their heavy robes, breathing softly in the security of our sacred temple.

As I looked around in the darkness, I noticed that the perimeter of the circle glowed with an eerie, yet pleasant, blue green light, which was not really apparent when the candles illuminated our circle earlier. At first, I though it was my imagination, but as I looked around, there wasn't any question, the circle was actually glowing. "How did they do that," I asked myself quietly, not wanting to wake the others, yet at the same time mystified by the experience. I stood quietly observing the phenomena for a few minutes or so and then decided to file my question away for another day.

When I'd finished watching the celestial glow, I made my way gradually around the sleeping forms of my coven mates and walked to the stone altar in the north. Surprisingly, it wasn't really that cold outside, considering the flimsy material my robe was made of, and I found that I actually enjoyed the briskness of the wintry night, now that the wind had disappeared without a trace. When I reached my destination, I knelt down before the array of knives and wands and the chalice that stood there and reviewed all of the strange objects temporarily residing on the standing stone. There were glass and wooden jars filled with unknown herbs and several vessels of colorful liquids scattered here and there bearing handmade labels, marked with strange and illegible symbols. There were also a variety of personal amulets and other ritual objects made of stones, crystals, and other natural objects, belonging, I assumed, to various members of the coven, mixed together with several woven woolen cords apparently made of rough spun yarn. As I leaned forward, I noticed that there were also the remnants of many previously burned candles, memorialized in intricate patterns of colored wax that ran down the sides of the rough hewn stone. Some were no more than a stain, washed by years of rain and sun, while others were brilliant and recent, perhaps from the Samhain I'd missed or maybe even the more recent Yule.

I paused to reflect on my initiation and the special night that accompanied it. Then looked once again to vastness of the wintry sky and said a little prayer asking the Lady for her love and support. I asked that she acknowledge the commitment I'd made in pursuing the path of the Witch, and that she give me a sign that she approved of my initiation and that she would remain at my side as I continued on my journey.

As I finished my request, a brilliant shooting star streaked across the sky, disappearing somewhere between the juncture of Spica and Mars in the constellation Virgo to the south. And I knew that the flaming arrow pointing to the young warrior starting his journey from the place of virginity signaled, at last, that my initiation was complete. I thanked the Lady one last time, as I started back toward my sleeping comrades, and then remembered something in Ron's earlier counsel.

He had told me that unlike my journey at birth, I would remember everything that I experienced within the womb this time, and that I would carry it all forward with me into the world from that day on. He was so right. For in making the transition of *wa da na*, and seeing the shining arrow pointing to the fiery Mars, I now saw for the first time how it was that I could serve the Lady.

The world I lived in was in turmoil right now and all of the young people I knew had risen up in one way or another to try to do something about it. Some wrote songs about change or protested against injustice, while others participated in love-ins, or took to the streets in riots. All of us realized that, as advanced communications brought the world closer together, making it a smaller and smaller place, old values geared toward a particular dominant race or any specific religion just wouldn't work anymore. Millions were considered second class citizens right here in our own country, even though we were supposed to stand for freedom and equality, and our generation had decided that it just wouldn't stand for it.

It hit me at the end of my initiation that the philosophy and spirituality behind what I was learning might help right the things that were wrong in our country by presenting a new way of looking at things, the same way that Spica, the brightest star in the heavens, was illuminating the path for the virgin, as she sought her way through the last moments of winter before the soon to blossom spring. And, while I might not be a great warrior like Mars, who could change the world overnight, I *was* someone who knew that there were other ways to win a battle besides just using might.

And so, as I stood in the still glowing circle, I made the decision to teach the principles of the Lady and to share Her values with anyone who would listen, in the hope that, with Her help, I might somehow make a difference. I understood that I wouldn't be able to teach this wisdom openly as Magic because of prejudice and misunderstandings about who we are, but I was sure that if I brought up the ideals behind the Magic in conversation, and pointed out how they could be applied to daily life, that those listening would see the sense of it all, the way I had as I went through my training. I felt called to perform this work and felt sure that the Lady would back me, and my mind buzzed with the possibilities for the future.

I nodded my head silently toward the rising moon, acknowledging once more the Lady's presence, then returned back to my chosen spot on the soft damp ground and curled up next to two of the slumbering forms. I didn't wake up again until the sun had risen high into the crisp February sky.

CHAPTER 12

The Wand

Shortly after my initiation, Stephanie took me out into the wilderness to cut my wand. We had to find a place that had willow trees growing, and we eventually chose a place near Bow Creek.

There were many willows there along the small winding stream, and I searched for several hours to find a tree that would meet my special needs. Stephanie guided me gently in my selection, pointing out trees here and there that met the necessary requirements.

"It needs to be a tree that's just beginning to come back to life," she said. "The trick is to find a branch that's about the same diameter as your index finger and that has no forks in it. It should be slightly green, like this," she said — pulling down a slender limb from a tree on our right that had a warm vibrant light green hue showing through its tougher outer bark. I examined the rejuvenated branch, whose bark reminded me of a newborn baby's skin, soft and pliant and full of life, and I could physically see and emotionally feel the awakening that was taking place within. As the new sap rose through the supple limb, it brought with it renewed life and a promise of new and wondrous things to come, and I knew from both Ron and Stephanie's training that this was the connection I wanted to capture in *my* wand. For it would be the wand above all other tools of the Witch, which would symbolize my new life after initiation and, particularly, my personal connection with the Goddess.

"The final length should be about the same as the distance from the tip of your elbow to the end of your middle finger," Stephanie went on, meandering through the trees like a wood nymph, never seeming to get caught in the hanging briars or stung by the towering nettles that blocked her way.

"That way, it will have a direct connection with you, or as we say, an equal measure," she continued on.

I walked through the woods in a far more clumsy manner than my elegant Priestess. Try as I would, I couldn't seem to avoid the brambles in my way, and it irritated me that every turn of the creek, brought yet another barrage of welts from the invisible nettle thorns as their tiny syringes of acid assaulted my arms. Stephanie turned and laughed as she listened to my complaints, informing me that being at one with nature didn't mean that I had to personally commune with every bush and thorn. I actually had the sense that she was enjoying my hardship, which irritated me even more. Finally, she turned around and approached me with an empathic look on her face, and I sensed that what she had to say was genuine.

"I apologize for laughing at you," she started in earnest. "It's just that I remember when it was like that for me, too. I used to get cut up something terrible when I first started, and I couldn't even begin to imagine ever walking through the woods without some mishap or other. But I promise you, things will change over time. It just takes a while for your spirit to get a sense of things, and then it'll all get easier. Think of a small child who's just learning to walk. When she takes her first steps, she falls over and over again. And even once she's finally able to retain her balance, she ends up running across the room a few times, right into a wall. But gradually, as she gets in touch with herself and her surroundings, she eventually becomes quite stable. In fact, if she chooses that course, she may even one day become a ballerina and move with incredible grace in ways that an ordinary person couldn't even imagine. That's how it will be for you, too, some day."

"Well, I hope it comes soon," I replied, "cause if it keeps up like this, I'll be lucky if I survive for a couple of more years."

Steph laughed in her delightful way and smiled. "Just remember that the Goddess has given us everything we need to navigate the world we live in. The ballerina's grace may be practiced, but the Magic of it all is that the potential for that grace was there long before she was even born. Always remember that Magic teaches us that there is absolutely nothing you can't do in the context of the universe we are all a part of, if you draw upon that initial spark that the Creatrix instilled in each of us in the beginning."

I considered my Priestess's counsel, and while I didn't understand it entirely, I felt that there was truth in what she said. "Thanks for the advice," I responded sincerely, and then wryly said, "I'll try to remember your words of wisdom while I'm still in the falling down stage, and hopefully I'll be able to run across the room and smash into a wall or two before too long."

With that, I continued my search, and I finally found an acceptable branch with the necessary new growth that also felt "right" to me.

Moving forward, reverently, I knelt down at the base of the waiting tree, finding comfort in the dark and fertile soil that surrounded it. The earth yielded gently to me, changing its shape and form as I worked my knees into a comfortable position below the willow's lithe and limber form. Once I was settled, a slight breeze teased at the few remaining leaves left over from last Winter's mild passing, and Stephanie, sensing my desire for solitude, disappeared into the woods quietly like a fairy, literally becoming the forest itself — as her earthy cotton shift and flowing nut brown hair became the colors and textures of the land itself — and then she was no more.

Once she was gone, I turned my attention to the spiraling currents of air that made their way through branch and stone and lonely stands of moving cattail that beckoned me to join them in this shadowy and secret place. The tiny gusts — scarcely more than the soft breath of a lover curled asleep within your arms — tugged and caressed at the surrounding landscape, carrying with them that now familiar scent, which had become such a rich part of my spiritual awakening, composed of fading, moisture-laden leaves, clinging to the last remnants of their shape and form as they made the transition from plant to fragrant earth. And fresh oxygen-filled water, tumbling gregariously through secret eddies and moss-filled caverns — full bodied and sweet with unseen treasures gleaned as the water meandered through forest and dale. And then there was the mugwart, with its pungent just-rained smell, sweet, yet slightly medicinal — and full of prophesy.

I looked around me, taking in the narrow serpentine canyon, shaded from the busy world above. I noted the sharp bend below the cliff to the east where the bottom of the ravine dropped suddenly, twenty feet or more, creating a small waterfall that slid rather than cascaded down the steep moss covered slope, forming a silvery ribbon as the afternoon sun illuminated it among the nut grass, rye, and dandelion.

Where I stood, among the willows, the water moved quietly through the small grove of trees, which was located in an area where the canyon widened slightly a hundred yards or so downstream from the waterfall. From there, the tiny creek continued on, making its way eventually to a point half a mile down stream. There civilization had cut short its cheerful journey redirecting it through a lonely myriad of concrete pipes and channels deep below the earth, where it eventually exited into the sea twenty miles away.

Returning my attention to the task at hand, I faced the tree I had chosen and made the proper greeting to it in *Elban*, preparing to begin the ceremony.

"*Sha ma na gadaf gadou*,"[6] I whispered, drawing the symbol of recognition in the air before me with my right hand.

While I was conscious that the saying "May the water forever flow," was a traditional greeting to trees and plants, I also understood the deeper meaning lying beneath the surface of these words. They referred to the interconnection between the sacred springs and wells, and the Goddess, and places like this. As I contemplated these

---

[6] May the water forever flow

things, I recalled an evening at Stephanie's house several months ago, where she spoke of this particular greeting. The discussion particularly stood out in my mind because it was one of the *very rare* times during my instruction as a Witch that we talked about Magic inside of a house rather than out in the wilderness.

"*Na*, not only means water in the physical sense," Stephanie had said. "As you know, it also personifies the womb of the Great Mother, which is the place of beginning. As such, it is often exemplified by the *chalice,* which is also known as the *cauldron* and represents the sacred vessel where Magic is born. But more importantly, *na* means *connected.* To be filled with *na* means that you are intimately connected to the Lady, and as such, wishing someone to be forever filled with *na* is the highest compliment one can give another.

"The word *sha* also has several meanings. The common use among Witches is, *may,* as in 'may you be blessed,' however, a more refined meaning is, *by your will*, or more specifically, *by your connection (to Her).* The word *gadaf* simply translated means *forever.* Yet in earlier times the word translated as a *circle,* as in *gadaf da ralda,* the circle of life. You know, life — death, and life again. *Gadaf* also refers to a cycle — particularly one that repeats itself like the cycle of the seasons or the rising and the setting of the sun.

"*Gadou* speaks of the flow. Yet it does not really represent the flow of water. Instead, it addresses the flow of spirit. So, when you put it all together, what you're actually saying when you make this greeting is something like this: May the water forever flow to meet your thirst. And by your will and connection to her may you be a sacred vessel for her Magic. May you also be as a circle . . . . never beginning and never ending — but rather continuing as spirit . . . . forever!"

I knew the tree already understood all of this naturally. I also knew that it would be honored to be selected for the purpose I'd come for. I addressed the tree softly and in the most sincere of tones.

"Oh, mighty tree, I come to you in peace and friendship and to ask your help. You see, today is a very special day for me. I've come to cut my wand and I'm here to see if you'll let me take one of your branches to make it. I give you my word that I'll cherish it and protect it from harm and that I'll never forget you for the gift you give."

My request was genuine and heartfelt, and I felt the tree respond in kind with its consent. I reached in my pocket and took out the very first and most precious of my magical possessions — a piece of smooth white stone shaped into a rectangle, which was divided in half by a thin black line. In the center of the line directly in the center of the piece was a tiny ball of silver which was fastened to the surface by some unseen device. Ron had given it to me in the beginning, shortly after the coven agreed to allow me to join.

"This is a gift for you," Ron had said. I made it a long time ago and have gotten much pleasure out of carrying it in my pocket. It's very magical and there's a lot of symbolism involved in its creation. I found the stone in the creek where I first saw the Goddess. It's funny, there wasn't another white stone anywhere else in that area, and I've never seen another one there since. I picked it up out of the water and it was pretty much the shape you see now. I carved the line in the center to represent the balance of everything in the universe and particularly to represent balance in my life. I drilled a hole in it and put on the silver ball to represent the moon and the Goddess. Over time I have come to think of it as representing focus. See how the two halves converge on the black line in the center, kind of like everything on each side of the spectrum is coming together. And then from there, everything further focuses on the silver ball in the center. Kind of like a magnifying glass, huh?" I'd accepted Ron's gift that day, and my teacher's words had proved to be true. There was a certain sense of security and even pleasure whenever I reached in my pocket and held the amulet in my hand. When Stephanie had told me that I would have to give a gift to the tree to take my wand, I knew from her description what my gift would have to be.

"It needs to be something that is precious to you." she said. "Think of it this way, your wand will only be as powerful as what you are willing to give in return for it. Always remember, that to receive, one has to give first. No one can tell you what your gift has to be, but you'll know in your heart right away what it should be when you think about it."

Setting the white talisman on the ground next to me, I dug a small hole at the base of the tree with my hands. I placed the stone inside and buried it slowly feeling a pang of sadness at my loss. I knew that if I left something precious, the tree would in turn give a gift to me. I recalled the rest of Stephanie's lesson as I pressed the last of the dirt into the hole and packed it gently with the palm of my hand.

"Everything in nature is about balance. If you want nature to work with you, you must be willing to give as much as you take. That is why when we cut a tree, we plant another, and why when we see an injured animal, we work to heal it — even though we might at some other time hunt it. There are times for taking, and there are times for giving, and true wisdom is knowing when to do which."

Once I was done burying the stone, I stood up and reached for the branch I had selected. It was a slender limb about three feet long with just a hint of green showing through the bark. I ran my hand carefully from the thicker base of the branch down to the spindly whip like tip. As my hand slid over its surface, I could feel the wax-like new bark, slightly cool to the touch pass between my fingers. There were small elongated oval bumps on the surface where new buds and twigs would eventually emerge once the full potential of the tree was released in the early spring. I reached into the small leather bag I now always carried with me on my magical forays into the woods, and pulled out a hand crafted crescent shaped blade with a simple wooden handle. I also took out the small vial of sacred oil given to me at initiation and, opening it carefully,

I distributed a few drops onto the tip of my finger, and then transferred it to the sharpened edge of the knife. Bending the branch back slightly, I proceeded to score the bark all the way around the desired branch, taking care not to miss any portion of the cut.

"Always use a blade of silver to make the first cut," Stephanie had said several months before, when we were out collecting herbs for the coven. I distinctly remembered the short knife she carried that day, which was quite different than the one I now held. While hers did have a curved blade, it was much shorter than mine and more like a linoleum knife. However, its blade was etched with symbols and the dark wooden handle was shaped in the form of a bird with the head being the end furthest from the blade.

"Why is the blade curved like that," I asked examining the worn blade from a distance, noting the many scratches and no longer sharp edge. She tossed her hair over her right shoulder with a practiced flip of her head and straightened to her full height as though pulled by an unseen string fastened to her breastbone. I was now familiar with this pattern. When she flipped her hair like that and stood up straight, what she had to say was especially important.

"My knife is patterned after the crescent moon — but it also has to do with the first blades made of stone long ago. You'll learn more about that when we teach you how make the blade that we use to create the circle. The reason the handle looks like a bird is because that is one of the symbols that represent Morrigan who is one aspect of the Great Goddess Shee. The reason my blade is made of silver is because silver is the metal of the moon, and as such it is sacred to the Goddess. If you cut first with silver when harvesting plants for magical use, you are dedicating the purpose of your harvest to the Goddess and this is the way things should be — for it is she, who provides for us with all living and growing things.

"Once you've broken the surface, you can finish your cut with iron or steel, or whatever you like. Silver isn't really practical for cutting plants because it gets dull right away. So that's why you'll see me cut the bark first with this knife, and then finish the cut with another." I remembered asking her if this was the way it always had been done.

"Actually, it's not," she responded. Then she briefly explained that long ago Witches made the first cut with stone, but that that was something we would discuss later when the time was right.

Shortly after that, I forged my own blade of silver with Ron's help. I shaped a longer curve and made the blade a little thicker than Stephanie's, so that it was more proportionate to my hand. I'd used it several times before this, although never for such an important task.

I recited the ancient words of power and, with a snap, I severed the slender branch with a single twist of the wrist. I thanked the tree for its gift and carefully rubbed sacred oil on the remaining portion of the limb. Then with a small amount of moss from the creek, mixed with sage and comfrey for healing, I made a magical dressing for the wound and recited the spell for rejuvenation as I applied it:

"Aga nup, damtaal tadoo jalam walda, dukaat"[7]

While I was collecting the moss, I also found a smooth black stone in the shallow creek, which caught my attention, so I picked it up and put it in my pocket to make an amulet for tranquility to replace the one I'd lost. I thought that since I'd given up the special piece that was a gift from Ron, it would be appropriate to find something new to replace it. Over the last year, I'd found that collecting such things offered me a special connection to nature, and I hoped that in the future it would help to remind me of happy times like today and the cutting my wand.

Once I finished with the healing potion, I saluted the willow, thanking it for the branch, and I started upstream looking for my Priestess. I followed the path she'd taken an

---

[7] 'Old one, make her green again. Let it be so"

hour or so earlier, and came upon her waiting in a grove of castor bean trees, just beyond the waterfall.

"I cut my wand," I told her, as I worked my way through the tropical looking trees with their spindly ringed trunks and palm-like leaves. I noted a few beans still on the ground and made a plan to collect them at some other time. They were highly poisonous of course so I would take considerable care in their use, but they also had a number of positive uses that I had learned in my training, and I didn't have any in my collection.

"That's great," she responded flashing me a smile. Then she returned her gaze upward toward the rim of the canyon.

"There are some really old oaks up there," she went on. "We should climb up there and harvest some of the bark to represent the God in our incense for spring." I looked up the steep side of the embankment, which was nearly straight up and sixty or so feet high. It went on for as far as I could see, and I couldn't imagine climbing up it anywhere.

"It looks way too steep to me," I returned. "I don't think we can make it up there without going all the way back to the bottom of the canyon."

"The Gods will provide," she said, and she started toward the high wall ignoring my comment. When she had reached its base about thirty feet away, she motioned for me to follow, and then waited for me by a small group of man-high bushes growing at the bottom of the incline.

"Look carefully," she said, pointing into the nearby clump of chaparral as I joined her. Following her direction, I carefully examined the dusty green bushes and the accompanying canyon wall, and discovered a small ledge working its way up from there. It was about three inches wide, beginning behind the clump of chaparral we stood by and continuing up the side of the slope at about a forty-five degree angle. The tiny ledge appeared to stop about twenty feet further up, ending in another clump of bushes which hung tenaciously from the steep bank.

211

"I see a ledge," I said to Stephanie. "But it only goes up part way."

"Ah," she replied. "That's the mystery. Let's work our way up and see what we find."

Questioning her judgment silently, I started up the tiny trail. I had to face the cliff directly and shuffle sideways slowly to make progress. It was quite steep but, after a few steps, I discovered there were small hand holds carved into the gritty sandstone that paralleled the ledge about seven feet higher up. They were carved in such a manner that they wouldn't be seen from below, but if you reached overhead as you worked your way up, they provided quite a secure means of transversing the trail. Stephanie followed close behind, seemingly unafraid of the drop below us, which from my perspective was quite scary.

When I reached the clump of bushes at the top of the path, I was in for a delightful surprise. Just behind the brush before me was a small ledge just large enough for a person to kneel on, and behind it was the entrance to a tiny cave. It was obvious from the marks around the opening that someone had widened the entry with a shovel or some other tool.

"Why don't you crawl in," Stephanie suggested, now crowding me from behind. I hesitated for a moment, and then crawled into the short opening, barely making it through due to the low ceiling. After a few feet, the cave widened both in width and height, and, to my surprise, it was actually quite large, being about twenty feet in diameter and over eight feet high. The cavern itself appeared natural but it was obvious that a lot of work had been done by someone to make the most of the space. In the dim light, I saw a niche carved in the wall on my left with a half burned candle and a box of matches next to it. At Stephanie's prompting, I walked forward and lit the candle.

The smell of sulfur burned my nose as the match ignited, illuminating the room with a pulsing glow. Once I lit the candle, which sputtered intermittently with dampness from the underground exposure, the light in the room slowly began to even out. Stephanie and I stood in silence for several minutes waiting for the sputtering light to stabilize, and then once it did, I began to explore the room. The soft glow of the lone candle permeated the chamber revealing several shelves carved into the soft sandy walls. There were several bottles and jars filled with herbs and what appeared to be ritual supplies and half a dozen extra candles. Aside from that, the room was bare.

"This is one of the places we come to, to do rituals or to just be alone." Stephanie said. "None of us comes here very often any more because we use the cave at Stony Point, which is a lot closer for us, but sometimes it's just nice to have a change."

"Did you guys make this cave?" I asked.

"No, we found it about five years ago when we were looking for herbs. Actually, it was Jack who found it. We did do some work on it, though, making handholds and widening the ledge a little. Someone else had already been in the cave a long time ago because there was soot on the ceiling and an old fire circle in the middle. But here's what's really cool," she said as she took my hand and led me to the very back of the room. She pointed up, and I saw that there was a natural crack that looked like it was made by water, and it was clear that it exited to the outside somewhere higher up, because you could see light reflecting from somewhere farther on.

"That goes up to the top," Stephanie said. "It's a pretty tight fit, but we can both get through there. You put out the candle, and I'll lead the way. Just follow me."

I blew out the candle and after a moment or so; I was able to see in the dim light of the room. There was some daylight entering from the entrance we'd come in through, and I could also see a little bit of light from the crack in the ceiling above us — now that I knew where to look. Stephanie worked her way up into the crack using small crevasses and protruding rocks as handholds and steps. I waited a minute for her to get a little ahead, and then I also started up into the chimney.

213

It was damp and close and I had to contort my body to make it around several bends in the tunnel. There was one place, just before I reached the exit, where the tunnel flattened out somewhat and I had to lie down on my stomach and literally slither through like a snake. I could feel the weight of tons of sandstone above me and thoughts of this all caving in on me filled my imagination. Anyway, I finally made it to the exit, which was more vertical than horizontal, and I had to shimmy on my stomach to get through that to the outside.

The tunnel opened out onto a flat area about three feet wide and ten feet long just under an overhang near the top of the canyon. I followed Stephanie across the shelf, and we both climbed up around the edge of the overhang, exiting onto a golf course that was above. It was really interesting that you couldn't see the tunnel from the top because of the overhang, and the little area we climbed up from the shelf just looked like it dropped straight off down the canyon.

"There are the oaks I'm talking about," Stephanie said, pointing just beyond a sand trap at the edge of the green. We both walked across the grass, apparently alone on the course until we got to the large trees we were heading for. Stephanie pulled some already loose bark from the larger of the group and put it into her leather bag, thanking the tree for its contribution.

"We'll use this to represent the God in our spring incense," she said. "I wanted to show you the cave, but I also wanted to get some bark from these trees, because this was one of the first places I ever came to do Magic when we moved here. Jack and I used to come up here before they built the golf course and sit on the grass at night. You could see all the stars in the sky and there's no one around after dark. It was a great place to meet and we did rituals here a number of times even after the area was 'developed' – – as contractors say. We were glad that they didn't cut down this stand of old oaks. After we moved to where we are now, it was just a little too far for us to come, although we did come here for Beltane a couple of years ago."

214

As we talked, we gradually worked our way across the golf course which turned out to be a short cut to where we had parked the car. On the trip home, Stephanie went over the instructions for making my wand, and I listened intently. When she dropped me off, I went right into my room, and immediately went to work on the branch following her instructions.

I carefully stripped back the bark removing it completely one strip at a time. It was an interesting experience doing so because it came off so easily. The bark of the willow was wet and slippery just under the surface, and it literally slid off the branch when you pulled on it. The remaining surface of the limb, once the bark was removed, had a highly polished appearance, accompanied by a very pleasing color, which was somewhat white, with a yellowish cast, much like the color of the newly risen moon.

There was also a pleasant smell emanating from the fresh cut limb, which was neither sweet nor medicinal, but rather damp smelling and soothing to the mind. I tasted the underside of the peeled bark as I had on my first lesson with Ron, experiencing a slight acidic taste that remained on my tongue for several minutes afterwards. I set aside the strips of bark to be used in healing rituals for the sick, and then tied them together with a piece of white yarn to symbolize their therapeutic use.

"In Magic," Ron had said, "we use the bark from the willow to make healing incenses and also to make potions used for the same purpose. We also sometimes use the strands pealed from our wands to weave special charms for the sick, especially in cases when they're critical. There's great Magic contained within the bark from your wand, but you must use it sparingly, as it can never be replaced once it's gone."

I scraped the sacred branch with a smooth stone in accordance with our handed down traditions, working slowly and carefully. Throughout the process, I concentrated on my desire for a wand that would be connected to the sacred light of *lazra meck*. I knew that without that connection, my wand would just be a useless

215

stick of wood, a conversation piece or, worse yet, something to put aside on a shelf. I continued the tedious process of removing any remaining inner bark from the surface until my wand shone as though polished by moonlight, having that same iridescent color and glow. I collected the unique shavings of inner bark, which came off in long slender curling tendrils — a little like ivory colored strands of corn silk — and placed them in a white cloth bag to dry properly. When they were done, I knew that they would be perfect for use in incenses Ron had taught me about, and to grind into salves mixed with witch hazel or thornbane to deaden pain.

After securing the shavings, I trimmed the bottom end of the branch so that it was flat and perpendicular to its sides and then slightly rounded the top end with some sandpaper to make it more attractive. Once that was finished, I lit a candle that I had dedicated to the purpose at hand and had saturated with sacred oil. Then with great care, I warmed the ends of the wand with the radiant flame, and then dipped them quickly into the molten wax. I had been taught that this would seal the wand's freshly awakened sap forever and keep it from cracking or splitting as it dried to its final form.

Once these things were done, I called upon the Great Mother to watch over my newly made wand, and then I set it outside to dry for the required nine days in a box filled with Bane of Soltra, mugwart, and dwale. Stephanie had explained that each of the herbs held a special gift for the wand, imparting wisdom, prophecy, and a connection with the world beyond. Once the branch was dry, I bored a small hole into the larger bottom end with the tip of my silver blade as Stephanie had instructed, and set the wand aside until Spring Equinox when the coven and I would convene in a magic circle to purify it, consecrate it — and give it its new magical life.

CHAPTER 13

The Spring Equinox, Magical Chalk, the Origins of Easter, and the Consecration of My Wand

It was on the Spring Equinox in 1967, that I finally consecrated my wand. Stephanie cast the circle that night in the same cave where I'd first met everyone at Stony Point nearly a year before. We had cleared the floor of debris and loose wood, and Derek and Eldon had swept the sandy floor, distributing the dirt in a smooth and even manner. Ron brought a small wooden foot locker which we used regularly to transport our coven supplies, and after emptying it of its contents, Nicky and R.J. set it out as an altar in the northern quadrant of the room. Once it was placed, Jack covered it with a white altar cloth which was decorated with several magical symbols, and James and Karen joined in, setting out the ritual supplies.

While they did that, Ron and I laid out a circle on the ground using pulverized chalk that he and the others had collected on one of their expeditions into the mountains.

"This isn't just ordinary chalk," Ron commented as we completed the powdery outline that defined our sacred space. "In fact," he said, "it's really very very special stuff."

"Why is it so special," I asked, wondering what was so different about this as opposed to any other particular chalk.

"This chalk is made by following a secret magical process that's been passed down by Witches for thousands of years," he replied in an authoritative but gentle voice, "and it actually allows us to see *lazra meck*. Not only that, but the process of creating and using this chalk, directly connects us with the ancient magical people who originally built the very first stone circles and other sacred sites in Europe. It also reveals much about our own magical connection to them and keeps alive one of the most ancient magical rituals practiced by man. It also helps us to better understand the deep layers that underlie just about

217

everything magical we do and confirms our belief that that which is obvious to us in our rituals and our Magic, is just a small part of what's really going on."

"You're losing me," I said, not fully comprehending what Ron was sharing with me and feeling a little overwhelmed at receiving such a long response to what I had expected to be a simple answer. My mentor paused for a moment as if weighing how to best answer my query, and then responded quietly to me in a low whisper.

"What you don't know is that this chalk brings illumination to our circle through the light of *lazra meck* in exactly the same way it did for our predecessors in the dawn of human history. And I'm not just talking in a metaphorical sense either; I mean it really makes our circles glow in the dark!"

Ron's words hit me like a bomb shell. The night of my initiation the circle had glowed with an eerie light just like he was describing and I realized that that was what he was talking about.

"So that's why the circle glowed at my initiation," I said. Ron threw me a surprised look and then questioned me. "You noticed that? I didn't think that you'd seen it because of the candles. They were so bright that night that the glow was pretty much overpowered by them."

"Actually, I didn't see it during the ritual," I commented. In fact it was almost morning before I noticed it at all. But once I did notice it, I was quite taken by it."

Ron smiled and raised his voice a little as he tucked away the simple cloth bag that held the remaining chalk.

"When you understand how that phenomena came to be," he said, "you'll come to better appreciate the complexity of both the process that created what you observed and the journey that those walking the sacred path for thousands of years before us have taken. In the end, if you're diligent and able to comprehend the depth of what we'll teach you about this chalk, you will far better understand the nature of the gods and the universe that we live in, and also better understand the truly sacred message that's intentionally woven throughout all of nature for us to discover. But even more importantly, you'll get just what it was that our ancestors were trying to accomplish to begin with and you'll be blown away when you see just how precisely nature and the gods accommodated them.

"Some people argue that everything we believe to be true magically is just superstition or coincidence. But most of the people making those observations have very little or no real knowledge of what Magic even is. The truth is that there are so many connecting coincidences relating to our beliefs that it is just not possible that they are not at least justified in part. But then I'm getting off the subject now and I'd like to get back to the chalk. Is that okay with you?"

"Of course," I answered.

"Well, you remember how I explained that Witches have been searching to understand the nature of *lazra meck* ever since the creation story surfaced?"

"Yeah."

"Well in the course of that process, a long time ago, some Witches noticed that the surface of the sea sometimes glows in the dark without any reflection from either the sun or the moon. You've probably seen that too right? You know when the foam glows on the crest of a wave even though the night's as black as pitch, or when you can see a blue green luminescence that seems to radiate from deep within."

"Yeah, I've seen that," I answered.

"Well, those early witches probably spent centuries observing that phenomena and trying to figure it out because that unexplained radiance matched right up with their own story of the light of creation, *lazra meck*, which made it particularly important for them to try and understand, right?"

"Yeah, I get that."

"Good. So, let's look at some of the factors that led them to explore that observation further and then I'll fill you in on the rest of the story as it's been shared from Witch to Witch since then, okay?"

219

"That sounds great to me," I responded with enthusiasm, following Ron out to the entrance of the cavern, where we were freer to talk with out disrupting the others.

"Well," Ron started, "first, the light they observed came from within the sea itself, which they often thought of as an earthly representation of the womb or the chalice of creation, similar to the way that they thought of the sacred wells. Because of this, it made sense to them that the magical light that seemed to emanate from within could be likened to the light of creation foretold in the creation story. Consequently, they decided to try to figure out how to capture the sacred light from the sea or to discover how to replicate it, in the hopes that they could use it in some way to be more closely connected to the Goddess and creation, like they had with the willow wand. Eventually, through the process of observation and probably lots of trial and error, they came to the conclusion that there was a relationship between certain types of shells and the mysterious light from the sea.

"Anyway, the story goes that one coven noticed that the blue green sheen on the inside of certain shells was similar to the color of the mysterious light that they had seen in the ocean, so they collected those shells and did a ritual to try to coax the *lazra meck* out of them. They did this by burning charcoal made from the sacred willow and then adding a portion of the crushed shells to the flames. It was their hope that by combining the sacred willow and the sacred shells together, that the combination of the two might somehow be coaxed to release their *lazra meck.* Unfortunately, the coven members were disappointed and their ritual ended in failure. Then someone got the idea that they had to reenact the story of creation in their ritual like they did in the creation of the circle, by telling the story of *lazra meck* and adding each of the appropriate elements to the mix as they acknowledged each stage of transition in the creation story that led to the creation of the universe and life itself.

"They began by starting in the center of their circle and then walking to the east as they told of the scream of the Mother and the creation of *lazra meck*. Once there, they lit a bowl carved from willow charcoal on fire as they acknowledged the transition from the unseen light of spirit into the illumination of visual light and the creation of the element of Fire. Next, they stopped in the south and added chalk, brimstone, and salt into the burning cup as they acknowledged the transition from spirit and illumination into the solidity and form of the element of Earth. After that, they continued on to the west, where they added water from the sacred well and the crushed shells that they had gathered from the sea, to acknowledge the element of Water and the womb that it represented. Then they carried the mix to the north, where they jointly blew on the smoldering formula in order to include the element of Air and to animate their creation with the breath of life. Then finally, they completed the circle and the story, returning the concoction to the altar in the center to be blessed by the gods. When the charcoal chalice exhausted itself and their creation cooled, only a white chalky powder remained.

"Once the ritual was completed, the participants took their creation into a dark cave to see if the *lazra meck* they were seeking would appear, but nothing in particular happened. Legend says they were quite discouraged and ready to give up and that they tossed the chalk they had made on the ground as they exited the cave. But then, the very next night, one of the Witches passing the cave noticed a glow coming from the entrance and went over to investigate. On entering the cave, the Witch was met by the light of *lazra meck* everywhere the chalk had been tossed.

"At first, everyone was very excited and they collected up all of the chalk and carried it deeper into the cave so the light would be more prominent, but then after a day the light faded and failed to illuminate again. It took a long time for them to discover that the original chalk had been exposed to the light of the early morning sun when it was low on the horizon and that it was only when that light penetrated into the cave, that the release of the holy light was initiated. Both the rising sun and the east where it first entered the horizon were considered to be sacred markers in the creation story, and the concept of illumination which was often equated with deity — was also equated with the spark of creation. All of these factors neatly fit with their expectations; and the culmination of so many powerful symbols showing up once their goal was finally achieved, confirmed to them the overarching nature of Magic and the support of the Gods in their quest."

"Wow," I exclaimed. "So they actually discovered exactly what they were looking for."

"Not only that," Ron returned, "but what they discovered evolved directly from the creation story, which is pretty unbelievable if you consider all of the possibilities. I mean, what do you think the chances are that someone could create a glowing chalk by only combining a few simple readily available items and following such a simple story? That's why I say that anyone who thinks this is all just a matter of coincidence has no clue what they are talking about."

"I agree," I said, beginning to see how big of a deal this all really was. "So that's how we ended up creating our circles with the chalk then?" I asked.

"Yes," Ron answered. "But it's not just our circles that were affected by the discovery. The chalk was also used at all of the ancient sacred sites and stone circles too. In fact, one of the greatest secrets the coven holds is that we know why many of earliest stone temples and underground barrows were designed to admit a single beam of sunlight on the Solstice, and a dozen other similar secrets relating to these ancient monuments. Even more powerful, is the fact that we know that the whole process directly connects with the Golden Key and leads to understanding the very creation of life itself. Even famous historians and scientists don't know that! But then that's another story for another time.

"The bottom line is that all of these things are connected and are part of the sacred path that we still walk today, and each of these pieces of the puzzle help reveal other layers that are still yet to be discovered. But for us, besides revealing the hidden secrets of the universe, they also serve to simply help us to understand why we worship the way we do and what each of the actions we take in the magical sense actually mean. There are lots of people in the world today who go through all kinds of rituals and religious devotions without a clue as to where their rituals come from or why they're doing them. In fact, a lot of them come from the same source as ours and they don't even know that either. Being aware of what you believe and why you believe it, is a critical part of pursuing the gods, and if you forget everything else I've taught you, at least remember that.

"There's so much more to be said about the chalk and the willow and all of these other subjects that we're talking about, but then those are stories to be told at another time and place when we're farther down your magical path. But for now I think we'd better get back to helping to set up for the ritual before we get too far off track."

"Okay," I said happily, totally excited by what he had already shared with me, and willing to wait till the time was right to learn the rest. "I'm really looking forward to hearing more about this," I returned smiling, and reached down to pick up a couple of small rocks to add to the fire pit.

Ron and I returned to the circle and helped the others finish setting things up. When everything was done, we all stepped back to review our progress. The altar looked great with the chalice sitting slightly to the left of center with its silvery surface perfectly reflecting the sacred symbols from the altar cloth below. Next to it and to the right was a small container of water taken from the seep near the creek where Ron had his vision of the Goddess. To the far right, carefully balanced on a piece of slate, was a simple bronze censor filled with sand. Next to the censor on the same pad were several pieces of charcoal made from a branch of willow that we'd also collected near the spring. Ron had invited me to participate a week before in the making of the charcoal which we created by burning long sections of willow boughs inside of a closed metal drum over a camp fire, and I remembered the experience vividly.

"The trick is to burn the entire piece with as little oxygen as possible," Ron had said. "This steel drum works great for that. You just take off the top like this" — pulling off the serrated lid, "and put the wood inside. You have to make a small hole in the top though so the smoke can get out, and it's really important that you light the escaping gas with a match once it gets going, otherwise, it could blow up! Anyway, this works a lot better than the old way, where we used to keep stacking wet wood all around as the fire burned, in order to try and smother the limbs inside."

Ron walked over to the small pile of wood we'd collected and grabbed a couple more small branches to add to the fire. When he found what he wanted, he turned and faced me.

"We use willow charcoal for other things besides just burning incense," he commented.

"Like what?" I responded.

He walked back over to the fire and pushed the new dry branches under the drum and then turned his attention to me.

"Well, you know that the willow's sacred to the Goddess right.?" he asked.

"Yeah, I know that."

"And that's one of the main reasons why we make our charcoal from it," he went on. "But then there's also a far more special reason beyond that," he confided, in a low voice that drew all of my attention. I was now quite familiar with my teacher's way of conveying important ideas, and I knew from his manner that a special story or lesson was about to come.

"And what is that?" I questioned, intrigued by the secrecy implied in his voice."

"Well, the main reason we make our charcoal from the willow is because of a legend that's been passed down through the coven. Basically, the story tells of a wise man who often gathered members of the early tribes together to celebrate the turning of the seasons. Supposedly, once he had them assembled, he would draw sacred symbols on the surrounding rocks, using colored clay mixed with water as a part of their ritual. The legend goes on to say that the Goddess, looking down on the celebration below, was pleased that the people had created the magical symbols for her, but that she was also disappointed that only two of the four elements, Water and Earth, were represented in their actual creation. So she sent a bolt of lightning down from the sky and struck the branch of a sacred willow, using the elements of fire and air to burst it into flame to get their attention. Most of the people who witnessed the event ran for the hills in fear, considering the fire in their holy tree to be a bad omen. But the wise man, who often sought counsel from the Goddess, went down to the spring instead to see what message such an unprecedented event might bring.

"As he watched the fire burn, a vision of the Lady appeared in the smoke above, and pointed to the smoldering tree. When the fire finally burned out and the vision faded, the man saw that the branch had remained intact in spite of the all consuming flames. He walked over to the tree to inspect what remained, and in doing so broke off a charred limb that transferred a black streak on to his hand. When he tried to wipe it off, the mark remained, and he took it as a sign that Goddess wanted her mark to be seen. He broke off a piece of the charred limb and took the charcoal up into the rocks where the ritual was being held and began to draw the sacred symbols once again with the charred hallowed branch. The legend goes on to say that from that day till this, all Witches since have always used charcoal made from the willow to create their sacred art. And it is also said that it always forms the base of any drawings or sacred symbols used in Magic, before adding any color or paint.

"From this story, we know that art is sacred to the Goddess, and that art made from willow charcoal is her first and most favored form. We even use ground up willow charcoal in our magical ink for the very same reason.

225

"So, that's why we use charcoal made from the willow to draw our magical symbols, and also why we use it in the censor to burn our incense. We believe that by using the branch of the willow in this way, we replicate the Goddess' personal request to include the elements of fire and air in our rituals. And we also complete our link with the sacred spring and the womb, and our connection with *lazra meck* too."

"That's a great story," I responded, enjoying the simplicity of it.

"It is," Ron answered back. "I don't know if it's true or not, but then who knows if *any* of the world religion's stories are true. It's always been interesting to me, how people from one particular religion will easily believe a story about some significant event in their own history, like an angel appearing from heaven, or a burning bush that talks, and then consider similar stories, like a Goddess who appears in a cloud of smoke, or a God who takes the form of a stag, to be completely ridiculous. Witches believe that there are truths within all of these stories, and that like the layers we know to be hidden within Magic, there is always more to the tale than what we first see. But in the end we believe that all of these stories serve to pass on the discoveries of what we've found to be holy, and at the same time, help us to explain the mysteries that we have yet to discover."

Returning to the present, I continued to review the large variety of paraphernalia donning the altar as Karen began to build a small fire in a rock circle behind the altar. On top and to the rear of the altar, sat a hand carved wooden container, filled with the incense we had all made together for spring. Each herb had been specially harvested in a ritual manner for the occasion, and the entire coven had worked together diligently to create the final result. We'd taken each of the plants, one by one, and crushed them in a large porcelain mortar while we all concentrated on their purpose. Each member took their turn in the process with the idea being that all of our energies and focus would be intricately intertwined with the final product. Stephanie told me that all of our incense was made this way and reiterated the importance of being involved in every step of the creation of our magical tools, oils, incenses and sacred artifacts.

"The power contained within any magical tool," Stephanie often said, "is only equal to the energy and effort stored within it. It is precisely the wisdom gained in the process of creating it, which gives it the power you seek. While it's true that part of the energy we draw on is already out there to tap into, an incense made without harvesting your own herbs and without full intimate knowledge of each plant's properties and personality, is about as valuable as a mimeograph of the Mona Lisa instead of the real thing."

Next to the incense and also to the back of the altar were two tall white tapers, placed on the outer edges, which sat in embossed silver candle holders of the type you'd place at a formal meal. In the front section of the altar, each of the members had placed one of their magical tools. Some had put down their magical knives and others their wands, filling up all the remaining space on the top of the wooden trunk. My wand in particular, I noticed, was elevated from the all rest, and held a position of honor on a carefully folded white cloth in the center of all of the others.

To the right of the altar, placed carefully on the ground, was an array of additional supplies. There were several cloaks, a large thermos filled with a special ritual drink made by the group especially for the Spring Equinox from seasonal herbs, fruits, and other seasonal foods, a large handmade book — which belonged to the coven as a whole, matches, a carton of eggs, a bottle of ink — made from plants and herbs collected by the group, which was then combined with powdered willow charcoal and soot from our altar candles — a crow quill pen, made by carving and splitting the end of a feather, and a clay pot full of fertile soil.

"OK, you guys," Stephanie called out, gaining the attention of all of the members. "It looks like were ready to start."

Everyone took a position in the southern portion of the circle behind the altar. Together we fanned out, forming a half circle facing the north. Stephanie moved to the center of the circle just behind the altar. She paused for a moment, turning slightly and making eye contact with each of us, and then turning back toward the center, she faced the altar. Once she was positioned everyone was silent. Jack, who was slightly to her right, moved up beside her and lit the two white tapered candles, first the one on the right and then the one on the left. Next, he lit the four candles at each of the cardinal points, beginning in the east and working his way *deosil* around the circle until he returned to the altar. Following that he held one of the pieces of charcoal over the newly kindled candle on the right until it caught fire, sending tiny orange sparks flying as small particles of carbon ignited, popped, and took flight — launched by the probing flame.

Once the charcoal began to glow, Jack laid it down within the coven's golden censor and poured a small amount of incense on the crackling coal. Immediately, a heady smoke billowed up from the burning brazier, filling the air in the cavern with a wonderful smell. The scent was completely different than previous incenses we'd used, having a particularly woodsy odor. It was pleasant and a little floral, but the thing I noticed most was its piercing earthy scent which penetrated not only my sense of smell, but left a distinct taste on the tip of my tongue.

"Knock na, knock goba, — By water and by earth and the sacred womb of the Mother," Stephanie called out, placing the tip of her blade in the vessel full of spring water, breaking the tension of the waters surface and disrupting the tiny flecks of minerals floating within. I felt chills travel up the back of my neck and shuddered involuntarily, like one of those times when we say "I felt a ghost pass," as she made the opening gesture. After a short pause, she stirred the mineral laden water carefully, three times in a sunwise direction, and then laid the blade back down on the altar between the glowing candles.

"*Knock djinn ralda... knock pa ralda,*" she went on — summoning the elements of fire and air — as herb-laden incense cascaded over the now brightly glowing coals when she added more sweet-scented fuel to the brazier. Stephanie lifted the smoldering censor high above her head, turning full circle as she invited the elements — filling the chamber with a fragrant smoky mist.

Setting the censor down, she once again picked up the blade and passed it back and forth three times through the rising smoke, taking care to be sure that every surface of the tool was thoroughly cleansed and purified. Once that task was finished, Stephanie lifted the shining blade toward the sky with her right hand, and then lowered it, letting it rest across her breast at a forty-five degree angle, as she made her way over to the eastern portion of the circle, pausing before the flickering candle that marked that direction. When she reached the place of *beginning*, all of the other coven members turned in place, facing the east also, so I too followed suit, mimicking their example. After a long moment of silence our Priestess took in a deep breath, and then exhaled slowly as she used the point of her magical blade to trace a simple rune in the air before her.

13: The Rune representing *Lazra Meck*

"That's the symbol for *lazra meck,* Ron whispered, explaining the significance of her action. "And now the creation of the circle itself actually begins," He said. I nodded my head, acknowledging that I understood his explanation and focused my attention on our Priestess to see what would take place next.

Leaning slightly forward, Stephanie bent down carefully and placed the tip of her sacred knife on the ground. Then she proceeded to trace the course of the chalk circle slowly in a sunwise direction. As she made her way determinedly around the perimeter of the room, a miraculous and, for

229

me, unexpected thing happened. At the point where the tip of the magical blade cleaved the sandy floor of the cave, I observed a blue white glow at the apex of the cut akin to the arc made by a welder. The ethereal glow was no where's near as bright as a welder's arc, but it was definitely present, and carried the same intensity for me as the former.

"*Lazra Meck,*" I whispered to myself, "the light of spirit."

I continued to watch in awe, nodding my head unconsciously in acknowledgment of the holy fire as she continued around the perimeter of our temple, passing each of the four directions and the candles placed at each juncture to represent the unseen *aesma's,* standing watch there. When the circle was fully cut and Stephanie finally returned to the *place of beginning,* she paused for a moment, tracing the sign of the pentagram in the air before her, and then continuing the gesture to include both a *deosil,* and an aeosil circle around it, finalizing the act. Once the circle of light was secure and the blade had completed its task, she returned to the altar in the center and set it down in its previous resting place, completing the first segment of the journey.

Next, she picked up the chalice and walked again to the east, acknowledging the *place of beginning* a second time. This time she made the sign for *lazra meck* with the silver cup, taking great care not to spill its magical contents. When she finished her salute, she reverently dipped the fingers of her right hand into the holy water and drew them back out, dispersing a course spray of water and earth along the outside of our chalk lined ring with her fingers. She continued to disperse water from the chalice as she walked slowly in a sunwise direction, until she'd covered the entire perimeter of our temple and returned to the center and the altar. Finally, she repeated the circular journey a third and final time carrying the censor instead of the chalice. She took great care fanning the rising tendrils of scented smoke around the perimeter until she had traced the entire circumference of our temple a third time, blanketing it with the elements of fire and air.

230

Once the circle was cut, each of us was purified one at a time by Stephanie and Jack in an alternating fashion. First with water from the sacred spring which Jack explained represented the spirits of both *na* and *goba* combined, because the water from the spring was filled with tiny particles of earth, gleaned from its long journey through the bowels of the planet; and next, with the smoke from the fragrant censor, in which incense representing the spirits of *djinn* and *pa,* fire and air, came together as one.

Once this process was completed, we returned to our places in the circle once again, and formed a crescent shaped arc, facing the altar and the north. When everyone was in place, our Priestess moved forward again and picked up the magical blade in her right hand. After a short pause to collect herself, she held the knife up to the sky, and calling out in a booming voice, recited:

"Alock ma shum neck meck..."[8]

shook ma ne mesk ba coomb..."[9]

"Ma baca chook."[10]

As she spoke, I visualized the primal place of beginning she described, as our Priestess told the story of creation in Elban.   She spoke of *Chakadah,*[11] the spirit scream of wisdom, which Ron had told me earlier in my training was like an utterance from the most primal of places, and had created everything that now existed.

"It's like the sound a woman makes when her child is born," he had said, as we walked one day in the hills. "Kind of like the Goddess screamed and the sound traveled at the speed of light across the blackness, turning into pure energy which then exploded and became the stars and the earth and eventually us," he went on. "When we cast the circle, we always speak first about the place where it all started.   Just imagine; no sound, no light, no form or existence, nothing living at all — just blackness.   Then a

---

[8] "From the depths of darkness..."

[9] "and the swirling mists..."

[10] "the Creatrix comes."

[11] The spirit scream of wisdom which initiated creation.

231

mist begins to form — which we believe is the Goddess materializing. And it slowly begins to swirl, gradually forming a spiral, and becoming more and more tangible as it moves toward the center. The center then becomes a tunnel, or if you would, a passageway, which as you know, we call *wada na* — the pathway to the womb. Finally, She wills herself into existence becoming the beginning and end of everything and, with her first sound, she gives birth to the rest of the universe. That moment in time, when that first primal scream broke the silence and entered the darkness beyond, is called *chakadah*. Afterward, once the sound had traveled away from the mother and became aware of itself, it changed form and became the very first light which we call *lazra meck* which as you know means the unseen light that illuminates even in the darkness.

"Why do we call it that?" I asked. "Doesn't all light, light up the darkness?

"Not in the way this light did," Ron answered. "*Lazra meck* is the light of spirit, not brilliance. It was the primal spark that first revealed existence. It's important to remember that in the beginning, there was only blackness and there wasn't anything to see, yet even so, that first light still revealed the knowledge that there could be more. *Lazra meck* does not illuminate its surroundings with brightness like a streetlight; in fact it has no physical manifestation of light in the way we know it at all. Rather it is the very essence of light, the principle that something *can* be illuminated, and the essential concept that all things can eventually be seen, known, and understood."

"Wow," I exclaimed! "That's really heavy stuff."

"There's even more to it than that," Ron went on. "*Lazra meck* is unique in the universe above all else, because it is everywhere at the same time. It exists both here and now in our physical world and also in the time before anything existed at all. It also exists in the future, even though we haven't gotten there yet, so its presence reflects the past, present, and future concurrently."

"There is so much to everything," I remarked, fascinated by Ron's explanation. "It just seems to go on and on and on."

"And that's the mystery," Ron responded, giving me his full attention now. "Every door opens another and so on and so on — and it just goes on forever. Once the creation took place, there was no longer a beginning or an end to any of it; just forever. That's why the circle is holy to us, because it symbolizes the sacred eternity of all this....."

"*Judanna-Naru, shum Sagchuti,*"[12] Stephanie called out – – transporting me back to the present as she invited the Goddess of the Witches.

I raised my palms to the sky with the rest of the coveners and joined her in the final word of her invitation.

"*Dukaat!*" — it is so!

Once the invocation was completed, everyone stood silent for a few moments, acknowledging the presence of the Creator and honoring the creation itself.

It was so wonderful to watch the whole creation of the circle and to see each phase of the ritual performed. And while I had been taught most of what would be taking place beforehand, experiencing it all first hand was far better than I had ever imagined. This was the first full ritual I had ever attended, and it was also my very first Sabbat.

"Patrick, are you ready to consecrate your wand?" Stephanie asked, beckoning me from the altar.

"Yes," I answered, moving forward to stand next to her as she looked upward and raised her palms toward the sky.

"Gracious Goddess, mother of all, whose love encircles the earth," Stephanie started. "I call to you in great joy. Before you stands a new Witch, ready to make his first magical tool — a wand of fire. Descend this night, O mighty Mother into our sacred circle, and lend your power to his spell. Let the light of beginning be his guide and let the Magic within the wand work his will. "

---

[12] Queen of Witches

At her prompt, I reached out and picked up my wand from the altar and held it up to the sky, repeating the simple invocation my priestess had taught me.

"Great Goddess and mighty God bless this wand and give it life. Let its connection with you remain and let it keep open the link between you and me. Grant me wisdom in its use and let me gain the knowledge to understand the ways of Magic.... *Dukaat!*"

Everyone in the cave repeated in unison.... "*Dukaat!*"

Kneeling before the altar, I opened the small bottle of ink and using a crow quill pen, I inscribed the symbols for the mystical power of *Na* from which the willow draws its sustenance. I also drew the symbol for *Djinn*, illustrating the illumination of *lazra meck* and the wand's connection with the first element: fire. As I continued with the pen, I used the runes of the Pritani[13] to inscribe the invocation that dedicated its purpose, and finished with the Theban Three[14] to seal the spell.

Figure 14: The Willow Wand with Runes

"Now you need to purify and consecrate it," Jack said when I had finished my task.

Following his advice, I dipped my fingers in the chalice and rubbed the cool liquid over the entire surface of the wand.

"*Knock na, kilar,*"[15] I said.

Ron stepped forward and handed me a small tin with the symbol for consecration drawn on the lid. I opened it and saw that it was partially filled with an unfamiliar incense. The contents, while thoroughly mixed, were

---

[13] An ancient tribe of the British isles
[14] A symbol representing the Golden Key and connection with the Goddess
[15] "By water, and by the sacred womb of the Mother — be pure."

coarsely ground, and in being so, revealed clues as to its composition. There were small bits of frankincense and dark resinous lumps which I recognized right away as the fragrant myrrh. Cut leaves of willow and crushed buds of the poplar also could be seen throughout the mix. Many other substances revealed their inclusion also, but they were too finely ground to identify. Even so, their vaguely familiar bouquet tugged at my memory.

I raised the small metal container to my nose, finding it sweet and spicy and unlike any I had previously experienced. I poured a small pile of the mixture over the waiting charcoal and a thin wispy smoke rose straight up. It didn't cloud out like the other incenses had but instead seemed to stay together in a long swirling tube. I had to bend over the censor in order actually to smell it, and when I did, I was pleasantly surprised. The scent was wonderful. It was a little sweet, reminding me of the smell of cotton candy that you buy at a fair, but with a heavier cinnamony weight to it. I picked up my wand again and passed it through the thready smoke, purifying it by fire and air.

"Knock djinn ralda, shook ma ne' knock lazra,"[16]

"Shook ma ne' pa ralda — kilar[17] Once the wand was purified, I pricked the end of my finger with a small knife — placed on the altar for that purpose — and squeezed three drops of my blood into the hole in the end of the branch. This, I had been taught was to connect my magical tool directly with me, sealing the bond between us, much like the American Indian custom of joining together as blood brothers. I sealed up the hole with the wax from one of the altar candles, taking care not to drip it down the sides of the wand. Then using the sacred oil, I anointed the tool thoroughly to give it life and purpose and to connect it with all who had done this ceremony before me. I'd learned from

---

[16] "By the spirit of fire and the spark of creation."

[17] "And by the spirit of air — be pure."

Stephanie that the wand was used to focus on our desires and that it could also be used to create a magic circle.

"This," She'd said, "will be your primary connection with the Great Mother in all your days to come. The wand is always the first tool created by a new Witch because the process of its creation connects us directly with her. Always remember what you've learned about *na* and the womb and its connection with the willow, for there are still secrets to discover there as you walk your journey as a Witch. And later on when the time is right, we'll also teach you more about the special blade we use to create the circle, which some people call *athame*[18] — and you'll make one of those too.

But for now, the wand will be fine to use to create your sacred space until the time comes to change to the blade."

"Dukaat," I said, returning to the present, as I held up my wand one last time completing its consecration and dedicating it before the gods.

"Dukaat," the coven repeated, and then for a time we all stood together in absolute silence.

Once the ritual for my wand reached completion, we moved on to celebrate the rites of spring. Stephanie brought out the eggs that were stored next to the altar and laid them out in a neat pile in front of the chalice on the altar cloth. Then she opened the bottle of herbal ink and placed the crow quill pen next to it. Nicky set out a clay pot full of dirt just in front of the altar and moved a bowl of seeds to the forefront where it could be easily reached.

"Spring is the time for planting," Jack said, and for the resurrection of the land. "In ancient times, people honored the Goddess of resurrection on the Equinox and it became known as the time of returning. In fact, one of the names given to the Goddess in those days was Eostre, which is where the name Easter comes from. I've always found it interesting that Jesus is said to have been resurrected at this time because it falls right in line with our

---

[18] One of the names used for a special magical knife, which is used to create the sacred circle.

236

understanding of birth, death and rebirth. Besides being a time for resurrection, spring is also the time for setting out our goals for the year and for making a commitment as a family to achieve them. Because of that, we're going to memorialize our goals by planting the seeds we've brought with us, as a part of our ritual. We'll let the seeds represent for each of us, the things we'd like to see come to bloom in our lives. So these eggs, which we've chosen to represent ourselves and the world we live in, will represent a larger seed — with the yolk being representative of the potential we each carry inside and also the potential available to us in nature. We'll draw sacred symbols on the eggs and consecrate them to connect them to the Magic, and then we'll break them open to symbolize our potential being released into the world. When that's done, we'll plant the seeds we've brought with pieces of the egg's shells, to connect our goals and desires with the spouting kernels. By mixing our shells with the seeds while at the same time intermixing them with each others' fragments, we will be acknowledging our goals and at the same time making a pledge to work together as a family. There is power in unity and that in itself will lend a special strength to our spell.

"I want each of you to take one of these eggs now, and draw the symbols of fertility on one side, and then add several symbols on the other side that represent something you really want to accomplish this year. They can be pictures of the thing you desire, or just a symbol that you feel stands for what you want. The idea is to solidify your dreams into something tangible, something you can see, so you can better focus on it."

Jack picked up the eggs from the altar, one by one. He purified them carefully with water from the chalice and smoke from the censor. Then he returned them to the altar cupping his hands over them face down, and he asked the Goddess to bless them and to help us with our goals. When he was finished, each of us selected an egg, and a small twig of willow charcoal to draw with, and we moved apart to different areas of the circle to draw the symbols of fertility, and to consider what other symbols we would use. Some made invocations to the Lady first and others began drawing right away, until each member gradually became subsumed into their own private ritual.

Stephanie walked over and stood by me because I was new, to help me with the symbols of the Sabbat. She handed me the bottle of magical ink which she brought from the altar and instructed me to use it instead of the charred twig, reiterating that the ink too, was made from the charcoal. I took great care in drawing the intricate pattern she described on the shell. And I was quite pleased with the end result which I admired for several minutes before moving on.

Figure 15: The Fertility Symbols for the Spring Equinox

When I indicated that I was finished with the fertility symbols, Stephanie then offered to show me how to draw the symbol for a successful harvest, which I added to the other side.

Figure 16: The Rune for a Successful Harvest

She also taught me the three runes for the Golden Key which I added to the white china-like surface as I rotated the egg in the palm of my hand.

238

Figure 17: The Runes of the Golden key: Achna, Rai, and Uuma

The ink was quite different than any I'd used before, having a distinct earthy scent and a slightly lumpy consistency when applied. It was dark purplish black in color like the juice of a ripe black cherry, but it rapidly transformed into an iridescent rich merlot once it dried. The surface of the color was filled with tiny shimmering flashes like minute sparkling diamonds, which added an ethereal cast to the symbols as the firelight reflected on their slightly luminous surface. The dried ink reminded me a little of an opal, seeming to contain an inner fire which added a particular mystical quality to the completed runes. The end result was quite pretty.

When I finished the symbols for the Golden Key, Stephanie went on to show me how to draw the sacred spiral which I'd seen previously on a number of our magical implements. "Spirals are a common symbol for us," she explained, using a stick from the firewood pile to draw on the cavern floor.

"But they're not always drawn in the same direction," she went on. "The sunwise version — one like this," she said, depicting a little clockwise spiral in the sand, which began in the center and spiraled outward, "is our symbol for *wa da na*.[19]

Figure 18: The Symbol for *Wa Da Na*.

This version represents the power of the Goddess available to us for use in Magic. We use this one quite often," she continued, "to add power to our magical tools and to

---

[19] The pathway to the womb.

memorialize our connection to the sacred. On the other hand, a spiral drawn like this," she said, drawing a counter clockwise symbol on the floor, which was exactly the opposite of the previous one, "represents a return to the mother rather than something coming from her. This one is called *mor' ga na*,[20] which means bird returning home or bird returning to the nest, or in our case, just going home.

Figure 19: Rune for *Mor' Ga Na*.

This particular spiral is drawn mostly at funerals or at Samhain celebrations, to represent a safe journey for those that have passed away. It's also sometimes drawn on tools or materials left over after a spell, just before we bury them. There's also a triple spiral, like this," she continued, drawing three more spirals which she joined together forming a triangle at their center. This version is called *ach' na Shee*,[21] and means a place of beginning or a place of spirit.

Figure 20: The Rune for Ach' Na Shee.

This one has more to do with identifying an actual sacred place or ritual site than it does with imparting specific Magic, although it's also a shorthand symbol for the triple circles we create when we cast our ritual space."

---

[20] A symbol used at burial places. *Mor' ga na translates as:* bird returning to the nest.
[21] A holy place, or a place of spirits

"I'm not sure I understand what you mean by the triple circles we create," I responded, "I thought there was only one circle around us."

"Oh no," Stephanie replied. Each of the trips we make around our sacred space form separate spheres around us. First there's the creating of the circle itself with the *lazra meck* in the blade, then there's the consecration of it with the water and earth from the chalice, and finally, there's the purification of it with the fire and air of the incense. More importantly, each of these actions correspond with the three runes from the *Golden Key,* which together symbolize the gateway to *wa da na.* That's why we carve the *ach' na Shee* spiral near our ritual sites, because the symbol creates a permanent circle there without our having to cast one. That way, our temple can remain in place indefinitely."

I finished drawing the additional symbols on my egg with Stephanie's help and then went to the eastern quarter of the circle to work on some personal Magic while the other members finished.

When everyone was done, Jack had us all return to the altar.

"Opening the egg and letting out its contents," he said, "is symbolic of our attempt to release our own potential into the world. I want each of you visualize *your* potential being unlocked as we open up these shells. Imagine your thoughts and your desires radiating and spreading all through the universe until they become reality. In Magic, we have a saying: 'A thought is like a tree; the more space you give it, the larger it grows.' Let your thoughts grow, and they will materialize into what you desire." We each cracked open our eggs and poured out the yolks into a shallow vessel.

We placed our broken shells around the edges of the fertile pot creating a unique mosaic of partial symbols and mismatched designs. Somehow, the final result had a unique beauty all its own, creating a pattern that was both chaos and harmony uniquely balanced within the vessel of hopes and dreams. Next, we each planted our seeds within

241

the container of soil, stating out loud the outcome that we desired to achieve. There was something especially comforting and even exciting in the act of identifying and vowing to take action on my goals, and I felt good knowing that the other members of my coven were making a similar commitment along with me. We each vowed, one at a time, to direct our energy toward one another's desires, lending finality to the spell. When we were finished, the coven formed a close circle around the small pot chanting, as our hands joined, and our bodies began to sway from side to side.

"By fire, by earth, by water, by air," they called out, the words echoing off the walls of the cave, creating a powerful yet haunting rhythm. I joined the chant as it grew in intensity and repeated it with the others over and over again. The words and ricocheting rhythms clashed against one another in the confined space, like atoms and electrons smashing together in an atomic reaction. The chant became chaos itself, primordial, a thing with a life of its own. When the intensity reached a peak beyond human enduring, the cacophony of sound stopped abruptly as if defined by a script, and utter silence prevailed. In that moment of transition, that instant between the chaos and the silence that followed, I felt a shudder rise within me like a surge of electricity. The vibrating jolt energized every nerve and fiber of my body, rising within me until I felt I would explode from sheer ecstatic bliss. Then instantaneously, like a bolt of lightning gathering, condensing, and releasing, it was gone, exhausted, and released into the universe.

Stephanie broke free from the circle and raised her hands over her head asking the Goddess to bless our desires and to help us in reaching the goals we had chosen. The whole coven responded as one with, "dukaat." After a moment of silence, Jack explained that we would take the pot of seeds with us when we left, and that each person would spend some time caring for it. We were each instructed to remember our commitment to one another's goals each time we cared for the plants and we all reaffirmed that we would continue to care for the seedlings until they made a harvest in the fall.

When the ritual was finished and the Magic completed, we sat down together and shared the food we'd brought and the magical drink we'd made. The drink was created from plants that we had collected in the forest previously, and I had been present during its making. Every ingredient of the drink carried a specific attribute relating to the Sabbat at hand, and the sum total of all the ingredients created a magical formula designed to impart the spirit of the season and the Magic within the plants — into our bodies and minds.

During the process, the story of each plant, how it should be harvested, and its specific attributes, were shared within the coven, and each of us was made to understand that understanding both the creation and purpose of the resulting elixir was paramount to the experience. Jack had told me that each of our sacred Sabbats had a special drink and that like this one, each was unique and related to the particular celebration at hand.

"Part of your magical training," Jack said, "will be to study the plants used to make our ritual drinks. Each plant and herb has some kind of special Magic within it and understanding those qualities and how to use them is very important. Not only do the drinks add Magic to the rituals," he went on, "some of them also provide us with protection against illness and diseases related to that time of year." Like everything else in Magic, the creation of the drink fit perfectly with everything else we did, and the reasoning behind it helped to reinforce our understanding of nature and our place within it.

When we'd finished our meal and the talking had subsided, Jack announced that we were going to make incense for the next seasonal holiday, Beltane. At his direction, the coven moved together into a circle on the ground, sitting cross-legged, and Derek went to the altar to gather the supplies we would need.

"Each holiday has special incense, just as it has a special drink," Ron said, as we watched Derek rummaging through the box next to the altar. "We harvest each of the necessary plants and herbs associated with the particular upcoming sabbat, and then we always combine them in ritual during the holiday which precedes them. Sometimes the drinks are made on the actual holidays where we drink them rather than beforehand, depending on that Sabbat's tradition, but the incenses are always made ahead of time at the previous ritual."

As Ron spoke, I thought back to our trip several weeks before, when the whole coven went together to harvest the very herbs we were preparing now. We went to a wonderful spot in the foothills above Sylmar, where a small creek feathered out into an alluvial fan, as it emptied into a tiny reservoir surrounded by several large farms. The area was quite swampy and presented a virtual playground for Witches seeking herbs. There were wild cucumbers, lacing the branches of willows and alders with their spiraling vines, as they twined in and out of the tree's branches like fairy tresses caressing a new bride. Nightshade and dwale dominated the higher ground, coaxed by bright patches of sunlight that filtered in — between occasional oaks and cottonwoods, and the whole area was packed with giant sycamores.

At the east end of the marsh, horehound and mint mixed with mugwart and marsh mallow, and the whole place was perfumed with anise and wormwood.

Stephanie explained which plants we were looking for, and then we walked along as a group to see what we could find. As the necessary herbs were located, we each took turns harvesting them, following a procedure similar to the one used for harvesting my wand. When it came to be my turn, we located the thornbane I was to harvest on a dry bank adjacent to the wetlands, and I approached the plant respectfully. The rest of the coven stood behind me, fanned out in a tight half circle, and lent their support to me psychically as I performed the ritual.

244

"Sha ma na gadaf gadou,"[22] I offered, nodding to the plant as I knelt down before it. I explained to the plant our need to harvest some of its leaves, and promised to honor both the plant and the leaves when they were used in our ritual to make the incense. I explained the attributes that I needed the leaves to convey, and asked the plants cooperation in that regard. Then I laid down a small gift, in this case, a parchment scroll with a spell for growth and fertility for the plant, and waited for a response. Shortly, after a few moments, I felt a reply. I unsheathed my crescent silver blade and started the first cuts by scoring each stem that I intended to harvest. Next, I carefully cut off the leaves, one at a time, and when I had finished; I covered each wound with damp creek moss, mixed with comfrey and sage.

I drew the symbol for healing in the dirt beneath the plant, and said my good byes. Then I rose and handed the herbs to Stephanie, who put them into a small paper bag, and labeled them to take home with us.

"Are you okay," Nicky asked, placing her hand on my shoulder and bringing me back to the ritual at hand.

"Yeah, I'm fine," I said, "I was just reminiscing about the day we collected the herbs to make the incense for tonight."

Nicky smiled, and nodded her head in understanding. "It's pretty cool how everything we do, ties into something else later isn't it?" She added.

Derek returned from the altar, with the bags of herbs from Sylmar. One by one, we placed them into a large marble mortar, and each coven member focused on the particular herb that was added, and on the purpose for which we desired it to serve. Once all of the ingredients were in the vessel, we passed it around the circle and each member took a turn grinding and crushing the contents. The idea, Ron had told me, was to have the energy of every member of the coven included in the end product so that the incense not only contained the proper herbs

---

[22] "May the water forever flow."

representing the holiday it was created for, but that it also contained the Magic and focus of the entire group.

"When this is finished," Ron said, it will contain all the energy and purpose conveyed throughout the entire process. It will have the energy and Magic of the ritual we did when we first harvested the plants, and it will also have the energy of this ritual when we bring all of the different components together. The end result is far more that just a nice smelling incense," he went on, "it's a powerful magical spell that continues to unleash its energy each and every time we burn it."

When the incense was completed, we put it into a large glass jar and packed it away for future use. When that was done, everyone followed Stephanie to the altar, where she performed the final rite to close up our circle. When the incantations were done and the area cleaned up, we started down the difficult path back to our cars.

As I worked my way down the steep trail, climbing through the giant sedimentary rocks, I noted that everything seemed quite different than it had the first time I'd come here. Before, when I'd met the coven for the very first time, I was somewhat uneasy and a little frightened by my surroundings. But now, as I negotiated my way down the secluded rocky trail, I felt safe and at home. Every rock, and every bush, seemed familiar; and I was completely relaxed as the coolness of the late night air caressed my face. I had enjoyed the evening immensely and I returned home inspired to do even more. After I returned, I laid in my bed awake until early morning, piecing together all of the things that I'd seen and learned at the ritual. There was just so much to take in, and even though I was now initiated into the coven, Stephanie told me that I had just barely scratched the surface. Finally, just before sunrise, I fell asleep out of pure exhaustion and didn't wake up again until long after the day was well underway.

Once my wand was completed, the doorway to Magic was wide open to me. I learned a little about each of the rest of the Sabbat rituals and their underlying meanings, and I committed hundreds of herbs and a myriad of magical potions to memory. Both Ron and Stephanie taught me a great deal more about the secret alphabets and the symbolic Witches runes, and I expanded my studies diligently, reviewing the history and the workings of Magic. As the coven worked its way through the seasons of the year and the rites of passage that exemplified them, they shared with me in detail the workings of nature and the nature of the Divine, and our friendships grew and matured. As before, each lesson built upon the last, and the wonderful stories and straightforward manner in which our oral tradition was shared, not only simplified the understanding of our religion, but it also showed me constantly how everything in nature was designed to guide us toward the Divine and to understand what our responsibilities were as the children of the Goddess.

"If you look closely at this water lily," Ron commented one day as we walked along a swampy area in Bouquet Canyon in the early summer, "you'll notice that the first thing your attention is drawn to is the single flower blooming in the center of a large and obvious leaf. Then, if you look closer, particularly under the water, you'll notice that the source of the leaf is a big thick root which begins to move downward and divides up into smaller roots as it progresses further below the surface. The farther down you go, the tinier the roots become and at the same time the more divisions there are. Eventually, if you follow the roots far enough, they actually disappear and the plant becomes a part of the water itself. In one way, this is how the practice of Magic is; we walk the path following the roots deeper and deeper until we eventually become a part of the whole of things. And hopefully, when we reach this stage, we become strongly rooted in our connection with Divinity. But there are also other important lessons to be discovered by observing the relationship between the roots and plant, which apply when we pursue the roots of our own beginnings.

"For example, if we were to observe a seed from the moment of gestation, we would see that it sends out the plant above ground while at the same time sending out the roots below to stabilize and nourish it. But once the plant seems safely on its way, with both root and plant intact, the seed itself (the very source of creation) is consumed and integrated into the whole. Once that transition takes place, no matter how far you travel down the root course, or up the plant, you will never find the beginning any more. Instead, you will only find what the original source chose to leave behind to remind us of its existence. That is how the Goddess is. She exists within each and every one of us and within every aspect of her creation, while at the same time, like the seed, having the inherent ability to recreate herself in her original form if necessary. Now don't misunderstand me. I am not saying that she doesn't exist as a whole anymore, what I'm actually saying is that the whole of her is infinite and that her creation itself is the body in which she dwells."

These types of lessons added greatly to my understanding of the world around me. Gradually as my training progressed I delved deeper and deeper into the mysteries of the ritual itself, slowly peeling back the layers, one by one like an archeologist on a dig. And like the archeologist, as I pieced together the tiny shards discovered in each successive layer, a more cohesive and understandable picture began to evolve. In fact now, when I participated in the casting of the circle — which originally appeared to be the fairly simple creation of a purified space in which to do ritual — I no longer just saw what I thought was a designated temple for us to stand in while we did our Magic — similar to an outdoor version of a traditional church. But instead, now that more than the first few layers were exposed, a much greater depth and understanding was revealed to me. And, from that new perspective, I now understood that the circle was a tangible reenactment of the story of our creation with all of the critical elements present. Even the chalk used to identify the circle's boundary carried far more within it than would be seen by an uninformed observer. And beyond that, I now understood that each element, be it the magical tools used in our practices or even something so simple as the oil we used to anoint ourselves, carried within it far greater symbolism and connection with the Divine than the uninitiated would ever understand.

∼୧୯ଈଓ∽

I was now moving through high school and many of the issues discussed in my classes took on a different meaning for me than they did for most of the other students. I remember sitting in history one day where we were discussing the Scopes monkey trial and the resulting battle between religion and science over creationism versus evolution. As I sat in the class listening to the discussion and the ensuing heated debate between students on one side or the other of the issue, I came to a new understanding of my own religion. For the first time, I came to the realization that *our* beliefs grounded themselves in a time that was before religion and science had split, and that we still comfortably embraced the two as one and the same. I was no expert on religion by any means, but because of my unique perspective, I could see that the split between science and religion was really more about those of one particular religious perspective trying to reconcile their own insecurities about their own beliefs. They did so, by choosing to disregard observable evidence of the possibility that it might cast doubt on some of their religious claims, rather that trying to see how that same evidence might be used to complement their faith.

It appeared to me that they did this, by mentally moving everything from the natural world that we can see, smell, touch, taste, and prove, into some quazi-testing facility said to be created by God and ruled by the devil, in which trick hallucinations, confusing performance tests, and moral

249

mazes ruled the day. It made absolute sense to me that if one took the perspective that everything that physically existed, and everything that we have been able to personally observe as human beings since the beginning of time, is in fact a fabrication created by God to test us, and not really a true existence, then it would have to hold true that what was discovered by the earliest developing religions as they unlocked the mysteries of nature, could not exist either, hence the need to separate and rename that unreal part of existence and religion, as science, and distance oneself from it.

The part of this perspective that was obviously flawed for me arose from my now keen awareness that many of the stories promoted as true by those who followed the Bible were in fact made up. It wasn't that the Bible itself was inaccurate, no one could be sure about that one way or the other, but rather it was the process whereby many of those who followed the Biblical religions chose to add additional stuff to their teachings which were not necessarily a part of the original scriptures. Stephanie used to refer to those additions as *riders*, after the technique used by politicians to attach some unpopular law they wanted passed in Congress to a law that everyone knew was a sure thing. By doing so, she explained, they were able to get the unrelated bill accepted even though it was unpopular, because to vote against it was to defeat the whole thing.

I was glad that our religion taught us to question everything and that it saw the process of doing so as being divinely inspired rather than being against God. For me, seeking to understand all of the things created by the gods just brought me closer to them, and the study of science, just made me recognize how much more complex and astounding creation really is. At no time during my education did debunking some religious myth shake my faith. In fact, in most cases, it strengthened it by making space for some important missing piece of the puzzle to fall into place, which brought me one step closer to understanding the true nature of the Divine.

The unique outlook offered by my faith, which sought not only just to refer to God or to pray to God, as I found in my experience in Christianity, but also opened up a whole way to come to understand the nature of God, which was the primary difference between my experience as a Methodist and my experience being a Witch. Also most of the people I knew during my Christian upbringing had a feeling of the presence of God when they went to church, but often forgot that connection when they cleared the doors on Sunday. Witches, on the other hand, had a tendency to experience God right here in everything all of the time, and did not think of deity as being off in some distant place, watching us from afar.

This way of looking at religion brought with it an amazing sense of wonder, and once that began to set in, things I'd never dreamed of began to fall neatly into place. It was as though I was working on a giant puzzle, for which someone had long ago lost the cover. I wasn't sure just exactly what the end picture would look like as I added one fragment after another, but as I carefully searched for and tried different pieces, I'd find one that neatly fit and there would be a tugging memory on the edge of my perception that fulfilled a place in my spirit as the things I learned came together. But the most exciting part of all was when I began to actually get a sense of where I was headed and discovered that the Magic I sought, went far deeper than I had ever imagined.

CHAPTER 14

The Golden Key, and the Athame'

The coven met again for Beltane, and then again for the Summer Solstice, in June. Every ritual was wonderful and inspiring and I learned something new each time we met. I really felt myself coming into sync with the cycles of the seasons and it brought a sense of peace to my spirit.

My book of magic was just about full and I had already purchased a blank book to make another one. At first, I had tried to organize my book into categories, separating spells, holidays and herb lore. But I soon found that that was a waste of time because there was just too much information coming in to possibly keep up, much less try to organize. Nicky told me that she had given up trying to organize her stuff after only a couple of weeks, and she suggested that I try making several different sets of books.

"The best thing to do," she said, "is to make one book to carry around with you for just scribbling notes to yourself or to make drawings of plants and stuff. Then make another more formal book, where you can later take your time planning and organizing things. Stephanie says you should write everything in runes so people who aren't Witches won't be able to understand them. She also says that by writing in runes, you will learn to memorize the symbols more quickly, and she was right. It worked really well for me, so you might want to try it too."

I tried Nicky's suggestion and things went well with my book of magical notes after that. I made three separate books, one smaller one to carry with me everywhere that I filled with sketches and notes and samples of the different plants I'd collected, and another one that I organized into special sections, which were devoted to different areas of study and that documented the rituals we performed. Then I also made a beautiful large book which was made from the bark of a huge fallen cottonwood tree that I bound together with red yarn and filled with pages of heavy parchment. In this book, I wrote everything in magical ink, using the language of the Witches and the runes I'd learned in my studies. I also drew intricate illustrations in my book, coloring them with the white of an egg, mixed with various colored dyes I'd learned to make from the plants in the forest. All in all, I'd amassed quite a collection of information, which I kept under my bed in a small trunk I'd bought at a garage sale.

By this time, I'd also put together quite a collection of plants and herbs and various implements used in Magic. Ron had taught me the proper way to dry plant materials and I had several dozen species hanging from the ceiling suspended by various colors of ribbon and yarn. There were jars filled with potions and salves and my knowledge of healing combinations grew substantially. I bought myself some candle holders and a tiny brass censor for burning my incenses. I didn't have a chalice yet, because Stephanie said it was not yet time to make it, but I did use a small plastic sugar bowl in the meantime, and it worked just fine. I did my own rituals and practiced Magic in all aspects of my life. I looked at things differently now that I was a Witch and the world was a far more sacred place for me.

Things were going great for the coven that year, and we all spent quite a bit of time together as a group. There were lots of walks in the woods and hundreds of discussions about Magic. Stephanie and Ron taught me more about the Elban language, and I practiced writing and speaking in it regularly. It was difficult to learn, because some of the words had multiple meanings, and depending on the context the meanings would sometimes change. I guess English is like that too although I never really noticed it that much, probably because it was the language I grew up with, and the changes just seemed more natural. In any case, we used Elban mostly for casting the circle and for certain spells relating to matters of high importance.

While Elban was the primary magical language spoken by the coven, we used another language called Theban to write things down. Theban was a language which K.D.,

Stephanie's Priestess, had learned from a friend in a different coven. Theban was made up of a series of interesting symbols, which mostly replaced the letters of our own alphabet. These Theban symbols were used like a code between us when we wrote letters to one another, so that other people outside of our group would not be able to decipher them. We did this primarily as a matter of protection, as there was great prejudice against Witches.

"I think if people became better educated as to what it is that we really believe and what our religion actually teaches, they wouldn't be so afraid of us," Ron said, on one of our forays into the forest. "There are a lot of ignorant people out there who aren't willing to even have a discussion with us to find out who we really are and what we actually stand for," he went on.

As he continued his rant, Ron chose the moment to use the surrounding landscape to further make his point.

"The gods created all of the plants and trees we see around us," he said, pointing to the abundant growth before us. "And yet if you look, you'll see that they're about as diverse and unique as you can get," he continued. "It's that very diversity — the mixture of their colors, characteristics, and growing cycles — that creates the beauty we see. If the gods had wanted us to all be the same, they would have made the world a gray and boring place. Therefore, it's important to remember that it is the very differences between us that make us unique and special — and it is the abundant flaunting of those differences throughout nature, that verifies to us that our creators have talent. To advocate acting in a manner that tries to make everyone the same, is against nature and against the creation itself. That is why all people must learn to respect their differences and to realize that by doing so, they are not only honoring their neighbors, but also the gods who created them."

I considered Ron's statement and it made perfect sense to me. Perhaps if people learned to appreciate one another's differences, we wouldn't have so many wars. After all, while not all wars were started because the "enemy looked or believed differently, far more wars were fought over religion and different perceptions of God than anything else. And that was just plain stupid.

❧⳥⳥♧

One day as we walked along the beach down near an area called Leo Carrillo, Ron brought up the subject of mystical numbers in our tradition. He told me that the time had come for me to expand my way of looking at things and that learning to understand the mysteries connected to certain numbers would help me to do so.

"There are many mysteries that are right in front of our eyes," he said, pointing out toward the sea. "The problem is that if we're not looking for them, they often go unnoticed. One of the greatest of these mysteries is the secret of the Golden Key. Now I know that Stephanie has already told you a little bit about it, but its time to give you a little more to think about.

"So, have you had time to consider the saying that Stephanie revealed to you yet? Have you thought any more about what it means?

"Do you mean 'Thrice three the golden key?" I asked.

"Yes."

"Well, I have thought about it, but I haven't really figured out anything new. What does it mean?"

"That's the mystery," he returned smiling. "You see, if I gave you the answer to the question, then you would be satisfied and think that was all there was to it. This question is much bigger than that. It holds the key to the greatest mysteries in all Magic, and the answer can only be found within you. It is the process of answering the question that is in itself the greatest mystery.

I found myself totally confused by this whole conversation and I told Ron that I felt so. He assured me that over time, both the question and the answer would become more apparent. He pointed out to me that every problem has a starting point, a place where you begin to

255

consider your strategy and come to a decision as to how you'll attempt solve it. He said that a good place to start solving this problem is by considering what I had already concluded in my conversation with Stephanie.

"Did you come to any conclusions in that conversation?" Ron asked.

"Yes," I answered.

"And what did you figure out?"

"That thrice three is nine."

"Very good, Ron said. Certain numbers play an important part in our lives. Others play an important part in the overall scheme of things. It just so happens that the number nine is one of the latter. In fact, we Witches believe that the number nine plays a fundamental part in helping us to understand the universe. This concept is not something new; in fact it is very very old. But I don't want to give away too much right now so let me just give you some advice. Study the number nine and make a list of the things you come across that relate to it. Keep your eyes and ears open and look for answers in every aspect of your life. When you've learned enough to ask the next question, one of us will give you the next piece of the riddle."

I made a vow to try and discover the mysteries associated with the number nine that day and set aside a special place in my book of magic to record my findings. Over the next several weeks, in fact, just as Ron had said it would if I started looking, the number nine popped up and I discovered several unique things about it. The first took place at school where I asked my math teacher Mr. Farr if he knew of anything special about the number nine.

"The number nine is the most unique number in the universe," he replied. I was surprised by his reply and I asked him why.

"We'll," he said, "multiply nine by any number you choose and tell me the answer.'

"Five times nine is forty five I answered."

"Add the four and the five and what do you get," he asked.

"Nine," I answered, feeling a sense of excitement stirring in the pit of my stomach.

"Try another," he said.

"'Seven times nine equals sixty three."

"And what does six and three equal?"

"Nine," I answered, getting the enormity of it all.

I wondered if Mr. Farr knew more about the number nine but I didn't ask him, mostly because I didn't want him asking me where all this was coming from. I went home that afternoon and immediately wrote down what I had learned. I could hardly wait to share what I'd found out with Ron and Stephanie and to find out if that was part of the mystery. I called Ron first, but he wasn't home, so I tried Stephanie instead. I told her what I'd learned, and she praised me for my discovery.

"That's very good Patrick," she responded, as I told her the news over the phone. "You're right; the qualities you've discovered are a part of the mystery. But don't get too excited yet, because that's just a scratch in the surface of things. The question you should ask yourself now, is which came first, the chicken or the egg?"

"Is that a Witch saying too," I asked?

"No," she replied, laughing. "It's just a good way to throw you another clue with out giving you the answers. Actually, I'd just like for you to focus on one aspect of what you've discovered so far. Do you think that it's a coincidence that the product of any number times nine always equals nine? Keep in mind our most basic rule — always look below the surface. The universe is made of many layers, and each layer you peel back reveals another. To discover truth, you must first be open to discovery itself. It is not until you choose to seek — that you will find what you are looking for. You have peeled back one layer now and opened a door to possibilities that you never realized were present before. The question is: will you be able to use what you now know to move forward from here. The secret to answering this call is to expand your imagination and to look more carefully at the complexity of the world we live in, in the same manner you just used to discover what you now know about the Golden Key. For as all Witches know, nothing is coincidence and everything is interrelated, for it all comes from the same beginning and therefore everything is a part of the same wondrous puzzle."

I assured Stephanie that I would continue my quest regarding the number nine, and that I would check in with both Ron and her whenever I felt I'd made progress.

❧ ⊙⊰⊱⊙ ☙

Around the last week in August, Ron suggested we meet up in the hills near Angeles Crest, which was a series of high jagged mountains above the San Fernando Valley. The view from the place he directed me to was spectacular. There was a cascading mountain stream filled to the brim with white turbulent water that threw a continuous spray of mist as it negotiated its way over sharp boulders on its trip down the gorge to the valley below. There were also thousands of large pines, a hundred feet tall or more protruding from the steep mountainsides like the quills of a porcupine — some straight and some at angles — documenting the course of a hundred years of tumultuous winds and stormy weather. Ron hadn't arrived yet so I left a note on my car and started up the narrow trail that followed the watercourse up the narrow trough. A short way up, I crossed the small wooden bridge Ron told me to look for and took the path to the right up the steep embankment. Cresting the slope fifty feet up, I came to the shallow pond where Ron said we'd have our meeting.

The pond was huge, more like an alpine lake, yet it was only ten or twelve inches deep. There were stands of cattails all along the edge, which stood completely motionless in the still morning air. The waters surface was like leaded crystal, smooth, glass like, and filled with silvery color. In its reflection I could see the trees and mountain tops replicated clearly in the ponds shimmering surface and visions of sky and cloud moved across the natural mirror in ghost like apparitions, giving a sense of movement, almost

258

life-like, to the still yet vibrant water. Behind me, as I turned around, was one of the most spectacular views I have ever seen. I stood on a granite knoll, seemingly on the edge of the world, overlooking a hundred miles of mountains and valleys.

Ron came walking up the trail and waved as he crested the rocky promontory.

"Have you been waiting long?" he asked, working his way around the edge of the water.

"Not really," I replied. "I just got here about ten minutes ago."

"Beautiful huh?"

"It's great. I can see all the way to the ocean. How did you ever find this place?"

"Just luck, although Stephanie says the Goddess leads us to these places so we'll have a place to hold our rituals."

"The pond is great," I said gesturing towards the shallow basin.

"Yeah, there's something about the way it reflects everything around, combined with the view of the valley below that makes you feel like you're floating in space."

As he spoke, I experienced a flashback to my near death experience. All of the sudden instead of standing on the rock knoll looking out over the valley, I found myself once again, suspended in infinite space just before the Lady offered me her hand. I shook my head warding off the on-coming vision and returning to the present. In those few lost moments, l realized there was a connection between this place and the doorway to the other side.

"This place is Magic," Ron whispered, not aware of my moment of revelation.

"We come here to do ritual when we can," he went on. "Unfortunately though, we don't make it up here too often because it's so far away. The lake's a great place to meditate and I've had a number of major visions here. Stephanie calls this place "crystal clear," because the water is always so calm and clean and because it's a place she thinks is connected to the Goddess.

"One of the reasons I brought you up here is to teach you about our magical knife, or as some people call it, the Athame'. The reason this particular location is a good place to begin will become more apparent once we start talking. So, what I'd like to do now is start, by having you tell me what you already know."

"Well," I responded, "I know it's the special knife we use to cast our circles. I also know that it takes a lot of work to make one, although I really don't know just exactly what that means. I also think that the blade is made of iron if I remember right, although I'm not absolutely sure about that either."

"That's a good start," Ron returned. "You're right about the casting the circle part and it does take a great deal of work to make one. You're also right about the blade being made of iron, although it has not always been that way — which brings us to why we've come up here in the first place. You see that white vein in the hill over there by the cattails?"

"Yeah," I answered, noting the white band in the hillside.

"That's one of the places where we get the chalk to make our circles," he continued. "There are also other veins we know about, but this one is particularly special because it has something that the others don't. Let's walk over there and I'll show you."

We walked around the edge of the pond past a large stand of cattails to the small hill on the other side. When we got there, Ron took a rock and scraped away at the two foot wide band of chalky dirt until he had broken out several small roundish hard stones that were mixed in with the softer chalky material. He cleaned the excess dirt off one piece and carried it to the waters edge. Bending down on one knee, he carefully washed the rock revealing a small purplish nodule with wavy lines outlining the contours of its surface.

"This is flint," he said. "You will usually find it any time you see white chalk like we see here. Anyway, watch this."

He set the small nodule down on a rounded stone near the waters edge and picked up another slightly pointed stone about the size of a fist. He struck the pointed stone against the flint, and after several hits, the flint cracked and separated flaking off a crescent shaped chip. He picked up the chip and held it up in front of me and said:

"See the shape of this flake? It's like the crescent moon. In Elban this chip has a name, it is called *ata — which* means 'sacred crescent'. In ancient times, being able to strike a piece of flint and make this shape was a highly honored and respected talent. All the early knives and scrapers were made using this process, and because of the importance of a blade in those times, the knife itself was also seen as sacred. Witches believe that the potential for the crescent within the stone is one of the first examples of knowledge hidden below the surface discovered by human beings and so the word *ata* also means 'to reveal that which is hidden'. When early man was creating these first sacred blades, they also discovered a second mystery within the stone. When struck a certain way, the stones gave off sparks and eventually brought about fire. As you know, fire contains *djinn ralda —* the spark of creation, and so the first blades were even more revered.

"Because of the complexity of the blade making, and the sacredness of the final result, Witches considered the act of creating a perfect blade as being guided by the Goddess herself. One interesting fact, by the way, is that it takes nine calculated strikes for an experienced flint worker to produce a blade. Of course there are many different types of blades, but making the most basic, requires exactly nine chips to be made. For the first Witches, it was a combination of the nine strikes, the fire within the stone, the sacredness of the blade, and the idea that intervention by the Goddess herself guided the hands of the artist — that moved them to use a blade to create their first magic circles."

"So, why don't we use stone blades to cast our circles now?" I asked.

"We'll, like everything else, there's a lot more to the story," he said smiling.

261

"After the knife was invented, people moved on to create the first axe. And the axe, once it came into play, changed life substantially for the early tribesmen. Once people had a way to chop and shape wood, they were able to make boats and to create simple houses. One observation made by early Witches was that to chop with an axe, one had to swing it in a perfect crescent. They called the crescent created by the swing of an axe, *acha* — meaning a sacred arc. By this time, they also recognized that a circle itself was just a continuation of that arc. No one knows whether the sacred circle came first or the understanding of the act of making an arc, but the two are definitely connected somewhere in the beginnings of time. Because of this, the word *acha* also became associated with a circle. In some of our Elban incantations, there are phrases like *alock ma ralda atacha chook chakadah* — which translates 'from the spirit circle comes wisdom'. And another saying — *atacha atan me'* which means 'to cut a circle'. The word *atan* means to cut and the word *me'* relates to something personal or shows personal possession of something. It is thought that the word athame' comes from several of these root words and signifies far more than just a knife.

"First it means to cut personally or to participate in the act of cutting something spiritually. It also means to create a sacred arc or sacred circle. If you move further back to its earlier roots, it means a sacred blade or a blade connected with the Goddess, and lastly, it means to reveal or discover that which is hidden. So, if you put all of that together, you end up with a knife that is sacred to the Goddess and is used to cut a personal spiritual space by creating a consecrated arc or circle. And that that circle, when created by the holy blade, reveals the mysteries and Magic that is hidden below the surface of things. As you can see, all of these meanings apply to our understanding of the blade, which is what makes it so special for us."

"Wow," I exclaimed. "I didn't realize it had such an interesting history. I guess there's a lot more to it than I first realized."

"That's definitely true," Ron answered. "But there's still more to the story.

"Some time, long after the discovery of the crescent within the stone, people began to discover the first metals. Most of the metals far out performed stone and were much less likely to break. Because of this new development, Witches began to make their sacred knives out of the metals of the times, instead of using flint. They probably used copper at first, then bronze, and eventually turned to iron, like we use today.

The earliest of these blades were forged into a crescent or curved shape, to continue the process of honoring *ata*, and many of those early blades can still be seen in museums and archeological digs throughout Europe and Asia. By the time the new metals came into play, some of the spiritual meanings connected to the earlier sacred blades became more and more obscure. Our legends tell us that our more recent ancestors on the sacred path, still spoke of the 'old ways,' and taught about the earlier stone blades and their connection with sacred fire. But they also reveal that the actual process of striking the flint and capturing the sacred fire within was no longer practiced for a period of time. Even so, Witches were still always aware that *djinn raldu* was associated with the creation and the use of the sacred blade, it was just that there was not the same direct connection between the fire within the stone and the knife that created the circles, anymore."

"But didn't they have to melt the metal and heat it with fire to shape it?" I asked.

"Yes they did. But that was not the same. While fire was used to make the blade, it was no longer actually contained within the blade, and that quandary was a difference that was difficult for them to accept. To solve this problem, Witches began to try and affix pieces of flint to the tip of the blade, using metal wires or sinews to secure it. When this didn't work well, they went on to try to actually forge a piece of flint into the tips of their blades in order to replace that which was lost. They actually melted the flint, which would turn to glass, and tried to pound the molten metal together with it. This process became the practice for some period of time; however it wasn't practical and didn't work well. Finally one day, a Witch saw a flaming meteorite strike the earth from the sky and he retrieved it. Seeing it as fire created by the gods, the Witch forged a piece of it into the tip of his sacred blade, once again reuniting the fire from the creation and the sacred blade. This process worked out very well and that practice has continued to this very day.

"Now all covens on the sacred path, make their athame's using a meteor collected from the sky, so that each one contains a direct and personal connection with the Goddess and with her heavenly fire. Besides making that connection," Ron went on, "the addition of the meteorite in the tip, also added another practical component to our blade. You see, when we cut the circle, we drag the blade on the ground all the way around the circumference. Over years, this abrasion with dirt and rocks and sand, would wear down most blades. But the blades forged with a meteorite in the tip, last forever."

"But where would I get a meteorite?" I asked, trying to imagine myself watching the sky for years waiting for one to hit.

"We'll make a trip into the desert to a special place I know," he replied. "There are meteor fragments there that can be found if you know where to look. It might take several trips to find one, but patience and understanding of the laws of nature will help us. The place we usually go is out in the Mojave Desert and we've had pretty good luck so far. But if that doesn't work, don't worry, there are still other options."

I had learned by now that the Lady seldom set tasks before me that I couldn't accomplish, so I decided to rely on my faith in her and I didn't push the issue further.

"Finding the meteorite is not the only difficult task", Ron said. "The forging and shaping of the blade takes a great deal of strength and the finishing of the iron is very tedious. Then there's the handle too, which has to be made from the branch of a tree that bears fruit. It too must be shaped and

264

worked. Overall, it will take you a long time to create your athame', but it'll be well worth the effort when it's finished!"

I was already well aware of the importance of creating all of the tools and ritual items with my own hands. Jack had taught me about the connection that is created when you make something yourself. I knew that part of the Magic and power of our sacred objects came from putting our own personal energy into them while focusing on our final intent for their use. This was the way it had been done for thousands of years, and I was well aware there is power just in the awareness of that. Ron went on to teach me that the athame' is also used to direct and focus energy for a purpose.

"See this circle," he said, as he traced a rough figure in the dirt near the water's edge. Think of this as the range of your ability to concentrate." Then he added a small dot directly in the center of the drawing and tapped on it repeatedly with a slender stick to draw my attention to it. "This is your final objective," he said. "You must learn to take all of this," he said, indicating the larger circle, "and focus it down to this," tapping again on the dot. "If you can learn to accomplish this, you will be able to use your athame' to create a proper circle."

I paused for a minute taking in Ron's diagram and then asked:

"How do I do that?"

"It's really pretty easy," Ron returned, looking directly at me.

"Here's your first exercise to help you accomplish that. Draw a circle on a piece of paper, as large as you can fit on it, and then put a small dot in the center like I did here. When you've done that, hang it on a wall in front of you and look at the overall figure. Try to concentrate on the dot and make the circle go away. If you practice diligently, you will find that the circle will begin to fade in and out and eventually disappear. Then only the dot will remain. When you've reached this point, you have learned to focus your thoughts on one thing and you should continue the exercise until you feel completely comfortable with it. Once you are able to do this on a regular basis, try to make the dot disappear also. When you can accomplish that, you are ready to focus all your energy and direct it through the blade. In this way, we use the mystical connections already attributed to the magical tool, combined with our own focus and desire to, as we say, put it 'out there'.

"Another thing you will experience once you've got your focus down, is that you will be able to see the flame of blue white energy emanating from the tip of your athame' whenever you use it to cast your circle. This is *lazra meck*, and it looks just like the light you saw emanating from the chalk we use for our circle.

"It's good to know what everything means," Ron continued, "and why we do things the way we do. Ultimately, the greatest Magic comes from a complete understanding of the process at hand, and not just from going through the motions." I considered Ron's words and thought back to what Stephanie had told me several weeks before.

"It's very important to understand the actions we take while creating a circle or other important rituals," she had said. "Just going through the motions, don't make no potent potions," she went on — laughing easily at the simplicity of her jest. As she often did, Stephanie used her great sense of humor and wit to make her point. But underneath it all, beneath the humor and the laughter — she was a very wise woman.

"Just what exactly are we doing when we cut a circle?" I asked Ron returning to his lesson.

"Mostly we're creating a sacred space to do our Magic as you already know, and telling the creation story." he replied. "But when we scribe an arc around the circle with the athame', the athame' also actually cuts a hole between the worlds and leaves the center, which is our temple, floating between heaven and earth. I guess you could say it's kind of like a church, but without any walls. As you know, we believe that a mountain top or a glade in the forest is closer to the gods than a building that shuts nature out. That's why the athame' is so important to us.

266

The blade is never used to cut anything physical, but instead only to designate sacred space.

"Is that the only way to create a circle?" I asked. "What if you don't have your athame' with you?"

"There are other ways to do it, it's just that using the athame' is the best way because of all the connections to the past and the spiritual significance attributed to it. You can also cast a circle using your wand, or for that matter pretty much any of your other magical tools. Sometimes, when I'm out in the woods and I feel like creating a circle, I just use my hand and visualize a circle in the air around me. Another way is to make a circle by interlocking the ends of your cord — which you haven't made yet — and then laying it on the ground in a circle and standing in the middle.

There's something else about the circle we should talk about," Ron said, seriously, "and that's the relationship between it and the Golden Key."

"What do you mean," I asked.

"What is the relationship between the circle and the number nine," he returned, giving me a sly look?

"I don't know," I said, trying to imagine a connection between the two.

"Well," Ron went on, "let's start with the four directions in the circle. What are they?"

"East, south, west, and north," I answered.

"Hum?" Ron considered. "So do you notice anything about the words or letters themselves that might relate to the number nine? Keep in mind that we aren't looking for the obvious like the red apple, were looking for that which is hidden."

I considered Ron's comment and then counted all of the letters in the four words. There were eighteen. I remembered my math teacher's revelation about the number nine and realized that the number 18 equaled nine. 1+8=9.

"The number of letters equals nine," I said, happy with my discovery.

"Very good," Ron commented. "Anything else?"

I looked at the words and tried to imagine some other correlation, but failed to do so.

"Nothing that I can see," I answered.

"Well, you're just beginning in all of this, so you probably wouldn't even know to look, but if we go back to the apple story, remember how discovering each layer leads to the next? Well that's the case here too.

I'm going to give you some help here to get you started. Try assigning each letter the numerical value it holds as to its place in the alphabet and you'll find something that will surprise you."

"I don't understand," I said.

Ron took the stick he had used to demonstrate the point and circle technique, and he started to scribe all twenty-six letters of the alphabet in the dirt. When he finished, he carved the numbers one through twenty- six above them.

"Okay, now add up the value of each word using the numbers that each letter equals."

I started counting one word at a time and when I finished I had: east = 45, south = 83, west = 67 and north = 75.

"Now add those together," Ron challenged me.
I totaled the numbers and got 270.

"Now add those three numbers," Ron said with a big grin.

"Nine," I said.

"You're learning," Ron chortled, patting me on the back as I got the message.

"That's unbelievable," I said, shaking my head.

"Oh, that's just the tip of the iceberg," Ron teased.

"Now let's consider the circle itself. How many degrees are there in a circle?"

"360," I answered, instantaneously realizing the significance as my mind quickly added the numbers together.

"So that equals nine also, doesn't it?" My mentor shot back, grinning.

"Yeah!"

"So how many degrees are between each of the directions," Ron prodded.

"90," I responded, beginning to feel anxious.

"And this is just the beginning," Ron exclaimed. There's just layer after layer hidden here. So a good question to keep asking yourself over and over again, is Stephanie's favorite riddle, 'which came first, the chicken or the egg?' This is a really important question for us to consider, because what we're trying to discover here is whether all of these hidden layers were created by us over time for some purpose, or if they are all just a coincidence — or more importantly, if the Goddess put them there for us to discover some great truth, and if so, what that great truth is?

"In any case, we'll have to stop here for now, because I want you to try to discover some of this stuff on your own, and if I keep giving you answers, you won't really get it."

"Why is it important for me to discover this stuff on my own?" I asked, wanting to better understand Ron's statement.

"Well," Ron started, "if you've ever watched students in a science class, you'll kind of get the idea. A teacher can tell the students over and over again, about some particular chemical reaction that they want them to understand. But if you let a week or so pass after the discussion, the students most likely won't be able to accurately recall it. On the other hand, if you give the students the necessary chemicals that lead to the reaction you want them to understand, and you tell them to start experimenting on their own, governed only by some basic guidelines that you know will lead them to the results you want to demonstrate, then the end results they produce, will stay with them for a lifetime. In fact, that's specifically why science classes do experiments in the first place, so the students not only won't forget what they've learned, but also so that they'll be able to use what they've learned, practically, in the future.

"But let's finalize our talk about the Golden Key before we get too far off track. The Key plays an important part in everything we do and if you aren't aware of its existence, you can't possibly understand real Magic and its use. But as I said before, that's something that I want you to spend some time thinking about on your own, before we talk further about it. Also, it's getting late and we'd better be heading home now, because the traffic will terrible in another hour or so and we definitely don't want to have to deal with that."

My mentor led the way as we walked around the edge of the mirror-like lake, and I followed him down the steep trail in a daze. There was so much to learn and so many mysteries to discover, and I just wasn't sure if I could take it all in.

As we approached our cars, a young hawk flew up out of the brush, gaining height as he floated upward on the rising wind currents. As he disappeared into the sunset I felt a kinship with the bird and his journey, for my journey also continued to propel me to a higher vantage point and carried me far away from where I had started. It was just like Ron had said when he taught me the lesson long ago about moving to higher ground in order to better see where you were going and how far you had come. And I realized for the first time that the Sacred Path itself *is* higher ground!

Chapter 15

The Magical Blade

The weeks rolled by and Magic surrounded every aspect of my life. Each new experience built upon the last and the elusive pieces of the mystical puzzle I sought to understand continued to fall into place. Fall blew in like a gentle but cool breeze and the cottonwoods and willows along the creek began their metamorphosis toward the dark times, preparing to return to the womb of the Mother. As Ron and I walked along the creek where he first introduced me to the forest, he told me that it was time to start work on my magical blade.

"It's time to look for a meteorite so we can start your knife," Ron commented casually, as though his revelation was a common occurrence in our discussions. I tried to hide my excitement but the roller coaster like sensation in my stomach made it impossible to do so.

"Really?" I stuttered, not expecting Ron's news.

"Yes," Ron said, sensing my excitement. "We have to start now or you won't be able to finish by Samhain, and then you'd have to wait another whole year before you could finalize it."

"Why is that?" I asked.

"The blade must be completed by then so that you can do the last ritual that's required to bring it to life, he returned."

"So what ritual is that?" I inquired.

"The blade must be placed into the ground within a sacred circle of chalk on Samhain so that it can reside in the womb of the Goddess for the dark times. This is the only way that it can learn the mysteries hidden there that give it the power to do its Magic. Then when the Winter Solstice comes and the Mother illuminates the chalk with the light of *lazra meck*, you can withdraw it as She initiates the cycle of rebirth. In this way, it becomes not only something created by you, but also a child of the Creatrix in its own right. Always remember, that the athame' is a living thing and that it is the most sacred of all of our tools. And once it's finished, its completion will affect all of your Magic going forward and it will add significantly to your journey on the sacred path for the rest of your life."

"So when do we start?" I asked anxiously, hardly able to contain myself.

"Saturday," he answered. "We'll drive out to the desert together, and that'll take at least a couple of hours. Then we'll hike from the road to a place I know where we've had some luck before. All in all, it will take us about three hours just to get there.

"The best time to look is toward the end of the day just before the sun goes down," he went on, "or after dark, using a flashlight. In any case, why don't you meet me at my house around noon, and we'll head out to the Mojave."

I agreed on the time and we continued on our walk. As we reached the end of the ravine and we climbed up over the bank, I noticed that the field where I first learned about Thornbane was now under construction. The whole area had been graded, and there were forms set out to pour concrete for what looked like forty or fifty new homes.

"It's really sad," Ron exclaimed, commenting on the construction before us, "to see our creek being invaded by progress. I hope it stops here. Jack and Stephanie say that one day the whole planet will just be a series of cities and streets and that there will be very little space left to connect with nature. If that's true, I'm glad that I won't be here to see it."

I too was saddened by the building in the area. They had already put a drainage pipe into the creek near one of my favorite places, which now spewed forth a pungent and unpleasant liquid. And now instead of the comforting magical scent of plants and trees and meandering creek which I had so come to love, there was an industrial stagnant smell permeating the area.

I paused at the top of the bank and turned back toward the creek, remembering all of the wonderful lessons I'd learned there.

"May the power of the Lady bless you and keep you safe," I said quietly, drawing a pentagram of protection before my beloved glade, and then I turned and followed my mentor, along the grassy berm back to our car.

When Ron dropped me off at my house, I waved as he drove away. "A meteor in the desert," I considered, and then made my way up to the house, fantasizing about the weekend coming up.

Ron picked me up around one o'clock in the afternoon and we drove for several hours. We eventually pulled over on the shoulder along the side of the highway at a place unmarked by any particular reference. Ron had been watching the mile markers on the side of the road, and he chose our destination according to that. There was no indication that anyone had ever stopped here before — no foot prints in the sand, no discarded bottles or cans on the side of the road, absolutely nothing to designate this particular spot from any one of a thousand others along the desolate highway.

"Are you sure that this is it?" I asked as we exited the car.

"I'm sure," Ron answered, starting out across the deserted desert toward some distant point on the horizon.

I followed my mentor, carrying a small day pack that Ron had brought with us, packed with the few supplies he'd said we'd need for our foray into the barren wasteland. There were two flashlights, some extra batteries, a couple of sandwiches, a large horseshoe shaped magnet, some matches, some string, a hand drawn map, and a compass. Ron also brought a large miner style canteen, which he carried over his shoulder while I carried the pack, and a small folding army shovel. Once I caught up to him, he started to tell me what we were going to do.

"Basically," he started, "meteorites are hitting the earth all of the time. We just don't see them for the most part, because we really aren't watching for them. And when they do land, they become almost impossible to distinguish because they are buried among the trees and plants and the thousands of other obstacles that block our vision.

273

That's why we come to the desert to find them. You see, out here," he indicated, pointing to the large expanse of sand in front of us, "there really aren't any of those obstacles in our way. And besides that, meteorites are usually black and shiny and they really stand out against the backdrop of all of this white sand."

"So why are we going to this particular place if they are hitting everywhere. Why didn't we just stop an hour ago on the side of the road and look?" I asked.

"Well, actually, they don't fall just anywhere," he responded, "They seem to be more attracted to some particular places than to others. I'm not exactly sure why that is, but Stephanie says it has something to do with the magnetic forces created by the earth. Maybe it's because they are made up of iron and they're drawn to the magnetic force in the same way that a magnet attracts metal filings."

"So how do we go about finding a meteorite for my blade? Will there just be a bunch of them lying around to choose from?" I asked.

"No, unfortunately not," Ron commented. Even though they are quite common, most of them are microscopic in size. The trick is to find one that is large enough to forge into the tip of your blade. Now we might get lucky and just find one lying right out in the open," he said pausing, "and that's what happened when Derek found his, but it generally doesn't work that way. What we need to do is to have you ask the gods to guide you and then have you pick a general area that you feel good about. Then, we'll tie a string to the magnet we brought, and you'll walk around dragging it in the sand and then checking it every little bit to see if it has picked up any little bits of metal. If it has, then we'll know that that's a good area, and we'll start searching the whole place inch by inch. We'll also do a little digging here and there just in case there might be something right under the surface. This whole area is constantly changing and the sand moves from one place to another all of the time. Also the rain is constantly uncovering stuff that's close to the surface, so these meteors are regularly being covered and uncovered all of

274

the time. The key thing here is to be thorough in your search and to have the gods on your side. I know it sounds hard, but just imagine how much harder it must have been for our predecessors. They most likely didn't have magnets, so they just had to follow their instincts in order to accomplish this, but then again, they probably had more time than we do to make this happen and were likely to have been much more observant regarding what was going on in the natural world.

After a while, we stopped and I went off by myself to do a brief ritual to ask for help in finding one of the travelers from the heavens. I drew a small circle in the sand with my hand and stepped inside. I asked the Lady to guide me in my quest and assured her that I would use my blade to accomplish positive things. I reminded her that she had asked me to serve her and that this quest appeared to be a part of that process.

As I stood in my circle, waiting for some kind of response, I turned toward the west and the now setting sun. There, about fifty yards in front of me was a tall twisted cactus highlighted by the sunset. And as I looked at it from the small circle I had created, I realized that long exposure to the wind had curved the top of the solitary resident into a curved arc. And from where I stood, observing it backed by the setting sun, it formed a perfect number nine, surrounded by a halo of brilliant light.

I took my vision as an answer from the Lady as to where to search, and giving thanks, I exited my simple but inspired circle. I walked over to the cactus, which no longer looked like the number nine once I changed my perspective, and dropped the magnet to the ground next to it. Using the cactus as a reference, I started walking in a spiral in a *deosil* direction, moving outward from the plant, but found nothing. Then Ron joined me, asking me what I was doing. I told him about the sign from the lady and he agreed that this was probably as good a place to start as any.

I continued my spiral as I walked, checking the magnet as I went for any sign of metal, until I was about twenty feet from the cactus; and then I hit pay dirt! As I pulled the magnet up from the sand, I noticed that one of the legs looked more bulky than the other. When I examined it more closely, I discovered that the end was covered with several minute black metallic pieces and a fine layer of iron dust.

"I have something," I yelled, holding up the magnet and waving it wildly in the air. Ron, who'd, walked off down a dry wash a hundred yards away, jogged toward me to see what the commotion was all about. When he got to the site, he took the magnet from my hand and looked at it closely, smiling.

"This is a really good sign," he said enthusiastically. "See these little chunks here," he went on, isolating a couple of small rice sized flecks with his finger nail. "These are actual meteorites, or at least pieces that have broken off of one. You should dig around here and if you're lucky, you might find the one that they broke off from."

I set the day pack on the ground to mark the spot, and went over to where Ron had set the shovel and the water. I opened the canteen and took a hearty swig and then offered it to Ron. Then I picked up the shovel and walked back to the pack — and began to dig around. The task was tedious. Basically, I would turn over one or two shovelfuls, and then run the magnet through the pile of sand, inspecting it for more fragments. The process continued, and I found little bits of iron dust, but no more of the actual fragments I had hoped to find.

The sun fully set and the landscape now took on a dark purple hue, with only a hint of the earlier blazing ball remaining as the fading orange glow merged with the horizon. Ron brought over one of the flashlights and I flipped it on, quite conscious of the rapidly diminishing warmth of the day. As I continued to dig, working my way out from my original find, a cool breeze began to move over the land, seemingly originating from nowhere. Surprisingly, as darkness fell, small sounds began to emanate from the desert, as though everything living and breathing had been waiting in hiding for the end of the day. There were even small flying insects, attracted by the beam from my light

276

that darted back and forth in the revealing glow. I turned over another shovelful, now fully beginning to doubt the confidence I had felt only hours before, as Ron opened and began to eat his sandwich.

"Would you like yours?" he asked, waving my sandwich toward me.

"Not right now," I responded somewhat desperately, realizing that we were running out of time. "I just want to do another four or five shovelfuls and then I'll quit," I answered.

I placed the magnet into the pile of sand I had just overturned and began to push it through the gritty earth in a manner that was now becoming quite familiar. As I pushed the magnet through, I heard a "clunk." I pulled the magnet out to see what I had hit, and attached to it was a beautiful meteorite nearly an inch in diameter. It was black and somewhat smooth and melted looking on one side, and the other side was almost crystalline in structure with little rectangular steps that shimmered like silver in the flashlight's beam.

"I found one," I cried, jumping to my feet with joy.

Ron ran over and inspected my trophy, turning it over carefully in his fingers as he grinned.

"Wow, that's a great one," he exclaimed. "That's exactly what you have been looking for."

Ron handed the meteorite back to me and I examined it even more closely. The metal was cold to the touch and quite heavy for its size, and there was something uniquely unearthly about it. As I looked at my find, I imagined the journey it had taken across time and space; and tried to visualize what its voyage had been like through the stars. I saw visions of wondrous planets and looming asteroids and great volumes of dark empty space surrounding it. And as I held it there in my grasp, I came to the realization in that moment, that beyond anything else I was aware of; this tiny piece of the heavens, this fragment of the ancient past that would join with me and my magical blade — had witnessed, and now held within its glistening form, far more knowledge of the creation, than the wisest of all men.

"Would you like that sandwich now?" Ron asked smiling, breaking the spell.

"Yeah," I answered truthfully, suddenly ravenous now that my quest had been fulfilled.

Ron and I sat down together in awe of the world we lived in, and I ate my sandwich in silence. When I'd finished, he gently suggested that we should start on our journey back home. We packed up our gear and made our way through the dark back to the highway where we had parked. I carried my meteor tightly in my right hand, afraid to trust it to the interior of the day pack, and I felt quite relieved when we finally reached the car with it still safely within my grasp. As we drove home, Ron laid out the steps that I would have to take to create the blade.

"The next thing that you are going to have to do," he shared, "is to select a piece of iron to forge. In ancient times, some people actually smelted their own ore in order to create a bar to forge from, but now we just find a suitable piece of iron to work with. You might find something lying around or you might choose to buy a piece, but either way, you will re-forge it into something new. The important thing is to make sure that it's iron and not steel or one of the other new alloys."

"How I will know if it's a piece of real iron?" I asked, knowing little of such things.

"Well, when you find something that you want to test, you can put it against a grinder and watch the sparks that come off of it. Iron makes kind of larger red orange sparks, and all of the steels make very fine bright white sparks. Most of the other metals make no sparks at all, or very few."

"How do you know all of this stuff?" I asked.

"I'm a Witch," he replied quickly. "Remember, that a big part of being a Witch is to work to understand the universe that we live in so that we can better understand what it all means. Things like understanding the qualities of metals and finding meteorites are all a part of the continual process of learning. To be a successful Witch, one has to understand the connections that link everything together, and if we didn't know how, why, and where meteorites fall and how to forge our own iron, how could we possibly make our own magical blades."

"That's a good point," I said. I just hadn't thought of it that way.

"Well," Ron said, if we can't even understand the simple processes that provide us with our basic comfort, tools, and personal needs, how could we possibly attempt to understand the gods and what it is they have in store for us. I think that religion today has gotten so specialized and has moved so far away from its own beginnings, that it has a tendency to move people toward ignorance rather than real wisdom and understanding. Simple concepts like, if you kill your neighbor because he's not like you — his brother will retaliate, have become lost in the shuffle of doctrine and scriptures, and religious persons who persecute others are always dumbfounded when someone goes after them for their particular beliefs. Witches believe that the better you understand the world and everything within it, the better chance you have of contributing to a world where everyone and everything fits. Nothing is perfect, but the closer you come to living those concepts, the closer we believe you are to God. But I'm getting off point here. We were talking about your blade, and how to forge it.

"Once you have found a piece of iron suitable for your blade, you must first put it in a bath of acid to remove any impurities from the surface. The best acid to use is muratic or hydrochloric, although sulfuric will also work. You can get these at a chemical supply house. You can also make your own from scratch by burning sulfur and bat manure and then mixing the resulting fumes with water, but unless you want to do that, I won't go into a lot of detail about just how to formulate that process. The bottom line here is that you want to dissolve any rust or impurities on the surface of the metals before you start forging so that you don't later force those impurities into the blade itself when you hammer it.

"Once you've stripped the metal of impurities, you'll want to decide on a design. The blade can be almost any

279

shape you like, but there are a few traditional things that you may want to include in its fabrication."

"Like what?" I asked, mesmerized by Ron's teaching.

"Well, for example, one way of forging the blade is to create a hole near the tip which represents the sacred circle and stands for the intersection of heaven and earth or as we say, the otherworld and the earth. Typically, the lower part of the blade below the midpoint of the hole is forged of iron and the top part, or the part from the midpoint of the circle up, is forged from your meteor. That way, the metals themselves actually replicate the principle you wish to convey — that in creating the circle, we call upon the energy of both the otherworld and the earth, to come together into a portal, to create a sacred space that's both between and, at the same time, connected — to both worlds. For our coven, this is an important part of the creation of the blade, because it reinforces the layers hidden within its construction, and at the same time continues the ongoing story of the sacred path. Another thing to consider is that many Witches carve runes or symbols into their blades so you may wish to take that into account also if you intend to do that. Other than that, you can shape it or design it any way you like."

"I remember that you told me that the handle is supposed to be made from a tree that bears fruit or nuts," I asked, "is that correct?"

"Yes," Ron answered. "You can use a number of different fruit or nut woods to make the handle, and all you need to do is to hold a ceremony similar to the one you did when you cut the willow branch for your wand."

"So what's the next step?" I asked, eager to get started as soon as possible.

"You'll have to build a forge, which I can help you with, and you'll need a heavy hammer and a few basic supplies. You'll also need to make a large supply of willow charcoal to heat it and you'll need a place where you can work undisturbed. Then it's mostly about forging the blade and filling it with your effort and energy. I'll instruct you on exactly what to do to actually forge the knife, and then you'll mostly be on your own when it comes to actually doing it."

Ron dropped me off at home, and I took my meteorite into my room and put it on my altar. I held it up and washed it with consecrated water from my temporary chalice. Then I passed it through the smoke of my consecration incense and anointed it with sacred oil. When I was finished, I sat it on my altar and then went over to my bed and just sat there staring at it. It was beyond my imagination when I first heard about the idea of having to find a meteor that I would ever be able to accomplish such a task, and now that it sat there right in front of me, I was absolutely stunned that I had accomplished it. A piece of wisdom that Stephanie had passed on to me earlier in my training came to the surface of my mind in that moment, helping to return some sense of reality to what otherwise seemed to me like a farfetched dream.

"There is no goal that we can't reach, if we just put one foot in front of the other," Stephanie said one day as we walked the hills looking for herbs. "It is always important to remember that all of this," she said motioning to everything surrounding us," was created to interact with and fulfill everything else in the creation. Because of that, there is an answer to every question, and a solution to every problem already built into the equation. Also, for us, that is us as human beings, all we were originally provided with by the Goddess when we were first created, were our creative impulses, our ability to walk to and explore our surroundings, and our intellect to be able to decipher and interact with them. Since that was all that was necessary to get us from the beginning of time where we had nothing, to where we are now with our TV's and our cars and our science and technology, there is little reason to believe that solving the universe's greatest mysteries requires anything more that just walking from here to there using our creativity to address the problems at hand, and then considering the possibilities before us – to resolve them."

In considering my Priestess' earlier words of wisdom, I realized that anything is possible once we set our minds to it. And with that realization, I laid back on the bed, content that I had within me the ability to confront and resolve anything and everything that life might throw my way.

෨ඏඕ෧

The heat from the glowing coals coaxed sweat from my forehead as I pumped air from the leather bellows into the flaming charcoal. The bar of iron, which was the center of my focus as I fed the hungry flames, glowed white hot under the intense heat.

"*Knock djinn ralda, shook ma ne' pa ralda,*"[23] I called out as the heat intensified around the glowing metal. I reached for the tongs and pulled the radiating iron out of the fire.

"Clang, clang, clang," rang the antique anvil as I swung the heavy hammer, flattening the bar, first on one side, and then on the other. I could feel the metal give, slightly at first and then gradually stretching and yielding under the force of my blows as I worked the glowing metal into shape. A flurry of sparks rose with each blow, popping and spiraling as they took flight, like fleeing demons driven out by exorcism.

"*Kilar.....* Be pure," I commanded with all of the authority I could muster, visualizing any impurities in the metal literally being driven out by the blows.

I returned the still cherry red blank back into to the coals, and added a measure of consecration incense to the now swirling inferno. On impact, the coarse mixture burst into flame instantaneously, yielding a cloud of pure white smoke so hot that the very scent of the herbs within it was decimated. Nevertheless, I added two more measures in quick succession, knowing that the contents of the mixture and the timing of the insertion were critical to the success of the project.

Once the smoke cleared, I added several more pieces of willow charcoal to the mix and drew the rune of creation for

---

[23] By the power of fire and the power of air.

the third time in front of the forge. The whole room radiated with the heat of the fire, and the taste of burning air, dry, hot, and purifying, caressed the tip of my tongue as I once again fanned the flames.

When the blade approached white again, I withdrew it and placed it on the anvil.

"*Knock lazra meck, alock ma acha neck malae, atacha chook chakadah,*"[24] I shouted, as I swung the heavy sledge.

The blade was taking shape now and close to the final thickness I desired. I laid it lengthwise on the anvil now, and delivered softer blows, working the high spots to even out the surface. As it cooled, I continued the process, first on one side and then on the other, until it was as flat and even as I could get it.

Next, I heated the blade again, only this time I just brought it to a dull cherry color in order to soften the metal. Ron told me that doing this would make the metal easier to work into the final shape. I set the newly forged blade to cool on a fire brick that I had salvaged from a construction site, and went to get a hacksaw. When the blade had cooled completely, I drew the shape that I desired on the metal with a pencil, and clamped the metal in a vise. Then, with great care, I sawed off all the excess metal outside of the defining line, and ended up with roughly the blade shape that I desired.

Once I determined I was pleased with the result, I added more charcoal to the forge, and worked the bellows once again to coax the heat back into an inferno. When the coals glowed appropriately, I fetched both the blade and a small leather packet and returned to the forge.

Unfolding the packet, I rolled my meteorite onto the workbench and placed both the blade and the meteor into the coals. When they both became fully heated, I pulled out the blade first and set it on the fire brick, and then rapidly pulled out the meteorite and set it on the anvil. Quickly and with care, I laid the tip of the blade over the meteor and

---

[24] By the light of darkness, and the sacred arc of the hammer, comes wisdom

struck it powerfully with the hammer. The strike joined the two as one as the metals flowed together under the power of the blow.

"Be one," I confirmed powerfully as the metals melded, joining forever the sacred fire of the heavens and the earthly blade.

I returned the knife to the forge again, this time only burying the very tip in the glowing embers. When the end reached a bright red, I removed the blade and returned it to the anvil for the last time.

"Clang, Clang, rang the anvil again as I hammered the tip to finalize the process, flipping it over repeatedly until it lost its glow.

When the blade had cooled completely, I brought out a large file and began to even out both the sides and the tip. When I was pleased with the shape, I started to also work the flat sides of the knife, evening out the hammer marks until the surface was smooth and even. Following that, I sanded the entire surface and sides with emery paper to a dull satin finish, finalizing that stage of the process. I examined the sacred blade carefully, removing any small nicks and scratches with a small stone, and then I held it up in front of me and smiled with pleasure as I approved the final product.

Once the blade passed my approval, I went to the workbench and retrieved a tiny chisel and my pencil. I carefully drew out the required runes on the surface, and then began to trace them with the small tool, using gentle strokes of the hammer on one end to cut the surface of the metal with the other end. It was fascinating to watch the runes appear, as the metal yielded perfectly to my calculated blows. When both sides were finished, I worked the entire surface of the blade once again with the stone, smoothing out any burs left by the chisel. Once that was finished, I set the blade aside and prepared to take the final steps to complete the blade portion of the process.

I filled the chalice with water from one of our sacred springs and said an invocation to enlist the aid of the element of Water in my ritual. Next, I crushed a small piece of brimstone and added it to the water to also enlist the aid of the element of earth. Stephanie had told me that brimstone was important to use in this ritual as opposed to just using water filled with minerals or salt, because the sulfur would have an effect on the surface of the blade that would protect it from rust over the years in addition to invoking the element of earth. She also told me that over time, the sulfur would bond with the surface and would make the carved runes stand out better on the surface of the blade. Once the brimstone was thoroughly distributed in the liquid, I added the three herbs that would complete the cycle, bane of Soltra, oak bark, and cinquefoil, and returned to the forge.

I placed the last of the Willow charcoal into the forge, and blew on it carefully to get it started. The fire had nearly gone out, and it was critical that the special blaze that had been initiated to create the blade in the first place be the same one that finalized it. Once I got it going again, I used the bellows to feed the flames for the last time, whipping them into a swirling inferno. Next, I added the last of the consecration incense to the flames to prepare them and placed the whole of the blade into the fire. When it reached the slightest shade of red, I removed it and thrust it into the holy water, focusing on my intention as I tempered the blade in the cool liquid.

"*Knock na ralda, knock goba ralda,*"[25] I called out, as I beseeched the elements to complete the cycle of purification, "*Kilar!*"

I removed the steaming blade and set it aside to cool for the last time. When the steaming stopped, I took the still warm blade and rolled it up in a coarse white cloth until I could create the handle and assemble the pieces. Then I sat back exhausted while I waited for the fire to burn out. An hour later, the charcoal was completely extinguished and I collected all of the now cool ash and placed it in a wooden box. I drew the symbols for protection and the

---

[25] by the spirit of water and by the spirit of earth.

spiral for *mor' ga na* on the lid and then sealed the remnants of the ritual with wax from a consecrated candle.

Figure 21: The Symbols of Protection and *Mor' Ga Na*

When the package was secure, I took it to the creek and buried it below one of the *aesma* there.   I thanked the ancient oak in advance for protecting the contents and then made the sign of friendship and greeting as I parted.

"*Sha ma na gadaf gadou* — may the water forever flow," I said nodding as I left, knowing that the wise old tree would protect my secret. I turned away from the giant oak and headed for home to a well deserved nights rest filled with haunting dreams and visions of my completed blade.

Chapter 16

The Black Handle

"I just can't seem to find anything," I said with frustration, after spending nearly a full day with my Priestess searching for the perfect branch for the handle for my blade.

"Patience is a virtue," Stephanie returned, smiling as she walked over by my side. She loved to use famous quotes to irritate me, and took every occasion to instruct me with them when I found myself in frustrating situations.

"I know," I shot back, irritated, "but we've looked at just about every single tree in the forest."

"When it's meant to be, your needs will be met," she said more seriously. "Perhaps we'll just have to come back tomorrow or try another place."

I left her side pushing my way through the brush to my right and ran right into an exposed root, which nearly caused me to fall. As I reached up to steady myself on one of the many branches overhead, I found myself staring straight at a medium sized gable oak with several smaller gnarled limbs that appeared perfect for what I was looking for.

"I found what I want," I called out excitedly, letting Stephanie know that I had been successful in my quest.

Moving in closer, I found a particular broken branch that was about sixteen inches long and around an inch and a half in diameter that looked just right

"Hurry, bring the pack," I called out to Stephanie, anxious to get started on the ritual before it got dark. Steph stepped through the brush and handed me the back pack, starting to speak.

"See, I told you."

"Don't lecture me right now," I cautioned, tired from the long day's search, "just let me do the ritual and cut a piece for my handle."

My Priestess nodded compliantly, and disappeared back through the way she'd come, leaving me alone to do the work.

I opened the pack and took out a tiny bottle of sabbat oil, a small keyhole saw, and the gift I had chosen for the tree. When all was ready, I faced the tree and made the proper greeting to it in *Elban,* preparing to begin the ceremony.

"*Sha ma na gadaf gadou,*" I whispered, drawing the symbol of recognition in the air before me with my right hand.

Figure 22: The Rune of Recognition.

I felt a sense of calm pass over me as the tree nodded in the breeze, and I relaxed realizing that I was almost done with the challenge at hand.

I went on to explain to the *aesma* why I had come and held my gift out for approval. It was one of the leaves of Bane of Soltra that was sent to me from K.D.'s garden, and for me, it was irreplaceable. Once I sensed that the tree had accepted my gift, I dug a hole at its base and buried the coveted leaf there to seal our pact.

Next, I untied the small leather bag that I always carried on my belt, and pulled out the same crescent shaped silver blade that I'd used for my wand. Holding the knife carefully in my left hand, I transferred several drops of the sacred oil to the blade's edge, using my right middle finger. Once the edge was properly prepared, I scored the bark all the way around the base of the branch in a circular motion, and then placed the saw in position to make a cut right within the consecrated score.

"*Alock ma shum neck meck,*"[26] I started, reciting the ancient words of power as I began to cut.

---

[26] from the depths of darkness

"*Shook ma ne mesk ba coomb,*"[27] I continued, working my way slowly through the resilient limb, finding it considerably more resistant and difficult than that that of the softer and more pliant willow.

"*Ma baca chook,*"[28] I continued finishing the cut, and pulled the short limb free.

The piece I'd cut for my handle was almost brown black in color and had several deep grooves penetrating through the bark. It also had several small burls, that is small nodules, on its surface which added interest to the slightly curved piece.

I placed my harvest in my back pack, and picked up all of my supplies. I rubbed sacred oil over the tree's wound, and pulled out a plastic bag filled with wet moss and sage. I gently covered the wound on the tree, and then drew the sign of healing over it.

Figure 23: Rune for healing

Once everything was done, I bade the *aesma* good bye, and then went in search of Stephanie to share my find with her. I found her examining a low growing herb, which she told me was five finger grass.[29]

"See the leaves," she said," pointing to them with her finger. "Each one has five fanned out segments just like this." She went on, "kind of like a little fan, you see?" The flowers, which come out in the spring, also have five petals as well."

I examined the shrub, which was one of many that were spread out along the fertile ground near the creek. It was woodsy with small red brown thready vines spreading everywhere, forming little clumps of green five fingered fans.

---

[27] and the swirling mists
[28] God, or "the Goddess" comes
[29] Also know as cinquefoil, or the "knight's herb".

Looking more closely, it appeared to be more of a ground cover than an upright shrub, with very few of the clumps raising more that several inches above the ground.

Figure 24: Five finger grass

"What is it used for?" I asked seriously, always interested in learning more about the inhabitants of the woods.

"It's a key ingredient of our sacred oil," Steph returned, clipping a number of vines and placing them in the large rattan purse she carried as she spoke. "I haven't seen this particular batch before, but we'll need some for Samhain, so it's great that I found it. Plus, it will save us a trip later which will be great considering how much we've still got to do in order to get ready.

"Do you want to know something really cool about this plant?" she continued, looking up at me with a smile."

"Yeah," I answered, fully interested in the new find.

"Well," she started happily, when the plant is in flower, and something threatens it, like a storm or cold weather, the leaves move over to cover the blossom like little hands until the threat is gone. Then when everything is safe, they move back away in order to give the flower room to grow. That's one of the reasons it's used in the oil in the first place, to protect us from some of side effects of some of the other plants that are used in the process, and to make sure that our journey between the worlds is safe until we return to this plane."

"Wow," that's really interesting," I commented, never ceasing to marvel at what mysteries nature holds in store for us. "When are we going to be making the oil?" I asked.

"On Samhain," she explained, rising to her feet. Creating the oil at that time is one of the oldest traditions of our path. We collect the ingredients beforehand and then we mix them and slowly heat them throughout the day while we make the Sabbat drink. There's nothing better than the smell of simmering sacred oil mixed with the scent of *wassa meck balaam.*"[30]

"What's that?" I asked.

"*Wassa meck balaam?* That's the sacred drink for Samhain," she responded. "It means, 'drink to support the spirit through the dark times,' and we make it every year. But you'll see that soon enough," she went on, "because Samhain is just a short time away."

"Speaking of Samhain, do you want to see the piece I cut for my handle?" I asked.

"Of course," she smiled brightly, lighting me up with pleasure at her obvious interest. I took the piece out of the pack and handed it to her to examine.

"This is great Patrick," she said excitedly. This will be just perfect!"

Returning the handle to my pack, the two of us started back toward the parking area while Stephanie told me

---

[30] A hot drink made from crabapples, fruits, and herbs, mixed with fermented elderberries and rum grog.

stories about earlier Samhains' that she'd participated in. I loved to listen to my Priestess as she talked and always got a great deal out of her sayings and analogies. She never ran out of interesting things to tell me, and she seemed to know literally everything there is to know about the forest. She wasn't quite as technically versed as Ron, but when it came to conveying spiritual matters, she was unparalleled in our coven.

❧⟨℘℘⟩❧

When I returned home, I started right away on the handle for my magical blade. I cut the both ends off, making them flat and even, and carefully stripped the bark off down to bare wood. The wood was exquisite with a pronounced grain and a resilient surface tempered by many years of changing weather and exposure to more than its share of abundant sun. Once the bark was gone, I mixed sand with the crushed buds of the poplar and rubbed every surface thoroughly in the old way. Ron had shared the process with me when we hiked earlier in the month, explaining exactly what to do.

"First you must strip off all of the bark," he revealed, "making sure that not even the smallest fibers remain. Then you take damp sand from the creek and grind it together with balm of gilead, picked right after the Fall Equinox when it's first turning brown. You don't want to harvest it too early or too late," he emphasized, as the resin will either be too sticky or not sticky enough to do the job. The best way to tell is to crush one of the buds between your fingers to test it. If it leaves a sticky residue or has any liquid in it, it's not ready to use yet, but if it leaves only a dull film that creates resistance when you rub your fingers together, then it's just right. Once you've made a paste, spread it over the handle with a coarse cloth, and then rub it back and forth, sanding it as though you are using a piece of sand paper to finish it. It takes quite a while, maybe four or five hours to do it, but the end result is both magical and practical at the same time," he added. "Hilts made using this process have been known to have lasted for hundreds of years," he continued, "plus the balm is the fruit of the tree of life which imparts great Magic on its own. When you're finished, let the handle sit for a few days without cleaning it off, and then polish it to a high shine, using a piece of fleece. Of course, it's important to thank the tree for its gift when you harvest the buds, which you already know how to do and to be sure to focus on your intention on the handle while you are doing the work. If you follow my instructions correctly," he went on, "you will have something to treasure for a lifetime."

The process was much more difficult than Ron had made it sound. Once the sand was mixed into a paste with the balm, it stuck to just about everything. Rubbing the surface with it was somewhat akin to dragging rubber soled shoes across a freshly waxed floor, resulting in very little progress, and of lots of squeaking and noise. Even so, I continued to work the mixture in relentlessly until my hands became cramped and impregnated with the clinging mess and the cloth became stiff from the heat of the abrasion. When I just couldn't do any more, I set the handle aside, and did what I could to remove the resin from my now heavily stained hands. Even though Ron had told me in advance to immerse my hands in olive oil when I was finished, I had disregarded his advice and forgotten to buy any. However, I felt confident that dish soap and water would take care of the problem, but rapidly abandoned that idea when I found that the soap actually coagulated the resin and made it even more tenacious. Abandoning the detergent idea, I tried paint thinner next. I would have to say that this old time favorite had never failed me before, but in the case of the tree of life's balm, it was useless. Instead of dissolving the sticky coating, it just made the surface of it slippery, but in no way affected the adhesive action that had bonded it with my hands.

"No wonder hilts treated with this stuff lasts for centuries," I thought to myself, "there probably isn't anything in existence that can get it off once you put it on."

Finally, I gave in, and drove my car to the corner store. I forked over a dollar twenty-nine for a bottle of Italy's Pride and set myself to the difficult task of paying for it, because I couldn't get the dollar bill off of my hand. I left the store with the checker staring after me, and drove back to the house. I took down a heavy white mixing bowl from the cupboard, and filled it with the contents of my new purchase and then retrieved a brick red shop cloth from the garage and plunged my hands into the oil.

There must have been Magic in that oil or Ron definitely knew something that I didn't. Almost instantaneously after I immerged my hands in the amber liquid, the resin released its grip. Within minutes after starting, I was able to simply wipe the stuff from my hands with the cloth, not only resolving the problem, but leaving my hands more soft and smooth than I had ever felt them before. There must have been something in the resin that was soluble in the oil, and something in the combination of the two that created a soothing balm. "Hmm," I thought to myself, "maybe that's where the term 'soothing balm' comes from." In any case, once I got my hands clean, I was definitely ready for bed.

Three days after treating the handle for my knife, I polished it with a piece of fleece I bought at the hardware store. Remarkably, the resin mixture came right off the surface, and the wood polished to a deep and beautiful shine. The wood also became more deeply colored now, ranging from a deep purple brown to a cherry tinged charcoal black.

Once I finished polishing the handle, I turned to the task of affixing it to the blade. First, I reduced the width of bottom first three inches of the blade from an inch wide down to a quarter of an inch, using a hacksaw and a file. Next I sharpened the narrowed base to a sharp point so that the entire base looked like a letter opener. Following that, I drilled a small three inch deep hole into the top of the oak handle, to provide a guide for the newly formed tang of the foot long iron blade.

Once the blade was prepared, I heated the tang to a cherry red, using a small propane torch. When it was fully heated, I picked up the blade using a pair of pliers and pushed it into the small hole in the handle. The red hot metal burned its way into the waiting oak, like a hot knife through a stick of chilled butter until it had penetrated more than half way down into the handle. I immediately turned the handle and blade upside down and struck the base of the handle with a hammer continuously to continue the process. With each strike, the tang moved upward, penetrating deeper and deeper into the wood until it eventually buried itself all the way into the hilt. Ron had told me that the heat of the tang would cause the wood to contract back away from the blade while it was still hot, and then that it would swell back tightly against it once it cooled, creating a snug and permanent bond. Apparently Ron knew exactly what he was talking about, because once the blade cooled, it became fixed to the handle so tightly, that it was as though both the iron and the oak were all made of one piece.

Once the blade and the handle were one, I turned to stoning the iron blade for the last time, as I had been instructed by my mentor. I used a piece of fine smooth quartz, and rubbed the entire surface until it shone with a dull sheen. Then to finish the job, I rubbed a small amount of sacred oil all over the blade and then continued the same over the handle as well.

I held up the finished knife, quite pleased with the final result, and reveled in the completion of the mystical tool before me. It seemed unbelievable to me that I had actually gotten this far, but then each step on the sacred path had been like that. I wrapped the sacred knife in a new clean white cloth, and tied three pieces of red wool yarn around it to secure it until Samhain when I would perform the ritual to give it life.

Figure 25: My magical blade, forged with the meteor I found

CHAPTER 17

Samhain

As the sun set in the west, Jack led the small caravan as we turned off the main highway and up a two rut four wheel drive road marked only by a small sign saying "Artesian Springs 6 miles." As I turned my station wagon to follow Jack up the steep fire road, Ron commented that the road ahead was pretty bad. He went on to say that none of the coven had been up to the site for a number of years, but that everyone was in agreement that this was the perfect place to hold our Samhain celebration and to finalize the creation of my sacred blade.

We continued to climb the sharp switchbacks, working our way higher and higher up the mountain and the road got narrower and narrower as we went. On our right, as we proceeded up the hill, the mountainside dropped off into a steep jagged canyon that was already deep enough at its base to bring queasy waves of uneasiness to my stomach even though we were still miles from the top of the mountain. We continued to drive, up and up through a series of treacherous switchbacks filled with manzanitas and chaparral and the highway below was gradually reduced to a thin thready line winding through miles of maze-like canyons and serrated peaks that were slowly turning various shades of purple in the receding light. Directly below us and to the north was a large reservoir nestled in the canyons. Its silvery surface reflected the surrounding terrain and added a perfect reference point to determine just how high we had ascended after turning up the dusty track. We could now see miles of mountainous landscape stretching far below from our bird's eye point of view, and the grandeur and unequaled beauty of natural wilderness truly revealed itself in the rapidly fading light. Eventually after crossing a steep mountain brook, which transversed the road near the top of the peak, we came out onto a concave depression surrounded by a grove of giant oaks at the apex of the summit as darkness began to set in. My headlights revealed a tiny valley only a hundred or so yards across and at its center was a small artesian spring that literally spewed forth from the rocky floor. The plentiful stream of water bubbled up through a crack in the rock and then flowed into a small rivulet across the circular clearing, eventually cascading over the steep precipice that led to the bottom of the canyon nearly a mile below.

The evening was cool and crisp and the sky was clear as glass as I exited my car and walked around the small clearing. Haunting scents reminiscent of my first walk with Ron back when I first learned about Magic, filled the air as I took in the smell of oxygenated water mixed with the earthy smells always found around creeks and springs. And as the darkness of night fully set in, I welcomed the company of the mugwart and the high mountain sage whose unseen presence I knew from the very air I breathed. I also acknowledged the oaks that stood before me, adding their acrid scent of tannin to the mix. And finally I greeted the unexpected nut grass, whose crisp clean scent I wouldn't have expected to find at this elevation, but who was clearly present in this magical place.

All of these scents, mixed with that of decomposing leaves and the deep fertility of the earth, greeted me as I walked through the tiny glade. Above me, hundreds of October stars began to reveal themselves through the indigo void, each crisp and clear, like tiny spheres of white hot steel, all clearly visible on this moonless hallowed night, and I was glad we had brought our heavy cloaks with us to protect us against the chill of the descending night. Mine was deep royal blue wool, lined with heavy black satin, and Nicky had made it for me for just the cost of the materials.

"So, what do you think?" Ron asked, approaching me from behind.

"It's perfect," I answered, awed by the beauty and sheer magic of the place.

Ron and I took our time laying out the perimeter circle, tracing its diameter with the special magical chalk we'd made. The chalk had been set out in the sun for the entire day, and it now glowed with an eerie luminosity stolen from the fiery orb as we spread it like sparkling fairy dust to define our sacred space. I watched the powdery border radiate its faint blue green hues as it reverently released its ghostly glow, my mind filled with visions of life beyond the veil and our connectedness with the mystery of death and the *dark times* to come. The eerie glow also reminded me of my early lesson with Stephanie about the celebration of Samhain. The combination of that memory joined with the remoteness of our ritual site and the pending chill in the air, once again brought alive the sense that something beyond this world was waiting to greet us just past the borders of our tiny refuge.

Once Ron and I finished laying out the circle, Eldon gently set out carved jack-o-lanterns at the four cardinal directions and carefully lit each one with a match in order to give us more light for our work. The end effect was astounding. As gentle breezes worked their way through our secluded glade, light from the carved pumpkins literally brought the surrounding forest alive with spectral movement. At any given time, one could see wispy shadows darting back and forth between the surrounding rocks and trees, in shapes born in the darkest imagination of the earliest of human beings. If ever there were a setting perfectly matched to meeting those who had passed from our world to the place of death, this was it.

"I'm going to walk down to a place further below us to meditate for a little while," Ron stated, bringing me back to current reality. "Just relax for a bit and watch the others get set up and try to feel the weight of the winter moving in."

I took Ron's advice and stood back, reviewing our site and noting the simplicity of construction. Our altar was simple, just an ancient stump — the only remains of a once great tree. Eldon had placed a plain black cloth over the center of the stump and was laying out our chalice, censor, and two black tapers. Stephanie stood to his left, carving away on a thick black candle, which Ron had told me was for depicting special moments with deceased loved ones that each member wished to commemorate in our service. Also on the altar to the front of the chalice, laid a large black crow feather with a tiny carved skull attached, which Jack had explained to me represented the Goddess of the Gate of Skulls, who was in charge of travel in and out of the spirit world. I also recognized the runes written in black ink down the prominent quill, which stood as an invocation to either speak from, or to open those gates, and I repeated them to myself as I considered each symbol and its meaning: *Caile' nai marigwyn na neg maru.*

There were also photos of lost loved ones decorating the altar, including several supplied by me. As I watched, R.J. placed a small cauldron on the altar and then began to place large colorful fallen leaves all over the surface. Even in the diminished light, the fall colors added a certain festiveness to the otherwise dark decor, once again reminding me that this was not only a ceremony to commemorate those we'd lost, but also a celebration during which we would be able to spend actual time with them once again.

Also, each of us had placed our magical tools on the altar, and there was an assortment of wands and blades filling nearly every inch of the altar's surface. And in the center, was a simple stand that I had made out of copper, and on it, in the place of honor, was my finished knife, waiting for consecration.

"Let's put the flowers over here," Jack interrupted, as he and Nicky carried a big bouquet of roses over to the altar, contributed by each of us in the coven in honor of those we'd lost. I walked over to my coven mates and asked if there was anything I could do to help, as they arranged the flowers around the base of the altar.

"You can help him get some wood together for the fire," Jack suggested, nodding toward Derek who was gathering stray leaves and twigs by candlelight.

I walked over to Derek, giving him a nod of recognition as I approached.

"Can I give you a hand," I asked, automatically starting to pick up small branches to add to the cache.

"Yeah, grab a few of those larger ones there, so we can get some good coals going for later."

We both continued to collect wood in the dark until we'd amassed a small pile near the northern watch tower, then we moved on to help Ron and R.J. with the food. Everyone had contributed to the feast and we were now setting it up on a small table that Jack had brought. Stephanie had brought rolls with butter and honey to accompany them. Derek brought a bucket of chicken from some fast food place that I had never heard of, which smelled wonderful as the steam escaped from beneath the ill fitting lid, and Ron contributed potato salad and chips to go with it. I brought a pineapple upside down cake, which I'd actually baked myself. There were also olives and sweet pickles and a macaroni salad too. Jack was the only one that didn't contribute to the food, as he had contributed most of the candles and ritual supplies for the night. But what I was looking forward to most was the hot sabbat drink which everyone told me was the best one of the year. I didn't get to help make it this time because I had to help with some last minute Halloween preparations at home, but Jack had opened the two gallon thermos just before we left, and the steaming beverage had filled the room with its wonderful scent. Ron had told me that it took hours to make, and that it was composed of crabapples and herbs and other fruits, mixed with fermented elderberries, rum grog, and honey. He'd also told me that in addition to warming us up on the chilly night, it would also protect us against sickness and disease.

Once the tasks at hand were done, everyone gradually congregated toward the altar. The circle glowed noticeably now as the fullness of night dominated the sky and the group grew respectfully silent in its presence. This was the first Samhain ritual I'd ever attended, and I mostly watched the others for cues and followed their lead. After a period of silent meditation, the ritual began.

At Stephanie's direction, we spread out in front of the altar and joined hands creating a half circle facing the north. Our Priestess then stepped forward quietly from the

301

group and with a gentle gesture, she picked up her magical blade and brought it first to her lips and then raised it to the heavens in salute. Next, she placed its tip into the chalice full of spring water and recited the incantation for purification.

"*Knock ma lazra neck ma ata me'*,"[31] she commanded..."*Kilar!*" She paused for a moment in intense concentration as if to impart her desire into the liquid, and then stirred the water in the cup three times in a *deosil* direction to finalize the spell. Next, she walked to the east and, placing the tip of the blade on the ground before her, she began to scribe a *deosil* circle around us, moving from *aesma* to *aesma* until the circle was complete. Next she placed the blade on the altar and picked up the chalice and held it up before her.

"*Knock na, knock goba*,"[32] she called out, as her voice echoed off the rocky promontory to the south and ricocheted through the twisting canyons below, diminishing with each successive refrain. "*Kilar!*"

Then she walked the perimeter of the circle carrying the chalice, purifying the circumference with its holy liquid as together we visualized all negativity leaving our temple. When she returned, she opened the carved wooden vial of incense on the altar and added some of its contents to the already glowing willow coals.

"*Knock djinn ralda... knock pa ralda*,"[33] she continued — summoning also the elementals of fire and air as she prepared to purify our space for the third and final time with the incense made of dwale berry and mullein, mixed with thornbane and mandrake.

The scent of the mix was heavy and earthy and left an unpleasant taste on the tongue as the spiraling tendrils rose from the glowing censor. I knew from my training that these were not the typical herbs used in incenses for other Sabbats and that they were in fact very powerful magical

---

[31] by the power of my sacred blade
[32] by water and earth
[33] By the spirit of fire, by the spirit of air

components designed to open the portal between the worlds of the living and the dead. Each had a specific connection with the task at hand, and only this exact formula yielded the results we sought.

"This recipe is one of the oldest known to man," Ron had told me several weeks before as we had gathered the herbs for tonight's ritual, "and it has been used for thousands of years to connect those who are living with those who've gone beyond," he continued. "In fact, each of these ingredients were so commonly used by our ancestors that they now grow right next to every one of our sacred sites in Europe and have done so for thousands of years. Even Christ was said to have been bathed with a tincture of this potent combination during his crucifixion, to open the doorway for his spiritual transition."

Stephanie continued the casting of the circle, bathing the border with sacred smoke, as she added intention to the purification. I felt an involuntary shudder as I watched the rising smoke spread out into ghostly shapes that hovered closely within the confines of our circle, dancing around us in the faint blue light.

Once the cutting and purification of the circle was complete, Stephanie approached each of the four directions, inviting the *aesmas* to our celebration, one by one. Beginning in the east, she retraced each step of the story of creation and the journey of the first light until her journey around the perimeter was complete. When she reached the east for the last time, she paused for a moment, facing the place of beginning. As she stood there, she drew the sign of the pentagram in the air with her blade, starting upward from the lower left point until she had completed the star. When the first figure was complete, she continued with her blade in a *deosil* direction, tracing a circle from the point where she'd completed the pentagram, all of the way around the hovering star. Next, when the second figure was finished, she simply reversed the blade to scribe a circle in the opposite direction, completing the third and final figure, which finalized the seal and sealed our sacred circle.

303

Ron had taught me the significance of the seal before my first Sabbat ritual following my initiation. He explained that its symbolism was a part of the Golden Key and that there were hidden messages within the sigil to be discovered later. He also explained that the trinity symbol was always used to seal the perimeter of the circle before turning inward to the center to call down the God and the Goddess, because it served as a seal to meld the beginning and the ending of the arc together into a continuous figure that went on forever, and because it also marked the place where lazra meck came to recognize the sacred path back to the Mother.

"That's why we also draw this symbol in the air when we leave the forest after our lessons," Ron had told me," because it serves to signify that the path we were walking on that day during our lessons, leads the seeker to the Creatrix.

Stephanie acknowledged the completion of the circle and turned to the center and the altar before us, to tell the story in Elban and to invoke the Mother. We all stood there quietly for a moment, frozen in time and space, taking in the unique beauty of the place we had chosen for our ritual. Then Stephanie nodded her head, and we all stepped back in reverence, while our Priestess, who raised her hands to the sky, opened herself up to be filled with the spirit of the Goddess.

"*Alock ma shum neck meck, shook ma ne mesk ba coomb, ma baca chook!*"[34] she called quietly — recalling for each of us, the place where everything began and the birth of the Mother.

"*Chook Shee; Shee wada na, Judanna-Naru, shum Sagchuti,*"[35] she continued.

A gentle breeze began in the north as she spoke. You could hear it far off in the oaks, perhaps a quarter mile away or so. A soft fluttering of leaves — dancing intimately with one another as the wind worked its way through the

---

[34] From the depths of darkness and the swirling mists, God comes!
[35] She is here, Goddess of the womb, Queen of Witches

304

intricate maze of branch and twig and leaf. I knew as soon as I heard that sound, that the wind would raise in intensity — and it did. By now, I was familiar with the signs and sounds of Magic, and this was to be Magic of the highest order. The branches in the nearby trees began to creak and bend under the weight of the awesome unseen force. As it approached us, the wind came in a gust from the north as it majestically cut through the trees, like a wave of wind on the prairie, parting a field of wheat. Then it made a wide turn off into the west, continuing down the canyons as it made a sharp whistling sound that transitioned into various haunting chords as it worked its way through the mountains. The gale repeated this process several times, with the effect being that we were in the center of a powerful storm which spiraled around us, yet left us untouched. Stephanie stood quietly before the altar, seemingly unaffected by the gale. Her soft features stood out against the blackness of night, framed by the moon-like glow of the luminous circle. Flickering candles added to the effect, lending a shimmering radiance to her long hair, which now sought flight on the ebbing currents of air.

As the howling wind continued, the increasing chill of the October night came along with it, making each breath visible before me. I recalled Ron telling me earlier in the week that the wind at night was power, and if that was true, I thought to myself, especially considering the intensity of tonight's gale, then this was going to be both a very powerful ritual and also a very cold night! I was glad to have my warm cloak, and was definitely looking forward to the warming sabbat drink we had prepared for later.

"Great Mother... *Ari-da-na*, shining mother of the womb," Stephanie continued, "you who are the beginning and the end of all things, we ask that you join us here tonight as we celebrate the end of the cycle of the seasons and the beginning of a new year. We also ask that you open the gates for us tonight, *shaktoom wa da na*,[36] so that we might once more join with our loved ones who have gone beyond,

---

[36] open the portal to the other world

as we celebrate and feast in their honor. We also call upon you O' ancient horned one, God of the forest and the sacred grove. Be here with us tonight, and let the Magic of the land and the creatures of the wooded dells and the babbling brooks, join our dance."

With that, our Priestess stepped forward and picked up the panpipes from the altar and raised them to her lips to complete the summons. Soft vibrant tones emanated from the intoxicating tubes as she gently blew the melody of invocation. The music was haunting with a quality unlike any other sound I'd ever heard and I truly felt its call as it coaxed all of nature to join us.

Stephanie had shown me the pipes once before, when she'd taken me on a walk down to the creek last spring. We had just rounded a bend in the creek when she told me to stop before a stand of dried out reed-like stalks interspersed with tufts of new green growth here and there on the edge of the river bank.

"These are purple spotted hemlock." She'd told me, pointing to the dried bamboo-like plants which were obviously the remnants of the previous year's foliage. "They're highly poisonous," she went on, "but they also yield one of our powerful magical tools, the musical pipes."

"Why do we call them purple spotted," I asked, not seeing any purple anywhere?

"These new plants," she said, bending down to point to one of the tiny hemlocks seedlings just starting to grow, "will be over six feet high once they mature. As they get older, they'll develop purple spots all over the stalks, which make them quite easy to identify. Later, when the foliage part of the plant dies, the purple disappears, but the stalks remain and dry out just like those you see here.

It's important to note the differences between the hemlock and other similar plants that grow in the same area so you don't get them mixed up. Over the centuries, some people have confused poison hemlock with parsley or carrots, or even dill or anise — with deadly results. Whenever you see plants with finely divided little leaves like these, use caution in handling them until you are sure exactly what it is you are dealing with."

With that, Steph paused and removed the leather satchel she carried over her shoulder and opened it. When she reached inside, she pulled out a set of simple Panpipes made up of nine varying sized tubes joined together with red twine.

"These pipes have been made by us for thousands of years," she said, placing the pipes slightly beneath her lips and blowing gently over the top of the longest of the tubes. A clear deep resonating note filled the air, carrying with it a poignant vibrato tone that touched my heart. The sound was breathy and fleeting, and definitely filled with Magic.

"The pipes are used to invoke the God, and to call all the creatures of the forests to our gatherings," she went on. "They are also used to create music for certain rituals and dances that we do and they play a big part in our history. Some say that the poisonous nature contained within the plant, actually intoxicates those who hear its music, and there is in fact some truth to that. In fact, I've always thought that the story about the Pied Piper of Hamlin, revealed among other things, that secret nature of the pipes, passed on as so many other magical traditions are, through folk lore and nursery rhymes."

"How can the pipes intoxicate people," I asked, drawn by yet another mystery of the Sacred Path.

"Well," Stephanie explained, "the stalks of the hemlock have a soft thick inner pulp that remains inside them after they've dried out. Here, let me show you what I mean."

She walked over to one of the stalks and snapped it off, bringing it back over to me and showing me the inside of the stem. There was a soft pithy marshmallow like material inside the stalk clinging to the outer skin, which was quite thick but still left the tube noticeably hollow.

"That pith," she continued, contains a very weak concentration of the poison that's contained in the plant. As it gradually dries out and begins to decompose, it creates a very fine dust on the inside of the stalk that goes airborne when you blow into the tube. When that happens, both the player and the audience, if they're close enough, are slightly affected by the chemical components of the plant, which makes them feel slightly heady and a little unworldly."

"Wow," I exclaimed, "that's really cool!"

"The hemlock has lots of other interesting traits and it's used in a number of our rituals in different ways which we'll talk about later. But just to give you an idea, its magical powers were used by the coven in the Middle Ages, to overpower certain "wasting diseases," like cancer and such, and it has a number of other good uses that go far beyond its potential to poison someone." But handling hemlock requires great care, something you will learn as your lessons progress. Even touching it can be deadly if you don't know what you are doing."

Shortly, the music stopped, bringing me back into the present and the ritual at hand. Once she had played the musical invocation to the God, Stephanie returned the pipes to the altar and then turned and faced us all.

"The circle is cast and we are now between the worlds!"

Once our space was consecrated, Derek started a small fire and we all gathered around it to ward of the chill of the night. Earlier Ron and Jack had dragged over a six foot section of a fallen tree trunk by the fire pit, and now several of us sat down on it. The rest of the coveners sat cross-legged on the ground on the other side of the fire, and they began the "song of the coven."

The song is a story telling time where our Priestess or Priest explains the history of the current Sabbat. It is also a time when other coven members are asked to share the history of our coven in general, and to share the stories of others who had walked the sacred path before us. The idea is to reinforce each covener's knowledge of our magical history, and to continue the age old tradition of sharing our Magic through oral rather than written tradition. Ron had explained to me the importance of this process long ago, and I was keenly aware that far more was actually being transferred through the telling of the stories, than just the facts being spoken.

"Human beings convey many subliminal messages when they're sharing stories," Ron had told me on one of our frequent expeditions into the woods. "There are gestures and innuendos that just don't translate the same when you commit them to pen and ink," he went on. "And besides that, there also seems to be some sort of ancestral memory that we all have deep in our subconscious, which appears to turn on whenever we hear mystically or spiritually related tales. When that happens, the stories we tell connect us with a deep and ancient internal wisdom or ways of understanding, which opens doorways into our past that are not normally readily available in our day-to-day perception of the world. Stephanie used to tell me that it was as if the Goddess had installed some locked magical diary deep within each and every one of us when we were first created. And that while that diary seems to contain many of the secrets of creation and the spiritual history of our people, in her great wisdom, the Mother, set the locking mechanism up in such a way that we can only have access to it a few pages at a time, under the most sacred of circumstances. And that, in its simplest form, is what the sharing of the song at each new Sabbat is really all about. So, I think you can see why it's so important to share the stories over and over again, because it's our only way of guaranteeing that the special Magic locked inside each of us, as we travel the sacred path together, doesn't get lost as our journeys move from generation to generation."

As we sat there in the midst of our sacred space on this Samhain, Stephanie shared the story of the Sabbat with us all, touching on the same points she had shared with me long ago in the creek bed. I was especially struck by the part of the story in which she talked about how our ancestors could literally feel the onset of the dark times at this time of the year, and how it made them feel as though they were on the threshold of the gateway between the world of the living and that of the great unknown. That hallowed place, where only those who had crossed the bridge into the cauldron we now call death resided, and where the womb of the Lady, waited like some spiraling web of spectral light, to transport us on to a new, and yet at the same time continuing, existence.

Stephanie's rendition of the story of Samhain and the way she articulated the perceptions and feelings of our most ancient of ancestors, captured almost exactly the current feelings I experienced, as I sat on our remote mountaintop, removed from the protective cocoon of the city's concrete and asphalt fortifications and the multitude of armed forces that kept us safe every day and night from both the unknown and the unseen. And in that moment, as Stephanie shared her powerful story, I found myself literally transported back into the dawn of humanity, alone with my own small fragile tribe of kinsmen huddling together in awe of the great unknown before us, waiting for some great and powerful shift to take place. And as we sat there in the light of our small fire, I could literally feel the tension build, as though we were sitting in the basket of some ancient army's catapult which was being wound up by the strength and sweat of a hundred men and women, and knowing that at any moment, that creaking, bending, tension loaded devise, would either trigger and release with palatable results, or shatter into a million pieces. And even after our Priestess finished with her story and we moved on to other ritual preparations, the tense anticipation remained. It was as though there were another shadowy world gradually merging with ours, a world that became more and more concrete and present with each new gust of the Sabbat's icy wind.

CHAPTER 18

Sacred Oil and the Consecration of my Blade

As the darkness deepened, Ron laid out the ingredients to make the sacred oil, and Derek added a few more sticks to the now well established fire. Jack, sensing the time was finally right, placed the coven's heavy iron cauldron into the glowing coals and filled it partially with water from the mountain's artesian spring. Karen, following suit, immersed an ochre colored ceramic urn filled with freshly pressed olive oil into the soon to be boiling liquid, and we all waited for it to heat up. As the cauldron began to steam and bubble, Stephanie passed around the sticky buds we'd collected from the cottonwoods earlier that day, and we each took our turn crushing the outer shells of a handful of the balm, and then adding our portion of the sweet-smelling mass to the urn full of slowly warming oil. Throughout the process, as each member added their buds and Magic to the mix, the rest of the coveners sang the low chant of creation in Elban, and the oil began to bubble. When the last of the buds were added, Ron handed out a smaller portion of the five finger grass, and each member added their contribution of that herb too, to the now fragrant mix. Following that, came a pinch of Bane of Soltra, and just a touch of the Bane of the Hen, until the oil turned golden red and rolled slowly from the heat of the boiling cauldron.

"Never allow the oil to boil directly from the heat of a fire," Ron instructed me carefully, "or ever allow it to be stored in anything made of a metal other than silver," he went on. Always heat it in a vessel made of glass or clay, and heat the vessel with boiling water from the cauldron. If you deviate from this, the oil will be ruined, and its Magic will be useless."

"Also, the oil should be made right at the time when the worlds are coming together at Samhain," Stephanie added, "and it should always be done in a circle or space fully prepared for ritual,".

When the addition of the herbs to the oil was completed, we left it to cook in the bubbling vessel, and the sweet scent of the simmering concoction wafted through the air, lending a pleasurable sacredness to the small circle on the mountain.

Once the oil was in motion, several of us began to lay out the food for the Sabbat, and to set up for the Feast of the Dead. R.J. and James created a table by spreading out a heavy blanket on the ground, and Ron, Karen, and I, laid out all of the food items in a pleasing display. At the same time, Stephanie, working alone, placed a folding chair in the northern quadrant of the circle and covered it with a black cloth to create a place for the coven members to sit and meet with those who'd gone beyond. Ron had told me about the black chair earlier in the day, and I knew that it was a special ritual place that was set aside specifically for us to speak privately with our beloved dead. It was a place Ron told me, "to resolve our grief and to finalize unresolved issues involving them, as well as to meet with them again. For those who have parted before us, can still be here with us, at this special time of year."

"Think of it as a private place where you can sit and talk with someone who's gone beyond, who you feel really compelled to connect with," Ron went on, "Like your departed Grandmother or even a favorite pet that you miss terribly.

Once the food was laid out, Karen began laying out the plates for each of the coven members, placing an extra one at the head of the table for those who had passed away.

"That's the place of honor," Ron explained, as Karen laid a wreath of flowers around the last place setting, "and we'll each share a portion of our best fare there to show those who come to visit tonight that we haven't forgotten them."

"It's kind of like inviting your family over for Christmas dinner," Karen added, "so it's important to lay out your best, just like you would if they were still alive and attending a special meal like that."

While a group of us were setting out the feast, two of the other coveners dug a couple of holes in the northern quadrant of the circle about four feet apart, and inserted two six foot posts into the ground to represent the gate posts between the worlds. Once the posts were firmly seated in the ground, everyone worked together to cover them with spiraling strands of orange and black ribbon, and to hang a strand of orange and black crepe paper across the gateway, to form a visible barrier. As we erected the gate, Jack explained that it represented the portal between the merging worlds, and that we would ceremonially cut the strands between the decorated posts later in the ritual, when we were ready to invite our beloved dead in to join the feast.

After the initial work on the posts and gate were finished, Ron and Stephanie went on to weave in several black crow's feathers and a handful of tiny carved skulls — like the one fastened to the feather on the altar — into the ribbons on the gate posts, while Jack painted mystical symbols and Elban runes on the stretched crepe barrier.

Figure 26: Runes for the Samhain Gate

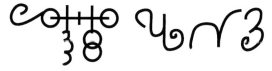

All of the inscriptions were applied using a mixture of our special ground chalk and sacred water, and they glowed intermittently with an eerie luminosity between the rising and ebbing light of the circle's small fire. When the posts and gate were finally completed, Stephanie hung a piece of weighted parchment on the twisted strands of crepe, and artfully inscribed the invocation to the Marigwyn on its yellow mottled surface, using a twig of charred willow.

"Caile' Nai Marigwyn, Na neg Maru,"[37] the invocation read, imploring the Lady of the gate of skulls to open her doors.

"Always use the charcoal to inscribe any important runes in your rituals," Ron instructed me as we watched the others at work. "And the same can be said about the special chalk mixed with water from the sacred springs," he went on. "By inscribing our magical symbols that way, all of the elements will be present in your runes and invocations, and at the same time, *lazra meck* is allowed to continue its journey throughout every component of the process. All of these customs help carry forward the Magic of our ancestors, and open doorways of understanding that otherwise would be missed."

Once the gate was finished, everyone moved back to the altar at Stephanie's request, and she proceeded to explain what would transpire next.

"Now we'll open the gates to the otherworld and let the feast and ritual begin," she announced. Then she stepped forward to the altar and picked up her magical blade with her left hand. At the same time, she opened a small vial of sacred oil with her right, and holding it between her thumb and middle finger, she slowly turned it upside down, allowing a tiny portion of the topaz liquid to coat her middle finger. Replacing the open vial on the altar, she proceeded to carefully rub the magical oil on each side of the blade, whispering an invocation in Elban as she did so.

"In the old days," Ron whispered, "the oil used to be kept in a special silver vial with a tiny hole in the top that was specially designed, so that when someone held it in their hand during ritual, the oil would automatically rise up through the hole and produce only one drop to be used at a time. The idea was to conserve the oil and at the same time to keep it from becoming contaminated or evaporating over the years. We've tried to create a vial something like, but we haven't been able to get anything to work yet. Stephanie told us that K.D. used to have a container like that, and

---

[37] Calling on the goddess of the gate of skulls, to open the doorway.

that it had a serpent coiled into the rune of wisdom wrapped around it, from whose mouth the oil came through, but that was long ago, and she never learned how it worked."

When the invocation was finished, Stephanie raised the consecrated blade, saluted towards the north, and then walked slowly around the altar and approached the gateway. When she reached the portal, she stood there stoically, apparently gathering strength for what was about to follow.

As if on, cue Karen stepped forward to the altar, and picked up the hand carved cylindrical wooden container that held our Samhain incense. Ron had explained to me previously, that the container was specifically made of wood, so that the difference in temperature between our homes where we stored the incense, and the damp forest where we did our rituals, wouldn't form condensation inside the container and cause the ingredients to mold.

Karen poured a significant portion of the special incense over the glowing charcoal, and a cloud of scented smoke immediately appeared in response. As Karen walked past me, I noticed that in addition to the heavy scent that I'd noticed earlier, the incense also had a piercing electrical smell to it, and reminded me somewhat of the smell associated with an electrical fire, although more pleasant than that.

Karen moved forward to stand next to Stephanie, and under the Priestess's direction, proceeded to fan volumes of the sacred smoke back and forth across the magical gate. Then, Stephanie stepped forward and offered an invitation to the departed dead, and asked them to join with us in our circle and to partake of our sacred feast.

"Departed ones, loved ones; you who have gone before us, and who know the mysteries of death. We invite you here on this sacred night, when the worlds merge and barriers dissolve, to join us as we celebrate the turning of the wheel and welcome in the New Year. We ask your presence at our feast that we might honor you and ask your wisdom in our divination, that we might be prepared for

315

what is to come. We invoke you in love and honor you in our presence, dukaat!"

"Dukaat," everyone repeated!

Stephanie slowly and purposefully raised her blade above her head with both hands and I could literally feel the tension in the act as the muscles in her forearms began to twitch uncontrollably under the self imposed isometric tension.

"*Ach-na, Rai, UU-ma,*"[38] she started slowly, stretching the words of the Golden Key, as her chant intensified her intention and her focus on the gateway.

"*Ach-na, Rai, UU-ma,*" we all repeated loudly, following Stephanie's lead.

"*Ach-na, Rai, UU-ma,*" she repeated again after a short pause, louder and slightly faster this time, with more emotion and more intensity in her delivery.

"*Ach-na, Rai, UU-ma,*" everyone responded in return, our voices now echoing throughout the canyon as we fully joined in her invocation to add the Magic of the legendary key to the act.

"*Achna, Rai, UUma,*" Stephanie shouted from the top of her lungs. "Open the gateway." she commanded."

In unison, we repeated her commands.

Her arm swept down in an arc, and the blade sliced cleanly through the rune filled crepe. A gust of wind blasted through the circle from the north as the barrier parted, and I felt the presence of many unseen beings rush through the opening from the otherworld.

"Can you feel it?" Ron asked, looking at no one in particular.

"It's unbelievable," Karen responded, "they are everywhere!"

As I stood there, mesmerized by the experience, I felt the presence of many people crowded within our circle. It was as though you could catch just a glimpse of them, a flash of light, a shadow where no shadow should be, the feeling that someone was right there behind you, breathing down your

---

[38] The three primary sacred words associated with the Golden Key

neck, but when you turned around, no one was there —
just the forest and the shadows, and whatever waited
beyond the light of our small quickly dwindling fire. It was
actually a little scary, and I kept close to Ron, waiting to see
what was next.

Jack called us all to the table, and we sat down around
the meal, far more quiet and serious than before the gate
was cut.

"Each of you should dish up your plates now," he said
instructively, "and when you're done selecting what you're
going to eat, make sure that you take a little of everything
that you've chosen and put it on the special plate for our
loved ones, so that they can join the feast along with us"

Everyone selected their food, and one by one, they made
their way to the place at the head of the table. When Ron
took his turn, he retrieved a small plastic dish from his
things, and placed it next to the plate of honor, and there
were tears in his eyes.

"This plate is for my cat, Pumpkin, who just died a
couple of weeks ago." He paused for a minute and placed a
piece of chicken from his plate, and then quietly said, "I
miss you Pumpkin," and returned to his place at the table.

My heart resonated with his sadness, and I immediately
thought of my own cat Midnight who had died a number of
years before. Until this moment, I wasn't even conscious
that that old wound was still open. Tears also formed in
my eyes in sympathy with Ron, and a vision of my own cat
flashed across my memory in response.

I got up from my place at the feast, and added another
small piece of chicken to Ron's offering and whispered a
heart felt message to my cat too. It was strange, I hadn't
thought about Midnight for several years now, but in this
moment, she was directly present in my heart, and my
unresolved grief was right there in front of me.

When I sat back down, Stephanie reached across and
touched my hand.

"It's okay," she said softly. "That's what this is all
about."

Each of the coven members added to the plates of honor, and then we all proceeded to tell stories about the people and animal friends that we were honoring while we ate. About half way through the feast, Jack explained that it was time to ritually acknowledge our losses, and with that, he rose and approached the altar. First, he lit a small pile of dry grass and kindling that had been placed in the cauldron, and got a tiny fire going. Then he picked up one of the colorful fallen leaves that R.J. had laid out on the altar, and using the coven's crow quill pen and magical ink, he wrote the name of his grandmother on the leaf's surface. Then he carefully laid the leaf into the flames and spoke out his grandmother's name, Merriam, as the leaf caught fire and its smoke rose up into to the heavens. Everyone in the coven repeated Merriam's name in remembrance of her and a silence followed. Following that, Jack picked up another leaf and wrote down the name of a friend who had died from an illness. He repeated the process of burning the second leaf and when he'd finished his ritual and everyone had acknowledged the second person, he said a prayer for them both, and then walked over to the black chair in the north, and sat down to speak with his beloved dead.

After a while, when he'd finished his conversations, he returned to the group, and rejoined the feast.

Next Stephanie got up and recorded her dead. Then one by one, we all repeated the process and took our turn in the black chair.

When it came my turn to sit in the black chair, I wasn't sure what to expect. I sat down slowly, and looked out into the shadows beyond, waiting for something to happen. I hadn't lost anyone that I could bring to mind, so after a time, I called out softly to my cat Midnight, and waited. A few moments later, a cloudy mist formed about three feet in front of me, and then I heard a meow. The sound didn't come from the mist in front of me; instead, it seemed to come from somewhere in the woods just beyond the edge of the circle. I called out again, "Midnight?" Again I heard the Meow. I was stunned and not sure what to do next. Then I felt a presence in the mist and so I leaned forward and just

318

started to talk to my cat. I told him how much I missed him and that I wished he hadn't died. As I spoke, the mist began to move along the ground very gradually, and I had a sense that my cat was right there in front of me even though I never actually saw it. Then I'd swear I heard purring for a few seconds, and then it was gone, both the mist, and the feeling of my cat's presence. It was very eerie and yet comforting all the same. I stayed in the chair for a while, just treasuring the thought that we could connect with our loved ones after death, and then eventually got up and returned to the feast.

When the feast was finished and everyone had honored their dead, Stephanie announced that it was time to complete the sacred oil. We all moved to the fire, which was nothing but coals now, and watched as our Priestess removed the bubbling ceramic urn from the cauldron. As she carried it back to the altar, I could smell the amazing scent of the magical herbs, which had now combined into a wonderful aromatic liquid, dispersing throughout the circle in a transient steam of mist.

The newly made oil still rolled gently from the heat of its container as she laid it on the altar, but the bubbling had now stopped. Then, at Stephanie's request, we all stepped forward and formed a tight circle around the altar and the steaming liquid.

"As you all know, the oil symbolizes the connection between us and all who've walked the Sacred Path before us," Stephanie started. "Now is the time to join that which is carried forth from all covens past with that which is in the now and the present."

She reached forward, and carefully picked up the coven's vial of sacred oil from years past and opened the lid. She passed it around to each member, and asked each of us to pour three drops of the oil into the urn of steaming liquid. "We always add some of the old oil to the new, each time we make a new batch. In this way, we always include some of the Magic and the energy of those who were in the coven before us, and our legacy is passed on throughout the centuries to come. This is an ancient tradition and it

319

carries with it not only its connections with the past, but also the very Magic of each and every Witch who's walked the path before us. There's tremendous power in that, and that's one of the reasons why our oil is so sacred."

She then instructed us to recite the words of power from the Golden Key and to draw the sacred pentagram over the oil after we did so, as she stirred the old mixture into the new.

When everyone was finished adding their power to the spell, Stephanie closed the vial of the original oil and placed it back on the altar. Then she asked Ron to retrieve six small mason jars he had brought for the purpose and to set them on the altar. When the jars were all set, Stephanie carefully picked up the warm oil and skillfully divided it up between each of the six containers.

"There is a container of oil for each of you, and one for the coven," she said. "Take this with you to use for your Magic throughout the year". When I received my jar, I closed my eyes and felt the warmth of the extraordinary liquid within. It felt comforting and welcoming and warmed my hands against the chill of the cold October high-country night. My thoughts turned to K.D. and Thomas, and Michael and Celia, and to the many others who had been in the coven before me. I tried to picture Hadsley, and Tim, and Larin and wondered about the many others whom I would never know. I imagined that it had been the same for each of them in their time, knowing only a few of those who preceded them, and yet feeling connected to those who were far beyond their perception. And I also wondered about those who would follow in *our* footsteps. Would there still be forests for them to wander and would our traditions survive the changing world? Would there be coveners far in the future mixing our oil with theirs and wondering about me? What would their world be like? All of these things were on my mind as I stood there, and I fully realized in that moment the full range of Magic that was actually inherent in the translucent talisman that was our legacy from the past.

320

"Now it's time to consecrate Patrick's blade," Stephanie announced, as she motioned me to come forward.

I approached the altar and picked up my blade as Ron and Stephanie had instructed me to, and held it up for all to see. Then I placed my fingers into the chalice, and lightly covered the handle and blade with the purified water.

"Knock na, kilar,"[39] I said forcefully.

"Kilar."[40] everyone joined in.

Then I poured a small portion of Samhain incense into the censor and I ran the blade through the thready smoke, as I asked the elements of fire and air to join in my purification.

"Knock djinn ralda, shook ma ne' knock lazra,[41]

"Shook ma ne' pa ralda.... kilar!"[42]

"Kilar," everyone repeated.

Then I opened the still warm jar of oil, dipped my fingers into the newly created liquid, and coated both the blade and handle of the knife, as I recited the consecration of the sacred blade.

"Knock ma aga chakadah gadou,[43]

bt ma ch rowam neck ma aga,[44]

Ki chuti!"[45]

"*Ki chuti,*" Everyone returned!

When the consecration was complete, I carried my finished blade to the east, and raising it up with both hands to the sky, I called out to the *aesma* there.

"*Aesma neck djinn, fay lazos jalam ma ata acha me'*[46]

---

[39] "By water and by the sacred womb of the Mother, be pure,"

[40] "Be pure!"

[41] "By the spirit of fire and the spark of creation."

[42] "And by the spirit of air.... Be pure!"

[43] "By the ancient wisdom that flows,"

[44] "and by the heart spirit of those who've come before us."

[45] "be alive!"

[46] "Guardian of fire, bring light to the blade that creates my sacred circle."

When the invocation was finished, I lowered my knife and carefully scribed the rune of fire into the air before me.

Figure 27: Rune for Fire.

Completing that, I raised my blade in salute, and proceeded *deosil* around the circle to the south. When I reached the candle designating that direction, I raised my knife again, and addressed the second *aesma* there.

"Aesma neck goba, fay chakadah shan'hari ch taal tadoo, jalam ch ata acha me'."[47]

Lowering my knife for the second time, I scribed the rune for earth before me, and continued around the circle to the west.

"Aesma neck na, dam wadda jalam ch ata acha me' "[48]

Again I scribed the appropriate rune, saluted the aesma of the west, and continued on to the north. When I reached that direction, I raised my blade for the last time, and addressed the Aesma there.

"Aesma neck pa, ralda neck pa, jalam ch ata acha me' "[49]

I traced the rune of air in front of me and saluted the final guardian. Then I walked to the east completing the circle, and turned inward to the center and the altar where I'd started. I stated my intentions and explained to all of nature and the gods the purpose intended for my blade. I told them that I would use the knife for Magic, and that I would only use it to promote good. I also committed myself to always do my best to honor nature and the path I had

---

[47] "Guardian of earth, bring the knowledge of solid things and green growth, to my blade that creates the sacred circle."
[48] "Guardian of water, give birth to my knife that creates the sacred circle."
[49] "Guardian of air, spirit of breath, give life to the knife that creates the sacred circle."

chosen, and to continue to pursue the mysteries of the Lady, and to share her wisdom with all who would listen. I also asked that the blade be given the power to bring about necessary changes and to focus my desires, and that it should serve me as a tool to cast our circles for ritual.

When I'd finished at the altar, I turned around to face the coven and nodded, signaling that I was finished. Stephanie stepped forward extending her hand, and I handed her my consecrated knife. She turned slowly and faced the coven and held the blade before her, speaking in a soft yet determined voice.

"The circle is complete and the ritual is fulfilled, and the blade waits only to be awakened. The light of the Mother resides within it and all of nature knows its power. This blade carries the song of the coven and the wisdom and knowledge of our ways, and in making it, Patrick has learned of many deep mysteries along the way. Let us honor now its holiness and the journey taken by Patrick to create it, and the journeys of all who've walked the path before us. For it is in this connection, the thread that weaves us all together in spirit and understanding and the sharing of the mysteries, that the key to our purpose is revealed. So let us all now come together to witness the surrender of the blade to the Mother herself, as it makes its own journey under her guidance, to be forged for the final time within her womb. And let the power of that journey transform it into a new and vibrant living thing when she renews all life upon the earth at Yule."

Stephanie then turned and laid my consecrated knife back upon the altar and picked up her own. Once she had hers securely in hand, she walked slowly to the edge of the circle and cut a doorway through the magical barrier surrounding us by tracing an opening to the outside world. As the portal was completed, the wind subsided as if on cue, and the entire forest grew strangely quiet and still. It was as though time stood still for the moment, and all of nature had settled down in honor of my sacred quest. When the doorway was complete, the coven began to chant in Elban, and Stephanie nodded toward me, indicating that it was time to surrender my blade to the Lady.

Ron had taught me more information about the process several weeks before, and I felt a pain of anxiety at the thought of giving up the very tool that I had put so much work into to create.

"As I said when I first told you about the athame'," Ron had said, as we walked through a field of chokecherry trees on one of our weekly excursions, "you'll have to surrender your knife when it's finished."

"Just what will I have to do," I had asked, wanting to know more about what would happen.

"Well," he said, catching my eye as he spoke. "When your knife is completely finished and you've properly consecrated it at Samhain, the coven will create a doorway through the circle into the forest. Then, you'll walk to a place of your own choosing where two paths meet, and you'll thrust your knife, blade first into the dirt, and leave it there until the time is right to retrieve it."

"But why would I want to do that," I asked, wondering what the point would be in burying the knife that I had put so much time into, or in abandoning it in a place where someone might find it or something might happen to it.

"Our path teaches that we must trust in the gods to instruct and care for us, and that we must learn to understand and befriend all of nature in order to have the mysteries revealed to us. By surrendering the blade to the gods and nature, we fulfill this. We believe that if the blade is right for us and meant to be ours, the Mother will fill it with the light of creation when we demonstrate our absolute trust in her. We also believe that she'll bestow upon it a life of its own, which will better serve our needs and increase our connection to her if we leave it in her hands. And we believe that nature itself, if we've properly established our relationship to it, will keep anyone or anything from harming or taking our sacred tool while it sits vulnerable in the forest. In fact, that's exactly why we place the blade in a place where two paths meet."

324

"I'm not sure I understand exactly what you mean," I asked, "why a place where two paths meet?"

"Because by doing that, we are making sure that our knife is accessible to all who might pass by. Everyone knows, that a crossroads or the intersection of two trails is a place that both people and animals gather or stop or make decisions. Consequently, we place our knife where it will be most vulnerable and in full view of passersby, and then we trust in nature to distract any would-be violators of that trust."

"But how would nature distract someone from seeing my knife?"

Ron laughed. "Remember back when you first started and you and I walked the path together down by the creek for the very first time?"

"Yeah."

"Did you notice the thornbane, or the sacred springs, or the willow, or the position of the sun in the sky, before I pointed them out to you?"

"No."

"Why do you think that was?"

"I'm not sure."

"The reason you didn't see them, even though they were right there in front of you, is because you were distracted by nature as a whole, and because you were disconnected from it. Nature is full of significant mysteries that are right out there in people's faces, yet because they aren't seeking them, and they aren't in harmony with them, they just walk by unaware of what's available. And it's *their* direct disconnect with nature, combined with *your* intimate connection to it, that will keep your blade safe."

The chanting behind me increased in intensity, and all of my training came together for the moment at hand. I turned back facing the altar, and then slowly walked over and picked up my blade and a small cloth bag of sacred chalk. As I turned and walked toward the portal Stephanie had opened, I reassured myself by recounting all that I had learned. I *was* connected to nature, and I *did* trust the Lady, and so my mood changed as I made my way through

325

the doorway and down the mountain to find a place to leave my knife. I nodded to the trees, whispering greetings as I passed by, and recalled my experiences with the elementals as I breathed in the crisp cold mountain air.

They were all there, I could smell them. The water in the spring, the fire in our circle, the damp sweet smell of fertile earth, and the cool refreshing scent of fresh air.... all there to witness and lend their aid to my sacred ritual.

I continued down the slope, intersecting a faint trail, and headed toward the canyon edge as the chanting of the coven became fainter above and behind me. As I approached the rim, another trail came in from the side intersecting mine, and I knew this was the perfect place for my purpose. The crossing was right on the edge of a precipice and the scene below was breathtaking and beautiful. I stopped for a moment, feeling the sheer majesty of the place, and then held up my blade to the stars.

"Gracious Lady, you who met me on the edge of death, and held my hand, I ask that you be here with me now. Watch over my blade, and fill it with your sacred light, as I surrender it into the mystery of your womb. Let it be a tool to create my circles, and to focus my desires into fruition, and let its Magic remain constant throughout my life."

I knelt down into the soft duff and placed the tip of my knife against the fragrant earth, focusing all of my energy into the task at hand. With a powerful thrust, I pushed the blade deep into the fertile soil and finalized the ritual with a "*dukaat!* I felt a powerful emotional shudder throughout my entire body as the hilt contacted the ground, and I immediately released my grip in response. Next, on my knees, I opened the bag of chalk, and poured a small circle of it around my knife. Once that was done, I then raised myself back up onto my feet and looked at the buried blade and the glowing chalk. I made the sign of the pentagram over the protruding hilt, and then turned confidently back up the trail toward the circle above me, knowing that the fate of my blade was now out of my hands and beyond my control.

326

When I reentered the circle, everyone congregated around me and congratulated me on a job well done. We continued our ritual, and celebrated with our ancestors and lost loved ones far into the night until it was almost dawn. When the circle came to an end, and we'd said farewell to our invited ghostly guests, most of the coven worked together to pack up our things. The fire had gone completely out, and only a few live coals remained, glowing dimly, as they gradually relinquished the last of their comforting heat to the wintry night. Stephanie and the others stood together talking Magic within the confines of the shimmering chalk circle, which glowed prominently now, no longer having to compete with flickering candles and Samhain blaze.

"I'm going to take a walk back down the trail to where I buried my knife," I said, to no one in particular, and started back down the hill toward the place where I'd left my blade.

"I'll join you in a bit," Ron responded, looking my way momentarily before continuing in conversation with Stephanie and the others.

"Ok," I returned, pleased that we'd have some time together alone, and knowing that he would approve of the place I had chosen.

When I reached the canyon's edge, I sought out the narrow crossroads and paused quietly there to ponder the night. As I stood before the buried blade looking out over the deep valley and alpine lake below, light from the barest crescent of a new moon shone silver on the dark water far below. Just the slightest hint of apricot illuminated the horizon in the east, announcing the coming of a new beginning, and I was moved by the sheer splendor of it all. Above me, shrouded in mist, like phantoms from the ancient past, stood the hooded forms of my coven, now standing silently within a faintly glowing circle of ethereal light — in honor of this momentous occasion. In that moment, I considered all that had happened to bring me to this time and place and to this moment of accomplishment. The accident, meeting Ron, the walks in the woods and the wisdom of the forest. Learning about Magic and the coven, and our connection with the Lady and the Circle of Life. My initiation, the sacred oil, the wand, and finding the meteorite in the desert. And now the forging of the magical blade, source of legends and great tool of Magic going forward, when reclaimed and dedicated in its full power at the Winter Solstice.

After a few minutes, Ron joined me, and we stood silently on the edge of the precipice for a few moments, mentor and student, each appreciating the other in silence — and then he spoke:

"It's been a long haul and you've learned a great deal," he said seriously, respecting the journey I'd taken.

"Yes I have," I answered, fully aware of the scope of his statement.

"Even so," he started in that low voice that was now so familiar, "even all of this is still just the beginning," he went on.

I considered his words for a moment and then smiled knowingly, sure that I knew where he was headed.

He put his arm around my shoulder and we turned together down a thready trail that followed the rim of the misty mountains toward the east. We walked together side by side, teacher and student, Priest and Witch, as Ron began once again to reveal the wisdom of the ages and I struggled to take it all in. Our feet kicked up small clouds of fine dust like generations of those who'd gone before us, and the mists parted and the Magic of the Lady revealed itself in every step along the way. For some, it was just a simple winding trail in the forest, seemingly innocent and unobtrusive and leading nowhere in particular, but for me it was the *Sacred Path*, the doorway into the soul and spirit of humanity and the nature and understanding of the Divine. And as I walked with my friend and mentor, I knew that there was still so much more to learn.

Ron paused quietly by a large pine, as though pondering some deep spiritual revelation.

"What about it, my friend, are you ready to delve into the next layer?"

"Yes," I replied in joyful anticipation.

Witchcraft, Magic, and Ancient Wisdom

The journey continues...

Coming soon

Courting the Lady
A Wiccan Journey
Book Two:
The Boiling Cauldron
❧◌ℛℰ◌❧

Also

The Witch's guide to the Sacred Path
A practical workbook and study guide
For Book One

www.courtingthelady.com
••

Journey on the Sacred Path with Patrick McCollum

Upcoming Workshops:

Passing on the Magic

A full-day hands-on workshop about the origins of the Circle, the Wand and the Athame'. This workshop utilizes items collected from ancient sites, photos, and authentic ritual tools. It is the extended version of the workshop presented at Pagan festivals across the country.

Creating the Sacred Oil: A journey into the past

A full-day hands-on workshop where participants will create the Magical oil passed down for centuries on the Sacred Path. Participants will journey into the forest and learn to identify and harvest the necessary plants and herbs. They will then learn and perform all of the appropriate rituals and steps to create the oil, and ultimately take home, the oil they've made.

Creating the Magical Blade

A three-day hands-on overnight workshop, where participants will learn the full history of the magical blade and how to perform all of the necessary rituals to create it. Each attendee will then hand forge their own Athame's in the "old way," using meteorites and a charcoal driven forge. All participants will leave with a fully finished magical blade.

**Check out: www.courtingthelady.com
for workshop schedules and more information**

Sha ma na gadaf gadou

3 3 3